Architecture and Climate

Tracing the evolving relationship between the architecture and climate of Britain from the late sixteenth to the twentieth century, Dean Hawkes presents an original approach to the study of architecture and climate. Through detailed studies of buildings by major architects, the book deftly explores how the unique character of the climate of the British Isles has had a fundamental influence on the nature of buildings of all kinds and periods, in both country and city.

Based on extensive documentary research and on first-hand analyses of significant buildings, the book combines architectural history with the parallel fields of climate history and the representation of environment in literature and the fine arts. It spans the period in British architectural history from the late sixteenth to the twentieth century; from the buildings of the greatest architect of the Elizabethan age, Robert Smythson, to the work of his twentieth century near namesakes, Alison and Peter Smithson.

Beautifully illustrated with drawings and photographs, including a colour plate section, the book brings a historical dimension to the appreciation of the environment in architecture and, equally, introduces an environmental element to the study of the history of architecture.

Dean Hawkes is emeritus professor of architectural design at the Welsh School of Architecture, Cardiff University and emeritus fellow of Darwin College, University of Cambridge. His previous books include *The Environmental Tradition* (1996), *The Selective Environment* (2002) and *The Environmental Imagination* (2008). In 2010 he received the RIBA's biennial Annie Spink Award for excellence in architectural education.

For William and Mary

Dean Hawkes

Architecture and Climate

An Environmental History of British Architecture, 1600–2000

Routledge
Taylor & Francis Group

LONDON AND NEW YORK

First edition published 2012
by Routledge
2 Park Square, Milton Park, Abingdon, Oxon OX14 4RN

Simultaneously published in the USA and Canada
by Routledge
711 Third Avenue, New York, NY 10017

Routledge is an imprint of the Taylor & Francis Group, an informa business

British Library Cataloguing in Publication Data
A catalogue record for this book is available from the British Library

Library of Congress Cataloging in Publication Data
Hawkes, Dean.
    Architecture and climate: an environmental history of British
    architecture, 1600–2000 / Dean Hawkes. – 1st ed.
    p. cm.
    Includes bibliographical references and index.
    1. Architecture and climate – Great Britain. I. Title. II. Title:
    Environmental history of British architecture, 1600–2000.
    NA2541.H39 2012
    720′.470941—dc23
    2011021736

ISBN: 978-0-415-56186-0 (hbk)
ISBN: 978-0-415-56187-7 (pbk)

Typeset in Janson and Univers
by Florence Production Ltd, Stoodleigh, Devon

MIX
Paper from
responsible sources
FSC® C004839
www.fsc.org

Printed and bound in Great Britain by the MPG Books Group

1006239090

Contents

Preface

In the literature of architecture the importance of the relationship between climate and building is widely accepted, particularly in the discourse of so-called architectural science. The concern is to define instrumental relationships between the physical characteristics of climate and the nature of buildings. These explain how to design buildings that will keep their occupants warm in cold places and cool in hot places and that respond to the diversity of the seasons. This is all of immense practical value and has been given further impetus with the emergence, in the last couple of decades, of the concern to make buildings more 'environmentally friendly', indeed to be overtly 'climate-responsive'. The present book aims to expand the scope of the debate by bringing a historical perspective to bear upon the way in which buildings both respond to and, in some respects, give expression to the climate in which they are set.

The study is concerned with architecture in Britain in the four centuries from 1600 to 2000. It carries us, in a sequence of thematic essays, from the remarkable 'prodigy' houses of Elizabethan England to the work of significant architects who explored these questions in the latter years of the twentieth century. At the beginning of this period the condition of climate was a matter not just of subjective experience, but of rich description in the media of literature and art. In the seventeenth century the tools of meteorological observation were developed, as part of the emergence of experimental natural philosophy, and soon began to influence the relationship of climate to architecture. One of the important developments in the eighteenth century was the systematic collection of weather data, which became a common pastime of country landowners and parsons. At the same time, the environmental characteristics of buildings began to be codified, with the publication of formulations and tabulations of guidelines for elements such as the dimensions of window openings and fireplaces. Then the fruits of the Industrial Revolution, in the form of developments of devices for the improved warming and ventilation of buildings, enabled the builders of the nineteenth century to define a new set of relationships between architecture and climate, in particular with the disagreeable, polluted microclimate of the expanding cities. In contrast to this 'industrialization' of the architectural environment, the close of the nineteenth century saw the emergence of the Arts and Crafts phase of British domestic architecture. Numerous houses of immense quality were built that, in their form and construction, gave a new poetic expression to a particularly British conception of comfort and the architectural means by which this might be furnished. In the early decades of the twentieth century architecture entered a phase in which the technological expertise of structure, construction and environment was given new and explicit expression. These ideas were widely embraced by architects working in Britain, but were transformed by a particularly British sensibility to the influence of climate and by the characteristics of the British climate itself. The second half of the twentieth century was, in many respects, dominated by an approach to architecture that effectively disregarded the historic influence of climate, as mechanical systems for heating, cooling, ventilating and lighting were incorporated into sealed building envelopes. These designs were, by definition, hugely dependent on the consumption of energy sources derived from fossil fuels and, as such, came to contribute to the emerging environmental crisis. In exactly the same period, however, a deepening interest emerged in reconnecting architecture more intimately to climate in order to reap the benefits of the natural environment as a primary influence on the nature of buildings. The science of meteorology has now a vast armoury of instruments of observation and prediction that allow yet deeper understanding of how buildings might respond to and express the nature of the climate.

Of necessity, the scope of the book bridges the histories of architecture and meteorology. The research has encompassed extensive reading in these respective literatures. To bring a wider perspective to the project I have also delved into aspects of the history of art and of English literature. But, as always in research of this nature, the most telling sources are the buildings themselves, which stand as witness and record of the rich and constantly evolving connection of architecture and climate in Britain.

Acknowledgements

Many people and institutions have aided the research for and production of this book. I should particularly like to record my gratitude to the following.

Stuart Band at the Devonshire Collection at Chatsworth provided access to and invaluable advice on the account books for Hardwick Hall, and Philip Riden of the University of Nottingham helped my further understanding of these and other documents. Stephen Astley welcomed me to the archives of the Soane Museum in London to track down documents related to Sir John Soane's interest in systems for warming and ventilating buildings. I should also like to thank the staff of the following for supplying images: Cambridge University Library; the RIBA Library; the National Trust Picture Library; The National Trust for Scotland; the Codrington Library; All Soul's College, Oxford; the Yale Center for British Art; the British Museum; London Metropolitan Archive; English Heritage; the Tate Archive; the Royal Meteorological Society; the National Gallery, London; Leicester City Art Gallery; the Goodwood Trust; the National Gallery of Victoria; and the Fondation Le Corbusier.

Diane Haigh's deep knowledge of the architecture of the Arts and Crafts movement, and in particular of the houses of M. H. Baillie Scott, significantly informed the essay on that period of British architecture. Nicholas Bullock, my friend and colleague of many years, helped me broaden the background of my studies into the modern movement in Britain. My work on Alison and Peter Smithson received unique insights from conversations with Simon Smithson and his personal experience of life at Upper Lawn Pavilion. Simon and Soraya Smithson gave generous assistance in allowing access to the Smithson Family Collection and in furnishing invaluable images and documents. I must also thank Derek Sugden for invitations to visit his and Jean's wonderful Smithson house at Watford.

As with much of my previous research, the ideas for these essays have been developed and tested in lectures given to students in a number of schools of architecture. This is a process that I find particularly productive and, in particular, I am indebted to David Dernie, head of the Leicester School of Architecture at De Montfort University, and Richard Fellows, head of the School of Architecture at the University of Huddersfield, who have welcomed me as visiting professor. I am also indebted to Alan Short and Koen Steemers, who have regularly invited me to contribute to undergraduate and postgraduate teaching in the Department of Architecture at the University of Cambridge.

The production of the book has been smoothed along by the help of Francesca Ford, Laura Williamson and Jo Endell-Cooper, my editors at Routledge, and I am indebted to Amy Tillotson, whose meticulous work in seeking permission to reproduce the images has been a boon to me.

I dedicate the book with love to my son and daughter: William and Mary.

Dean Hawkes,
Cambridge,
October 2011

Introduction

In 1955 Nikolaus Pevsner broadcast a series of radio lectures, the Reith Lectures, from the BBC in London. These subsequently became his book, *The Englishness of English Art* (1). The first lecture had the title 'The Geography of Art'. In this Pevsner reflected on the validity of geography as a tool in understanding aspects of the nature of art and architecture. As part of the argument he examined the influence of climate on national character and, by extension, of the art of a nation, concluding that there is 'a whole string of facts from art and literature tentatively derived from climate'.

In the wider literature of architecture the importance of the relationship between climate and building is commonly accepted, particularly in the discourse of so-called architectural science. Seminal texts include Victor Olgyay's *Design with Climate*, Baruch Givoni's *Man, Climate and Architecture* and, a recent addition to the field, *Climate and Architecture*, edited by Thorben Dahl (2). The concern of these and numerous other books is to define instrumental relationships between the physical characteristics of climate and the nature of buildings. They explain how to design buildings that will keep their occupants warm in cold places and cool in hot places and that respond to the diversity of the seasons. This is all of immense practical value and has been given further impetus with the emergence, in the last couple of decades, of the concern to make buildings more 'environmentally friendly', indeed to be overtly 'climate-responsive'.

Here we have two complementary but quite distinct views of the relationship between climate and architecture. The first, from Pevsner, is firmly located in the humanities, the second, from Olgyay, Givoni, *et al.*, in the applied sciences. This distinction reflects the notion of 'two cultures' that was first articulated in 1959 by C. P. Snow (3). For over a decade, a theme in my writing has been to try and bridge this cultural gap in the study and understanding of the environmental function of architecture. The present book is a further instalment in this project. In *The Environmental Imagination* (2008) I explored the relationship of what I chose to call the *technics and poetics of the architectural environment*, through a group of essays ranging over the timescale of the nineteenth and twentieth centuries and, geographically, embracing western Europe and north America (4). My method is to explore specific themes within that framework in the hope that these would, individually and cumulatively, connect the worlds of, in the terms of the book's subtitle, the technics and poetics of the architectural environment. Here I attempt to work on a similarly broad canvas in bringing together the culture and science of architecture's relationship with climate.

Terms of reference

The present book is, in some respects, a development of the themes explored in *The Environmental Imagination*. Although buildings by Sir John Soane, Charles Rennie Mackintosh and the contemporary practice of Caruso St John helped to illustrate that argument, the works of many other British architects could also have served to support the thesis. Similarly, the link between architecture and climate was more implicit than explicit. Upon reflection, it seems to me that my argument could be fruitfully pursued by making a study of the relation of architecture and climate as this may be discovered in the history of British architecture.

In developing this line of research my aim has been to propose an alternative reading of the link between architecture and climate. In architectural science the method is invariably to represent buildings as a logical response to a pre-existing climate. This is, of course, the process that is observed in all practical circumstances. The climate exists. The building, in various manners and degrees, responds to this. But, in taking a historical standpoint, buildings may be seen, in some respects, both to represent and to interpret the climate that shaped them. What I am trying to show is that the meeting of architecture and climate is as much a question of history and culture as it is of technology.

This study is concerned with the architecture and climate of the British Isles and the timeframe extends from the last decades of the fifteenth century to the last decades of the twentieth. The nature of the British climate is comprehensively documented in terms of conventional meteorology. The Meteorological Office (5) is the principal source of contemporary climate data and there are numerous other substantial modern sources that are relevant to this study. There is also a vast resource in the field of climate history (6). In addition I have tried to draw upon the richness of English literature in providing insights into the representation of climate and its impact on human affairs (7). A further important source is the visual representation of the British climate in fine art, as painters have depicted both country and city (8).

The choice of this timeframe is, in part, related to the availability of meteorological records, but is mostly a matter of architectural history. To establish the ground of the study, I begin with Summerson's encyclopaedic *Architecture in Britain: 1530–1830* (9). In proceeding from the 'English

Renaissance' of the late Tudors and the Stuarts to the first decades of the nineteenth century, Summerson sets out an ideal framework for the present study. His narrative is carried through the study of the works of individual architects, and this is particularly important. There are important studies that examine the relationship between climate and vernacular building (10). My concern in this research, however, is to show that the influence of climate is also felt in the designs of those who consciously – perhaps self-consciously – practise the art of architecture. The account continues, from the conclusion of Summerson's study, through the nineteenth century and onwards towards the end of the twentieth, in order to capture other significant events in the unfolding relation of architecture and climate in Britain.

A final reference in helping to define the structure of the book is to the ideas and practices of the architects Alison and Peter Smithson. To characterize their response to the English climate, the Smithsons wrote (11):

> The stress is on the needs for immediacy of response and reaction to the changeable weather of England; the almost constant need for full or partial weather protection from one quarter or another, a need that can change several times throughout an afternoon . . . Northern Europe involves us inevitably in sun acceptance, amelioration of climate and, above all, of exclusion of rain.

For architects of any environmental sensibility this kind of perception would follow, almost unconsciously, from the experience of living England. But the Smithsons frequently brought historical observation into play in support of their insights and, on environmental matters, a frequent reference was to the buildings of their Elizabethan namesake, Robert Smythson. The coincidence of name may have had some bearing on their initial attraction to his work, but this would, almost certainly, have been primarily in response to the overwhelming presence and substance of Smythson's buildings. Peter Smithson made observations regarding Robert's great house, Hardwick Hall, on a number of occasions (12):

> In Hardwick New Hall there is a gallery which runs along the whole extent of the house. What's nice about (the plan) is that it indicates the thick spine wall, where the fireplaces are . . . and the perimeter bay windows that let in the light. . . . in the winter you have screens around the gallery against the fireplaces, and in the summer you moved into the bay windows.

I begin the essays that follow with a study of the Elizabethan houses of Robert Smythson and close with an account of the environmentalism of Alison and Peter Smithson.

Architecture and the British climate

At the end of the sixteenth century Britain was in the grip of the 'Little Ice Age'. Throughout Europe in the years from 1560 to 1600 temperatures were markedly cooler and winds stormier than any experienced in the twentieth century. Specifically, the 1590s was the coldest decade of the entire century (13). In 1590 Robert Smythson (14), in collaboration with Elizabeth, Countess of Shrewsbury, began the construction of one of the most remarkable buildings in Britain. On an exposed Derbyshire hilltop, 179 metres above sea level, arose Hardwick Hall (Plate 1). Elizabeth, or Bess of Hardwick as she is almost always known, first occupied the house in October 1597. The house is remarkable for many reasons, but for present purposes we should note the apparent contradiction between its location, form and construction and the extreme climate of the time. Hardwick, which is visible from miles around, quickly acquired the appellation 'Hardwick Hall, more glass than wall', and with its strict symmetries, flat roofs and enormous windows on all faces, would seem at first sight to defy climatic logic. But architecture is a complex business and one of the lessons of Hardwick and of other designs by Smythson, such as his remarkable Wollaton Hall near Nottingham and Bolsover Castle, close by Hardwick, is that nature and art may be reconciled in surprising ways. Behind their apparent formal abstractions these buildings reveal subtle accommodations to the climate and to the needs and complexities of human inhabitation.

The seventeenth century saw the development of scientific instruments for many purposes. Amongst these were the first devices for measuring and recording elements of the climate, and by the middle years of the century the first reliable thermometers and barometers had been demonstrated (15) and thus allowed subjective experiences to be supplemented by quantification. This was to have a significant influence on the understanding of climate and to promote the application of new knowledge to practical affairs. Christopher Wren was both scientist and architect (16). In 1936, Summerson wrote revealingly about the influence of Wren's scientific mind on his architecture, and more recently the question has been revisited at length by the historian of science J. A. Bennett (17). Neither, however, addresses the possibility that the scientist might have developed a particular appreciation of climate and that this might be manifest in the fundamentals of his architecture. In *Heavenly Mansions* Summerson provides an intriguing juxtaposition between an engraving of a 'weather-clock' devised by Wren, probably dating from 1663 or shortly after, and Loggan's engraving of the south façade of the Sheldonian

Theatre (1662–1663) (18). This coincidence of dates suggests that there is a case for interpreting Wren's architecture from a climatic viewpoint. The luminosity of St James, Garlickhythe, often referred to as 'Wren's Lantern', or of the great library at Trinity College in Cambridge (Plate 2) lend support to this reading.

Summerson defined the years from 1710 to 1750 as the 'Palladian Phase' of British architecture, writing, 'During this period . . . a set of distinct ideas as to what was good in architecture became widely held, and standards, based on the acknowledged excellence of certain architects and authors, were widely endorsed.' (19). The principal documentary influence on English Palladianism was Palladio's *I quattro libri dell'architettura*. Published in Italy in 1570, this was first translated into English by Giacomo Leoni in 1715–1720, followed in 1738 by Isaac Ware's more accurate translation, *Andrea Palladio's Architecture in Four Books* (20). In the First Book, Palladio provides explicit guidelines concerning a number of matters that are directly related to climate. Detailed prescriptions are given for the dimensions of windows in relation to the size of rooms in order to ensure sufficient daylight and to avoid too much heat or cold according to the season. Formulae are also given for the location and dimensions of chimneys. Bringing an architecture conceived in the climate of the Veneto to the cooler conditions of Britain meant that these relationships of solid to void, window to room were invalid. The pragmatic British easily understood this, and a defining characteristic of British Palladianism is the climatic fine-tuning that it demonstrates. This can be identified in the buildings themselves, at Houghton Hall, Chiswick House (Plate 3) and Mereworth, but theoretical consolidation may also be found in a number of eighteenth-century treatises by, amongst others, Colen Campbell, Robert Morris and William Chambers (21). Awareness of climate was widespread in eighteenth-century England as part of a growing interest in natural history, primarily amongst the gentry and clergy. Of these, one of the most celebrated was Gilbert White, the curate of the village of Selborne in Hampshire. The author of *The Natural History of Selborne* (22) kept, from 1768 to 1793, journals in which he recorded daily observations of rural life, always against the background of descriptions of the climate. These provide vivid evidence of the persistence of the Little Ice Age at this period, recording on 13 February 1784 that 'This evening the frost has lasted 28 days.' And, on 21 June, the summer solstice, 'Dark and chilly rain. Cold and comfortless.' But the summers could be warm, as, for example, when White recorded on 24 June 1786, 'Wheat is I bloom, and has had a fine, still, dry warm season for blowing.' (23)

The climate of a city inevitably differs from that of the surrounding countryside. In 1661 John Evelyn published *Fumifugium or The Inconveniencie of the Aer and Smoak of London Dissipated. Together with some Remedies humbly*

Proposed (24). There he described at length the horrors of the 'Hellish and dismal Cloud of SEA-COAL' that covered the city, the city of Christopher Wren. But even the campaigning authority of Evelyn failed to remedy the problem and by the beginning of the nineteenth century the problem was, if anything, even worse (25). By this time meteorological observation, whilst still largely undertaken by amateurs, was on a substantial scientific foundation. A major figure was Luke Howard, whose *The Climate of London* (1818 and 1833) not only collated extensive data on the climate of the metropolis, but drew precise comparisons between the city and the surrounding countryside (26). As cities grew rapidly and new techniques for building became commonplace, new relationships were forged between architecture and climate and, in particular, with the polluted urban climate. The design of newly conceived building types – the gentlemen's clubs, public libraries and the great museums – incorporated new devices for central heating, mechanical ventilation, and artificial lighting. These extended the practical hours of inhabitation of buildings, both by day and night and throughout the seasons of the year. They also made it possible to create cleaner and healthier environments within a building as a refuge from the conditions of the city without. In parallel with developments in practice, a number of important 'theoretical' texts by authors such as Walter Bernan, D. B. Reid and Charles James Richardson (27) were published. To the end of his life, Sir John Soane continued his experiments with heating installations, and these proved essential to his designs for the Bank of England and the Law Courts at Westminster. Following the disastrous fire of 1834, the ventilation of the rebuilt Palace of Westminster became the subject of considerable debate and dispute, at the centre of which was Reid in his role as a consultant to the architect Charles Barry (28). Many of the significant architects of the time readily incorporated these devices in their designs. Particularly important examples include gentlemen's clubs, such as Charles Barry's Reform Club (Plate 4), great museums such as Alfred Waterhouse's Natural History Museum and highly specialized structures such as the Reading Room at the British Museum (29).

Towards the end of the nineteenth century British domestic architecture gained an international reputation (30). Inspired by the theories of William Morris, a group of talented architects created an architecture that had its roots in both the traditions and contexts of vernacular building. Philip Webb was Morris's own architect in making the Red House (1859) and he and his exact contemporary, Norman Shaw, prepared the ground for the outpouring of remarkable houses by a younger generation of architects, including C. F. A. Voysey, W. R. Lethaby, M. H. Baillie Scott, Edward Prior, Parker and Unwin, and Charles Rennie Mackintosh (31). The majority of these houses were sited in leafy suburbs of the expanding cities or, in a number of cases, deep in the countryside made accessible by the development of the new commuter railways. In this respect they may be interpreted as marking a strong contrast to the buildings in the inhospitable climate of the industrial city. But climate, however benign, may be shown to have a strong influence on their form, planning and materiality. Voysey wrote emphatically that 'We are not Greeks, nor have we a Grecian climate . . .' and went on to offer a poetic interpretation of the significance of climate in defining the essence of an English architecture. '. . . a careful study of our climate makes us emphasise our roofs to suggest protection from weather. Large massive chimneys imply stability and repose. Long, low buildings also create a feeling of restfulness and spaciousness. Small windows in relation to wall space suggest protection' (32). A more specific climate response of Arts and Crafts architects was their commitment to achieving good orientation. For example, Parker and Unwin wrote, '. . . no sacrifice is too great which is necessary to enable us to bring plenty of sunshine into all main living rooms' (33). Similar statements may be found in the writings of Voysey, Baillie Scott and others, and their buildings consistently demonstrate their respect for the principle (Plate 5). In the field of climate science, the British Meteorological Office was established in 1854, principally to provide forecasts for mariners and, in 1861, began publishing daily weather forecasts in the national press (34). At the same time, the rigours of the Little Ice Age had now finally disappeared and there emerged a pervading sense of climatic well-being. It is, perhaps, significant that Jane Brown entitled her book on the partnership of Edwin Lutyens and Gertrude Jekyll, *Gardens of a Golden Afternoon* (35).

In 1929 Le Corbusier proposed a new relationship between architecture and climate when, in one of the lectures he gave on a visit to Buenos Aires, he declared, 'Every country builds its houses in response to climate. At this moment of general diffusion, of international scientific techniques, I propose only one house for all countries, the house of *exact breathing*.' (36). It has been shown, however, that, in this respect, Le Corbusier's practise frequently contradicted his rhetoric (37). Throughout his life many of his designs, from the white villas of Purism to the Indian works of his later years, were finely calibrated to specific conditions of climate. And an acute sensibility to matters environmental – to *milieu* lies at the heart of *Le Poème de l'Angle Droit* (38). The influence of the Arts and Crafts movement upon international Modernism has been widely argued in both early and recent writings (39). In most cases the connection between the two movements is seen in terms of the influence of the material and even moral theories of the Arts and Crafts upon Modernism. When, however, we consider the relation between Arts and Crafts and Modern architecture in Britain, the influence of the seemingly benign climate becomes strongly apparent. The beginning of radio broadcasts of weather forecasts was firmly established by the foundation of the British Broadcasting Company – later the British

Broadcasting Corporation – in 1922. A decade later, as a symbol of the new emphasis of climate in architecture, the Royal Institute of British Architects commissioned a 'Joint Committee on the Orientation of Buildings' to conduct a detailed study of how to maximize the benefits of sunlight (40). In buildings of many functions, and most particularly in design for houses, architects, including George Checkley, Connell, Ward and Lucas, Maxwell Fry, Berthold Lubetkin, Leslie Martin, and Sadie Speight, began subtly to transform the principles of the new architecture in response to the unique qualities of the British climate (Plate 6).

In conclusion, we come to the perspective that was brought to the relationship between architecture and the English climate by Alison and Peter Smithson. The Smithsons were major figures in the theory and practice of British architecture for some 40 years (41). Throughout their work ran a strand of awareness of climate in shaping the essence of architecture. This was manifest in designs for buildings in many climates, for example in projects for the Hospital of Santa della Scala in Sienna (1987) and the competition entry for the Bibliotheca Alexandrina (1989). But they expressed a particular engagement with specific nature of the English climate early in their work in the project for 'The English Climate House' (1957). Following this, it is possible to identify a deeply perceptive and expressive take on the relation between architecture and climate in a sequence of built and unbuilt projects for buildings of many types. The Smithsons' environmental sensibility is strikingly evident, although in contrasting situations in their designs for the Sugden House (1955–1956), in the suburbs of Watford to the north of London and their own weekend house, Upper Lawn Pavilion (1959–1962) in an idyllic rural setting in Wiltshire (Plate 7).

Notes

1. Nikolaus Pevsner, *The Englishness of English Art*, first published by the Architectural Press, London, 1956; republished by Peregrine, Harmondsworth, 1964.

2. Victor Olgyay, *Design with Climate: Bioclimatic Approach to Architectural Regionalism*, Princeton University Press, Princeton, NJ, 1963. Baruch Givoni, *Man, Climate and Architecture*, Elsevier, Amsterdam, 1969. Thorben Dahl (ed.), *Climate and Architecture*, Routledge, London, 2010.

3. C. P. Snow, *The Two Cultures and the Scientific Revolution*, Cambridge University Press, Cambridge, 1959.

4. The subject has been pursued in a series of books: *The Environmental Tradition* (1996); *The Selective Environment* (with Jane McDonald and Koen Steemers) (2002); and *The Environmental Imagination* (2008); all Spon Press/Routledge, London.

5. See the National Meteorological Library and Archive, Exeter. www.metoffice.gov.uk/corporate/library.

6. See, for example, H. H. Lamb, *Climate, History and the Modern World*, Routledge, London, 2nd edition, 1995.

7. Here a good point of departure is Jonathan Bate, *The Song of the Earth*, Picador, London, 2000.

8. See John E. Thornes, 'A Rough Guide to Environmental Art', *Annual Review of Environment and Resources*, Vol. 33, 2008, pp. 391–411. This outlines the ground in art from John Constable to James Turrell. Thornes' *John Constable's Skies: A Fusion of Art and Science*, University of Birmingham Press, Birmingham, 1999, is an extensive study of the relationship between Constable and the work of the important nineteenth-century meteorologist Luke Howard, who produced the first systematic taxonomy of cloud formations.

9. John Summerson, *Architecture in Britain: 1530–1830*, Penguin, Harmondsworth, 1953; 9th revised edition, Yale University Press, New Haven, CT, 1993.

10. See, for example, Paul Oliver (ed.), *Encyclopedia of Vernacular Architecture of the World*, Cambridge University Press, Cambridge, 1997.

11. Alison and Peter Smithson, *The Charged Void: Architecture*, Monacelli Press, New York, 2002.

12. Catherine Spellman and Carl Unglaub (eds), *Peter Smithson, Conversations with Students: A Space for Our Generation*, Princeton Architectural Press, New York, 2005.

13. Brian Fagan, *The Little Ice Age: How Climate Made History, 1300–1850*, Basic Books, New York, 2000.

14. Mark Girouard's, *Robert Smythson and the Elizabethan Country House*, Yale University Press, New Haven, CT, 1983, is the standard reference for the life and work of Smythson.

15. W. E. Knowles Middleton, *Invention of the Meteorological Instruments*, Johns Hopkins University Press, Baltimore, 1969, provides an extensive history of these and other instruments.

16. Lisa Jardine's *On a Grander Scale: the Outstanding Career of Sir Christopher Wren*, Harper Collins, London, 2002, is a detailed study of his work in both fields.

17. John Summerson, 'The Mind of Wren', awarded the RIBA Essay Medal, 1936, printed in *RIBA Journal*, 1936, and reprinted in John Summerson, *Heavenly Mansions and Other Essays on Architecture*, Cresset Press, London, 1949. J. A. Bennett, *The Mathematical Science of Christopher Wren*, Cambridge University Press, Cambridge, 1982.

18. Summerson, 'The Mind of Wren', Plates XI and XII. Knowles Middleton, *Invention of the Meteorological Instruments*, cited in Note 15, gives an extensive account of Wren's work in the development of 'meteorographs' in which he includes the same engraving.

19. Summerson, *Architecture in Britain: 1530–1830*, cited in Note 9.

20. See Robert Tavernor, *Palladio and Palladianism*, Thames and Hudson, London, 1991.

21. Relevant texts include Colen Campbell, *Vitruvius Britannicus or the British Architect*, 1715–1725; Robert Morris, *Lectures on Architecture*, 1734–1736; and William Chambers, *A Treatise on the Decorative Part of Civil Architecture*, 1759.

22. Gilbert White, *The Natural History of Selborne*, London, 1789, first published 1788–1789, Penguin Classics edition, with Introduction by Richard Mabey, Penguin, Harmondsworth, 1987.

23. Gilbert White, *The Journals of Gilbert White* (ed. Walter Johnson), John Routledge and Sons, London, 1931; paperback edition, Futura, London, 1982.

24. John Evelyn, *Fumifugium or The Inconveniencie of the Aer and the Smoak of London Dissipated. Together with some Remedies humbly Proposed*, printed by W. Godbid for Gabriel Bedel and Thomas Collins, London, 1661.

25. For the most extensive account of the climate history of London, see Peter Brimblecombe, *The Big Smoke: A History of Air Pollution in London since Medieval Times*, Methuen, London, 1987; paperback edition, Routledge, London, 1988.

26. Luke Howard, *The Climate of London*, London, 2 vols, 1818; 2nd edition, 3 vols, 1833.

27. Walter Bernan, *On the History and Art of Warming and Ventilating Buildings*, G. Bell, London, 1845. D. B. Reid, *Illustrations of the Theory and Practice of Ventilating*, London,

1844. Charles James Richardson, *A Popular Treatise on the Warming and Ventilation of Buildings Showing the Advantage of the Improved System of Heated Water Circulation*, John Weale, Architectural Library, London, 1837.

28. M. H. Port (ed.), *The Houses of Parliament*, Paul Mellon Centre for British Art/Yale University Press, New Haven, CT, 1976.

29. For a representative survey of buildings, see *Timeless Architecture* (ed. Dan Cruickshank), The Architectural Press, London, 1985.

30. This reputation was most emphatically signalled by the publication in Germany of Herman Muthesius, *Das Englische Haus*, 3 vols, Ernst Wasmuth, Berlin, 1904–1905. The first three-volume edition in English, edited with an introduction by Dennis Sharp, was published by Frances Lincoln, London, 2007.

31. An overview of the architecture of the Arts and Crafts movement may be found in Peter Davey, *Arts and Crafts Architecture: The Search for Earthly Paradise*, The Architectural Press, London, 1980; revised edition, Phaidon, London, 1997.

32. C.F.A. Voysey, 'Ideas in Things', in *The Arts Connected with Building* (ed. T. Raffles Davidson), Batsford, London, 1909.

33. Barry Parker and Raymond Unwin, *The Art of Building a Home: A Collection of Lectures and Illustrations*, Longmans Green, London, 1901.

34. 'Met Office celebrates 150 years of forecasting for the nation' www.metoffice.gov.uk/media/pdf/g/m/150_years_video_script_01.pdf. 1 August 2011.

35. Jane Brown, *Gardens of a Golden Afternoon: The Story of a Partnership: Edwin Lutyens and Gertrude Jekyll*, Allen Lane/Penguin, London, 1982.

36. Le Corbusier, *Precisions: On the Present State of Architecture and City Planning*, Crès, Paris, 1930; English translation, MIT Press, Cambridge, MA, 1991.

37. See Colin Porteous, *The New eco-Architecture: Alternatives from the Modern Movement*, Spon Press, London, 2002; and Dean Hawkes, 'Essay 2, Le Corbusier and Mies van der Rohe: Continuity and Invention', in *The Environmental Imagination*, Spon Press/Routledge, 2007.

38. Le Corbusier, *Le Poeme de l'Angle Droit*, editions Verve, Paris, 1955; facsimile edition, Fondation Le Corbusier/Editions Connivences, Paris, 1989.

39. See Nikolaus Pevsner, *Pioneers of Modern Design: From William Morris to Walter Gropius*, Museum of Modern Art, New York, 1949; revised edition, Penguin Books, Harmondsworth, 1960 (first published as *Pioneers of the Modern Movement*, Faber and Faber, London, 1936. See also Alan Powers, *Modern: The Modern Movement in England*, Merrell, London, 2005 (this book provides a useful survey of British Modern architecture).

40. RIBA Joint Committee on the Orientation of Buildings, *The Orientation of Buildings*, RIBA, London, 1933.

41. The Smithsons' lives and works are comprehensively presented in the two volumes *The Charged Void: Architecture* and *The Charged Void: Urbanism*, Monacelli Press, New York, 2002 and 2004, respectively.

Essay 1
Climate described

Introduction

> The western and northern parts of the United Kingdom tend to lie close to the normal path of the Atlantic depressions and are mostly cool and windy.
>
> The lowlands of England have a climate similar to that on the continent (drier with a wider range of temperatures than in the north and west). However the winters are not as severe as those on the continent. Overall, the south of the United Kingdom is usually warmer than the north and the west is wetter than the east. The more extreme weather tends to occur in the mountainous regions where it is often cloudy.

This statement from the present-day British Meteorological Office (1) provides a broad description of the climate of the British Isles that would have been recognizable to those living in Britain over the four centuries of architectural history that are the subject of this book. In that period there have been many deviations from the norm, which I will try to identify as the account proceeds, but this nicely sets the scene. We note a climate that is temperate and varies only within moderate limits.

An essential objective background to any historical study of the British climate is provided by the Central England Temperature (CET) series of records. These cover the period from 1772 to 2010 and were first compiled from a variety of historical sources by the meteorologist Gordon Manley (2) and have subsequently been maintained and updated by the Meteorological Office (3). From the earliest date the existence of these records depends on the availability and use of instruments by which the physical variables of climate could be reliably measured. The development of these began at the turn of the sixteenth and seventeenth centuries and they were soon in the hands of numerous amateur enthusiasts eagerly recording temperature, barometric pressure and rainfall in both city and country (4). Therein lies the origins of modern meteorology.

But climate has dimensions that may be captured by means other than the purely quantitative. The Elizabethan buildings of Robert Smythson were constructed at precisely the moment, at the turn of the sixteenth and seventeenth centuries, when the first meteorological instruments were being devised, but there is no evidence that these buildings were in any manner influenced by these early stirrings of modern science. They were, however, profoundly connected to the climate in which they were situated. There is extensive evidence that the climate of the time was keenly observed, recorded and interpreted, using means that were, in their various ways, as acute and influential as those of the new science that was to follow. An invaluable source is William Harrison's *The Description of England*, published in 1587 (5). There, amidst a discourse that spans topics as diverse as 'Of cities and townes', 'Of the manner of building and furniture of our houses', 'Of universities' and 'Of the food and diet of the English', we find a chapter, 'Of the Air, Soil and Commodities of this Island'. In this there is a deeply perceptive account of how best to locate a house in relation to the topography and climate of England.

At the time of Shakespeare the English language was richly able to encompass all aspects of human experience, and we shall see how the literary mode served, and continues to serve, as an essential and rich reference in the description and understanding of the climate (6). It is possible to trace a line of climate description in English literature that illuminates aspects of all four of these centuries. Indeed an entire field of environmental discourse has emerged as an important theme in literary criticism (7).

The great households of the sixteenth century were fastidious in the administration of their estates. In their household account books and their frequent inventories of contents we may discover extensive evidence of their understanding of and response to the climate in which they dwelled (8). These practices were maintained into later centuries and provide numerous insights into the ways in which buildings were inhabited as social customs evolved.

A further source of climate description is found in the fine arts. Landscape painting, as an independent genre, other than being the setting for religious, allegorical or portrait painting, is a relatively late development in the history of art. But in the seventeenth century, and in a direct relationship to the establishment of great estates in England, topographical painting became popular as landowners sought to give significance to their properties as extensions and expressions of their personal prestige. From that date to the present, depictions of both the landscape and the city have helped to capture the literal condition of the climate, both at its ideal best and to depict it in its worst states as a contribution to social criticism.

The quantitative record

The Central England Temperature (CET) record depicts the principal parameter of our understanding of and response to climate, that of temperature. The graph, extending over a period of more than two hundred years (Fig. 1.1), distinguishes the fluctuations of temperature year by year and allows an immediate oversight of large-scale variations. The beginning of the record in the middle of the seventeenth century was the mid-point of the period that has become known as 'The Little Ice Age'. This is now quite precisely defined as extending from the fourteenth to the nineteenth centuries and there is extensive documentary evidence of its nature and consequences from archaeological and historical records. An extended review of this is provided by Brian Fagan in *The Little Ice Age* (9). This shows that the last decades of the fourteenth century brought some of the coldest winters in northern Europe in the whole of this period, and this experience continues throughout the next two centuries until in the nineteenth century the temperature began steadily to recover. But, against this generally chilly picture, warm summers could frequently be enjoyed and, in a largely agrarian society, both the rigours and pleasures of the climate were readily experienced, outdoors and indoors, where the interiors of buildings were complex receptors of all the elements.

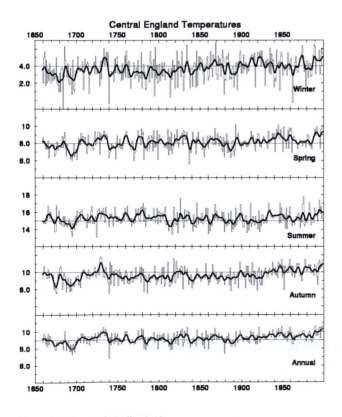

1.1
Central England
Temperature record (CET).

In the seventeenth century the quantitative revolution in meteorology was in full cry and the literature covers many contemporary sources. Christopher Wren with his sometime collaborator Robert Hooke made important contributions to the development of meteorological instruments. In 1662 Wren showed a tipping-bucket rain-gauge at a meeting of the Royal Society, and a version of this was later incorporated into a weather-clock that measured rainfall, temperature and barometric pressure, which was presented to the Society by Hooke in 1679 (10). Here, perhaps uniquely in this entire four centuries of history, we have architecture and climate embodied in the works of one individual (11).

By the last decades of the seventeenth century, weather observation had become a popular activity amongst members of the gentry and country parsons (12). A notable example is the 'Observations of Weather' kept by Sir John Wittewronge of Rothamsted for the years 1684–1689 (13). The winter of 1683–1684 is the coldest in the whole period of the Central England Temperature record. Wittewronge did not have a thermometer, but his written observations capture the nature of the cold. He did possess a 'weather glass' – a barometer – and made use of this, particularly in the winter months, when the primitive instrument would more easily detect the wider fluctuations. He also made careful observations of the wind direction, presumably using the weathervane on his roof.

Particularly valuable sources are a series of papers by, respectively, John Locke and William Derham, published in the *Philosophical Transactions of the Royal Society* (14). In the earliest of these Locke presents 'A Register of the Weather for the Year 1692, Kept at Oates in Essex'. This tabulates seven columns of data. First is 'D' for the day of the month. Next is 'H' for the hour of the day. 'Ther.' is the 'Thermoscope' reading of temperature, 'Bar.' is 'Mercury in the Baroscope' and 'Hyg.' is 'Moisture of the air', which was measured using 'the beard of a wild oat.' A wind column gives the wind direction in relation to the cardinal points and a numerical code related to the wind speed in the following terms.

1. When it just moved the leaves.
2. When it blew a pretty fresh gale.
3. When it was a hard and whistling wind.
4. When it blew a storm.

The final column is a general note on the 'Weather' in terms such as 'Frost, Fair', 'Cloudy, a little Rain next morning'.

William Derham's contributions extend over the period from 1698 to 1731 and are particularly valuable in presenting descriptions of the instruments that were used in the recordings of weather events first at

Upminster in Essex and, later, at Windsor. Derham's data are particularly valuable in providing a numerical record of the extreme winters of 1703, 1708–1709 and 1730–1731.

Gilbert White's *The Natural History of Selborne*, 1788–1789 (15) is one of the greatest literary descriptions of English rural life. The evocative account of village events is supported by the detailed descriptions of events, and in particular of the climate, in all its variety, as White recorded these in his journals, kept from 1768 to 1793 (16). The richness of White's description may be represented by the following brief extracts from his notes for the years 1787–1789.

> *Dec. 24.* Deep snow. The Bantham fowls, when first let out, were so astonished at the snow that they flew over the house.
>
> *Dec. 25.* The snow, where level, about one foot in depth: in some places much drifted.
>
> *Feb. 21.* Full moon. Barom. at Newton 28! No wind.
>
> *Apr. 1.* (Selborne) Daffodils in bloom.
>
> *May 18.* A thunder-storm at London that damaged houses.
>
> *July 26.* The fields are now finely diversfyed with ripe corn, hay & harvest scenes, & hops. The whole country round is a charming land-scape . . .
>
> *July 30.* Some workmen, reapers are made sick by the heat.
>
> *Oct. 22.* Much wheat is sown. The fallows are very dry; & the roads clean as in summer.
>
> *Nov. 27.* Some light snow. Boys slide on lakes.
>
> *Dec. 4.* The plows have been stopped by frost some days.
>
> *Dec. 14.* The navigation of the Thames is much interrupted thro' the want of water occasioned by the long dry season.
>
> *Dec. 15.* Therm' 20, 23, 17. Many have been disordered with bad colds and fevers at Oxford. The water in the *apparatus* for making mineral water froze in the red room. The wind is so piercing that the labourers cannot stand to, do their work. Ice in all the chambers. The perforated stopple belonging to the apparatus broke in two by the frost. . . . Shallow snow covers the ground, enough to shelter the wheat.
>
> *Dec. 20.* The frost has now lasted five weeks.
>
> *Dec. 30.* Ice within doors. Rime. Snow on the ground.
>
> *Jan 1.* Snow thick on the ground. Timothy begins to sink his well at the malt-house.

Although White provides only small scraps of quantitative information, it is important to note that, in the lineage of Wittewronge, Locke and Derham, he possessed and used both a barometer and a thermometer and these records help us to relate his vivid verbal descriptions to now familiar measures. Vladimir Jankovic points out that White tended to use his measuring devices primarily in instances of extreme weather, hot or cold, citing the events between 7 and 9 December 1784, when, as the temperature fell rapidly, White hung two thermometers, one by Dollond, the other by Martin, to capture the drama of the extreme temperature (17).

Only three decades after White's book was published, a new figure made some of the most important contributions to the development of meteorology in Britain. Luke Howard was a pharmacist who made comprehensive quantitative records of *The Climate of London* (18). These are significant in regard to the extent and detail of the records and, in comparison with most of the earlier records, bring the focus emphatically onto the urban climate, just as the process of urbanization was gathering pace. Between 1819 and 1827 Howard made daily observations, first at Plaistow and then at Tottenham. These were collated into monthly summaries, which gave daily values of wind direction, maximum and minimum barometric pressure, maximum and minimum temperature, evaporation, hygrometer (i.e. humidity) at 9.00 a.m., and rainfall. Explanatory notes and a monthly summary accompanied each table. The detail of these data exceeds everything before that date.

Howard is probably even more important for his work on the classification of clouds, in which he proposed the system, using the terms cirrus, cumulus, stratus and nimbus, that is the basis of the classification that is still in use today (19). Although he was no more than a competent amateur watercolourist, Howard used the medium as an essential tool in capturing and explaining his observations (20). This aspect of his work and its wider effects in fine art will be revisited later in this essay.

In 1854 the British Meteorological Office was founded as a department of the Board of Trade to provide a service to mariners. Its first director was Robert Fitzroy, who was captain of the *Beagle*, the vessel that conveyed Charles Darwin on his voyage to the Galapagos Islands (21). Over the last 150 years, the services that it has offered have expanded to serve almost all aspects of public and private life. The modern Met Office, with its advanced technology and extensive networks for observation and, now, simulation modelling, continues to play an important role in relation to architecture and the construction industry and offers extensive services at all stages of the design and construction of buildings in Britain and, indeed, further afield (22).

Climate in literature

> When all aloud the wind doth blow,
> And coughing drowns the parson's saw;
> And birds sit brooding in the snow,
> And Marion's nose looks red and raw,
> When roasted crabs hiss in the bowl.
>
> William Shakespeare, *Love's Labour's Lost*,
> Act V, Scene ii

> Shall I compare thee to a summer's day?
> Thou art more lovely and more temperate:
> Rough winds do shake the darling buds of May,
> and summer's lease hath all too short a date:
> Sometimes too hot the eye of heaven shines,
> And often is his gold complexion dimm'd;
>
> William Shakespeare, *The Sonnets*, 18

Descriptions of climate run through Shakespeare's entire corpus and this suggests the extent to which the elements in their ever-changing diversity were present in the Elizabethan mind. Even where the setting is an imagined world far from the British Isles the climate may be seen to be essentially that of England. The Athenians of *A Midsummer Night's Dream* inhabit a wood rich in vegetation common in England at that time (23):

> I know a bank where the wild thyme blows,
> Where oxlips and nodding violet grows,
> Quite over-canopied with luscious woodbine,
> With sweet musk-roses and with eglantine.
>
> William Shakespeare, *A Midsummer Night's
> Dream*, Act 2, Scene i

In the seventeenth century an entire *genre* of the country house poem acquired wide popularity. The most celebrated example is probably Ben Jonson's *To Penshurst*, published in 1616, but many other houses were celebrated in this form (24) and, in doing so, they are frequently placed in descriptions of place that convey a sense of topography and climate, as we shall see later.

In Christopher Wren's day the great diarists Samuel Pepys and John Evelyn fill out the background. Evelyn, in particular, was deeply engaged in the impact of the weather, notably the extreme winters, as he struggled to promote his vision of the garden and the forest as the saviours of society and the environment. In *Sylva*, his discourse on forest trees first published in 1664, Evelyn wrote:

. . . we find that the hot and warmer regions produce the tallest and goodliest trees and plants, in stature and in other properties far exceeding those of the same species, born in the cold north.

(25)

Evelyn's other work of the greatest relevance to our subject is *Fumifugum*, a tract on the polluted atmosphere of London (26). Here he develops what is probably the first study of the effect of human impact on climate – in this case the effect of the enormous consumption of 'sea coal' in the houses and factories of the metropolis, 'sea coal' being coal brought by sea from the north-east of the country.

Jonathan Bate has written that, in the eighteenth century:

Bad weather was a scandal to the modern Constitution. As Serres has remarked, the Enlightenment was one long attempt to repress the weather, to dispel the clouds of unknowing.

(27)

It is in this context that James Thompson's poem *The Seasons*, according to Bate a 'poem in praise of Newton', was published in 1730 (28). In a succinct analysis Martin Price captures the work's essence:

Thompson explored those areas (of climate, weather, of moral choice) where order was threatened and yet could be shown, in a larger frame, to have survived; in doing so he studied natural phenomena with a new closeness and a new feeling for their sublimity, and the result was the displacement of epic action by a descriptive counterpart.

(29)

In the poem the essence of each season is instantly established: 'gentle SPRING', 'refulgent SUMMER', Autumn is 'jovial' and Winter 'sullen and sad'. Here we may glimpse the vision of climate that lay behind the emerging Enlightenment sensibility in Britain.

This essentially eighteenth-century, lyrical, ruralist view of the climate survived as a literary theme to the end of the century and on into the first decades of the next. Jonathan Bate invokes Emma Woodhouse, in Jane Austen's novel of 1815, to represent a prevailing impression of well-being as she looks out over the view from Dodswell Abbey (30):

The considerable slope, at nearly the foot of which the Abbey stood, gradually acquired a steeper form beyond its grounds; and at half a mile distant was a bank of considerable abruptness and grandeur, well-clothed with wood; – and at the bottom of this bank, favourably placed and sheltered, rose the Abbey-Mill Farm, with meadows in front and the river making a close and handsome curve around it,

It was a sweet view – sweet to the eye and the mind, English verdure, English culture, English comfort, seen under a bright sun, without being oppressive.

(31)

This is a pre-industrial landscape, whose preservation in literary form is, to some degree, in defiance of the changes to both agricultural practices and to the wider implications of industrialization and urbanization that were beginning to be felt in traditional, conservative culture. Verdure, culture, comfort are precisely connected to a description of the English climate at its most agreeable, 'a bright sun, without being oppressive'. The cultural historian Jan Golinski has nicely summarized the manner in which climate came to be a symbol of national character:

The British weather came to be seen as an example of God's providential goodness to the island's people, His benevolence in bestowing upon them conditions that fostered the growth of agriculture and commerce. The national climate was represented as bound up with the character of the people and a condition of the progress of their civilization.

(32)

At the same date the state of the city and its climate was already beginning to exert an influence on the priorities of literature. Byron's *Don Juan* was written between 1819 and 1823 and there we find in the Don's impression of his first sight of London a new and predominantly negative representation of the urban climate:

A mighty mass of brick and smoke, and shipping,
Dirty and dusky, but as wide as eye
Could reach, with here or there a sail just skipping
In sight, then lost amidst the forestry
Of masts; a wilderness of steeples peeping
On tiptoe through their sea-coal canopy;

A huge dun cupola, like a foolscap crown
On a fool's head – and there is London Town!

(33)

Just three years before *Don Juan*, Byron's poem, *Darkness*, describes an extreme climatic event:

I had a dream, which was not all a dream.
The bright sun was extinguish'd, and the stars
Did wander darkling in the eternal space,
Rayless, and pathless, and the icy earth
Swung blind and blackening in the moonless air;
Morn came and went – and came, and brought no day,

(34)

The climate in 1816, the year of the poem's composition, was recorded, across Europe and the United States, as unusually cold. Byron was living in Geneva, where Jonathan Bate reports that it rained on 130 of the 183 days between April and September and the average temperature in July was 4.9° Fahrenheit below the monthly mean. In London the temperature at noon on 1 September was 47° Fahrenheit, in comparison with the monthly average for the previous September of 63° (35). Bate proposes that the 'Year without a summer' may have been the consequence of the eruption of the Tambora volcano in Indonesia in the previous year, 1815, with effects that lasted for at least three years, rendering Byron's poem, '. . . as contemporary as it is apocalyptic'.

The climate of London is a powerful metaphor in Charles Dickens' 'London' novels, where he demonstrates a keen awareness of the language of meteorological science as he sets the scene for his dramas. In *Little Dorrit* the microclimate of Southwark is given the most vivid characterization:

The morning light was in no hurry to climb the prison wall and look in at the Snuggery windows; and when it did come it would have been more welcome if it had come alone, instead of bringing a rush of rain with it. But the equinoctial gales were blowing out at sea, and the impartial south-west wind, in its flight, would not neglect even the narrow Marshalsea. While it roared through the steeple of St. George's Church, and twirled all the cowls in the neigh-bourhood, it made a swoop to beat the Southwark smoke into the jail; and, plunging down the chimneys of the

few early collegians who were yet lighting their fires, half
suffocated them.

(36)

In reaction to the increasingly disagreeable climate of the nineteenth
century city, it became commonplace for the new professional classes –
lawyers, bankers, stockbrokers – who made their livelihoods in the city to
reside in the healthier climate of the surrounding countryside. The new
suburban railways made this arrangement convenient, and wives and children
could flourish in houses and gardens set in clear, clean air and sunshine. The
most potent literary evocation of this arrangement is probably E. M. Forster's
novel *Howard's End*, published in 1910 (37). The book takes its title from the
name of the house that is the setting of many of the significant events of the
narrative. Many of the nineteenth-century *nouveau riche* built new houses in
the suburban countryside; others, like Forster's Wilcox family, took over old
houses and adapted them to their modern needs. At the beginning of the
novel Margaret Schlegel, a houseguest, writes to her sister Helen, who
remains in London:

> I'm writing before breakfast. Oh the beautiful vine leaves!
> The house is covered with a vine. I looked out earlier and
> Mrs. Wilcox was already in the garden. She evidently loves
> it. . . . She was watching the large red poppies come out. . . .
> The air here is delicious.

Three days later Margaret writes:

> Marvellous weather and the air is marvellous – views
> westward to the high ground.

Here is a representation of the English climate that reflects a new social order
that, although available only to a privileged few, under-pinned one of the
most productive and internationally acknowledged phases of recent
architectural history, the house designs of the architects of the Arts and
Crafts movement.

In the twentieth century the city continued to be represented in the
negative image of much of nineteenth century literature. T. S. Eliot's *The
Waste Land* depicts London still fogbound in 1922:

> Unreal City,
> Under the brown fog of a winter dawn,

A crowd flowed over London Bridge, so many,
I had not thought death had undone so many.

(38)

But, in those early days of modernity, more optimistic metaphors also had their place. Virginia Woolf's Clarissa Dalloway sets out to walk in London on a bright June morning:

> For it was the middle of June. The War was over . . . The King and Queen were at the Palace. And everywhere, though it was still so early there was a beating, a stirring of galloping ponies, tapping of cricket bats; Lords, Ascot, Ranelagh and all the rest of it; wrapped in the soft mesh of the grey-blue morning air, which, as the day wore on, would unwind them . . .

(39)

This is the context in which new ideas about architecture and the city would emerge. An architecture in which light, space and air would become important influences upon form, detail and material.

Only three years after the publication of *Mrs Dalloway*, Evelyn Waugh vividly depicted the response of modern architecture to the English climate in *Decline and Fall* (40). Waugh's purpose in describing Professor Otto Friedrich Silenius' design for 'King's Thursday', built to replace a much loved Tudor house, is more satirical than admiring, but nonetheless provides a glimpse of the environmental essence of the new architecture. The protagonist, Paul Pennyfeather, approaches the house for his first visit:

> The temperate April sunlight fell through the budding chestnuts and revealed between their trunks green glimpses of parkland and the distant radiance of a lake. 'English spring,' thought Paul. . . . And surely it was the spirit of William Morris that whispered to him . . . about seed-time and harvest, the superb succession of the seasons . . . But at a turn in the drive the cadence of his thoughts was abruptly transacted. They had come into sight of the house.

Next morning Paul awoke to the full, bright, environmental experience of the new house:

> The aluminium blinds shot up, and the sun poured in through the vita-glass, filling the room with beneficent rays. Another day had begun at King's Thursday.

Waugh's satire implies that this new architecture stands at odds with the enduring qualities of the English climate and landscape, but both his and Virginia Woolf's presentations of a bright, optimistic climate are in tune with the particular interpretation of architectural modernism that was to emerge in Britain between the wars.

Painting the climate

The Flemish painter Jan Siberechts (1627–1703) has a claim to be the founder of British landscape painting (41). His last known work, dated 1698, is a panoramic view of 'Henley on Thames' (Plate 8). With its dramatic light and double rainbow this is probably more a product of the artist's imagination than a true meteorological record, but nonetheless it captures the changeability of the English climate, even in the relatively benign situation of the Thames valley. Of direct relevance to the present study is the view of 'Wollaton Hall and Park' that Siberechts painted in 1695 (Plate 9). This shows Robert Smythson's remarkable house over a century after its completion, with numerous alterations to its immediate surroundings, but illustrating the agreeable, temperate microclimate that may be enjoyed in the south-east-facing garden, with its fountain and ornamental trees. Under a bright sky with high white clouds, the cultivated landscape close to the house shades into the wilder uplands of the distant Peak District. All this is unmistakably English.

Antonio Canaletto arrived in London from Venice in 1746, eighteen years after the death of Christopher Wren. Canaletto's many depictions of London show the city of Wren, with St Paul's surrounded by its palisade of city church spires. In many of these paintings London almost becomes Venice, with skies of the brightest blue and the river filled with a dense traffic of exotic craft. In the year of his arrival, 1746, Canaletto made two versions of a 'View of London from Richmond House' (Plate 10). Waterhouse declares that:

> He never painted better pictures in his life. The enchantment of Venetian sunshine was still upon him, the weather when he was painting them must have been fine, and the two most sparkling views of London that have ever been achieved were produced sprinkled with little figures as alive and full of London character as his Venetian figures were alive with the *genius loci*.
>
> (42)

Close scrutiny of these paintings suggests that the artist, in his first encounters with London and its climate, readily made the translation from the lagoon to the Thames. The tones are muted and the light, from a clear but hazy midday sky, casts gentle shadows. Wren's spires and the south façade of St Paul's reflect the gentle light and warmth of the northern sun. The figures in the foreground are comfortable without the need to seek shade, not a parasol is to be seen, and the seats placed against the garden wall are an encouragement to linger.

At almost the same date as Canaletto created this wonderful image, Thomas Gainsborough painted 'Mr and Mrs Andrews' (1749) (Plate 11). Here is a rural parallel to that serene depiction of London. The Andrews pose in bright light overlooking the rolling landscape of their estate. The signs of harvest in the foreground, the foliage just on the point of turning and Mr Andrews' hunting gun and dog suggest that this is late summer, but it is still pleasant to be out of doors. Just out of view we may imagine a Palladian villa, itself a translation of the Veneto to the English climate.

We encountered the meteorologist Luke Howard earlier in this essay, when we discussed his comprehensive study *The Climate of London* (43). Howard's enduring contribution to meteorology is now recognized to be his classification of clouds that he published in 1803 and which remains the basis for the system still in use today (44). In this work Howard's method was to make watercolour renderings of his observations of the skies, and, although these are barely works of art, they demonstrate the utility of the graphic method in this aspect of meteorological observation (Plate 12). In the early years of the nineteenth century 'sky studies' were made by a number of significant artists as they strove to bring a more scientific realism to their landscape paintings, the most notable of these artists being Turner and Constable (45). Thomas Werner suggests that Constable's are the most realistic representations of the English sky and attributes this, in the first place, to his native, flat Suffolk landscape, which is dominated by the enormous skies. In the 1820s Constable made numbers of 'cloud studies', which were primarily matters of record, not fine art, and were in some cases supplemented by written notes of the weather conditions at the time of their painting.

Gustave Doré's *London: A Pilgrimage* was published in 1872 (46). The 180 engravings in the book present a dark image of the city and are powerfully supplemented by Blanchard Jerrold's accompanying texts. On the day of the Oxford and Cambridge Boat Race, 6 April 1870, Jerrold provides perhaps the most detailed and vivid description of the London fog:

> We were well in to the morning and it was as dark as the
> darkest midnight. The two Pilgrims confronted one another
> Candle in hand, speculating on the turn of affairs would take

on the river, in presence of a completely representative London fog. It was choking: it made the eyes ache. It rolled into the house, as a visitor remarked, like a feather bed, at the heels of every arrival. For sky we had a deep yellow-orange roof across the street: and about the street red specks of light played, borne by lads and men whose voices seemed to reach us through woollen comforters. A fog almost equal to this had surprised us on an early journey – when a coffee-stall proved a most welcome illumination to us.

The practical effect of the fogs on everyday life in the metropolis was clearly entirely negative, as Peter Brimblecombe records in *The Big Smoke* (47), a comprehensive history of London's atmosphere, but there were some for whom the effect was an inspiration. The most notable of these, perhaps, was Claude Monet, who painted his 'London series' between 1899–1905. These evocative images show the river Thames, invariably seen through swirling mists. A striking example is 'The Houses of Parliament, sunlight in the fog' (1904) (Plate 13), which shows the Palace of Westminster from a vantage point within the site of St Thomas's hospital on the opposite bank. A recent study by Jacob Baker and John E. Thornes has revealed the meteorological accuracy of Monet's representation of the sun's position in this and others of the London series (48). They calculate that this image shows the sun in the late afternoon on a day in mid-March. Such analytical precision is interesting in establishing a 'scientific' dimension to the work of this great artist, but, for us, these paintings are more valuable in their more positive representation of London and its climate at the opening of the new century.

Just when Monet was about to begin the London series, Ebenezer Howard published one of the most important critiques of the nineteenth-century industrial city in *Tomorrow: A Peaceful Path to Real Reform* (49). In his 'Three Magnets' diagram, Howard compared the virtues and vices of the town and the country to show that the idea of the 'town–country', the Garden City, offered the virtues of each, without the vices. Amongst the disadvantages of the town he listed 'fogs and droughts, foul air, murky skies', while in the town–country citizens would enjoy 'beauty of nature, pure air and water, bright homes and gardens, no smoke'.

The Garden City is, in effect, the city of the Arts and Crafts movement, and the first Garden City, at Letchworth in Hertfordshire, has many fine examples of Arts and Crafts houses by architects including M. H. Baillie Scott and the partnership of Barry Parker and Raymond Unwin, who were the overall planners of the city, following a competition held in 1903. The new city attracted many radicals and idealists, amongst them a number of artists. One of the most notable of these was Harold Gilman, who was, with Walter Sickert and Spencer Gore, a member of the Camden Town Group of painters (50).

As their name indicates, these artists were primarily observers of the urban scene, and their works often touched upon the darkest aspects of life in the city, most strikingly in the so-called 'Camden Town Murder' series painted by Sickert between 1907 and 1909. In marked contrast to these scenes, some members of the group developed an interest in the Garden City. In 1909 Gilman moved to a new house at 100 Wilbury Road in Letchworth, designed by Parker and Unwin. In 1912 Gilman was away on a painting trip to Scandinavia and rented the house to Spencer Gore. In a period of four months between August and November, Gore made more than twenty striking paintings of the Garden City, including a number that depict Gilman's house (51). The example here was probably the first painting Gore made during his stay (Plate 14). With its clear blue sky, strongly contrasted tile roofs and full-blown, late summer English garden, this wonderfully illustrates the translation of Howard's vision into built reality and captures much of the ambience that was sought by the architects of the Arts and Crafts Movement in their combination of house and garden as a seamless whole.

Landscape painting continued to occupy British artists throughout the twentieth-century as painting moved into new modes and methods. A major figure in British art in the first half of the century was Paul Nash (1889–1946). Nash's greatest recognition is for the war paintings he made in both the First and Second World Wars. These depict the ravaged landscapes of the battlefield, but in the years between the wars and, briefly in the 1940s, he turned his attention to the English landscape, producing works that captured both the topography and the changing nature of the seasons (52). This is best shown in the series of paintings made in 1943 and 1944 at Wittenham Clumps, a group of small hills above the Thames valley in Oxfordshire. *Landscape of the summer solstice* (1943) (Plate 15) is a particularly relevant example of these. Nash's written commentary on *Landscape of the Vernal Equinox* (1944) reveals the artist's special insight into meteorological phenomena:

> . . . the idea of simultaneous sun and moon – a red disc and a white . . . on the one side . . . lit by the setting sun . . . while the other lies under the influence of the moon . . . Where the rival illuminations merge in the sky and over the distant view, the intermediate pale greens and green greys and subtleties of brown come into play to complete the full harmony . . .

(53)

Conclusion

In the twenty-first century the relationship between architecture and climate benefits enormously from the sophistication of modern meteorology. In Britain the Met Office provides extensive support to the construction industry through its online and documentary services (54). Research in the field of sustainable architecture and large areas of environmentally aware practice make use of comprehensive meteorological data sets. The value of all of this is inestimable, but in the pursuit of these admirable technological goals we should not overlook the continuing value of other dimensions of climate understanding that lie in the realms of fine art and literature. The works of, amongst many others, Andy Goldsworthy, Richard Long and David Nash, in their different ways, help us register the complexity and richness of British climate and it effects. Although an American, James Turrell's three British 'Sky Spaces', at the Yorkshire Sculpture Park, in the grounds of Houghton Hall in Norfolk (Plate 16) and in Keilder Forest in Northumberland, serve to provide us with a unique vision of the British sky in all its diversity. Turrell wrote about his work in Yorkshire, 'You realise that England is at sea, and this beautiful cloudscape, the greyness of it, was something spectacular to me, and also the fact that I could finally take this sky and give it the blue which is its due' (55). In literature, writers such as J. G. Ballard and Iain Sinclair provide deep, often critical, insights into the often dystopian topography and climate of contemporary Britain. Sinclair's *Edge of the Orison* (56), in which he re-travel's John Clare's 1841 journey from Essex to Northamptonshire, draws a particularly revealing comparison between the pre-industrial terrain of south-east England and its contemporary condition. W. G. Sebald brought the landscape and climate of the county of Suffolk vividly to life in *Rings of Saturn* (57), an account of a walking tour undertaken in 1992, and Roger Deakin's lyrical and detailed nature writing is a further rich source of insight into that county and places further afield (58).

Notes

1. National Meteorological Library and Archive, Exeter, *Climate of the British Isles*, Fact Sheet.

2. G. Manley, 'The mean temperature of central England, 1698–1952', *Quarterly Journal of the Royal Meteorological Society*, Vol. 79, 1953, pp. 242–261, and 'Central England temperatures: monthly mean 1659–1973', *Quarterly Journal of the Royal Meteorological Society*, Vol. 100, 1974, pp. 389–405.

3. D. E. Parker, T. P. Legg and C. K. Folland, 1992, 'A new daily Central England Temperature Series, 1772–1991', *International Journal of Climatology*, Vol. 12, 1992, pp. 317–341.

4. See W. E. Knowles Middleton, *Invention of the Meteorological Instruments*, Johns Hopkins University Press, Baltimore, 1969. An excellent exploration of the activities and achievements of many of these 'amateur' meteorologists may be found in Vladimir Jankovic, *Reading the Skies: A Cultural History Of English Weather, 1650–1820*, University of Chicago Press, Chicago, 2000.

5. William Harrison, *The Description of England*, reprint edition (ed. Georges Edelen), Dover, New York, 1994.

6. See William Shakespeare, *Complete Works* (eds Jonathan Bate and Eric Rasmussen), The Royal Shakespeare Company/Macmillan, London, 2007.

7. A key text is Jonathan Bate, *The Song of the Earth*, Picador, London, 2000. It is an interesting coincidence that two works in this field share titles with two earlier books on the architectural environment by the present author: Laurence Buell (ed.), *The Environmental Imagination: Thoreau, Nature Writing and the Formation of American Culture*, Harvard University Press, Cambridge, MA, 1996, and John Parham (ed.), *The Environmental Tradition in English Literature*, Ashgate Publishing, Farnham, 2002.

8. The original household account books for Hardwick Hall are in the archive of the Chatsworth Settlement. Inventories for Wollaton Hall for the years 1596, 1599, 1601, 1607 and 1609 are included in Pamela Marshall, *Wollaton Hall: An Archaeological Survey*, Nottingham Civic Society, Nottingham, 1996. See also Lindsay Boynton (ed.), *The Hardwick Hall Inventories of 1601*, The Furniture History Society, London, 1971. For a record of the domestic environment of the eighteenth century see T. S. Rosoman, 'The Chiswick House Inventory of 1770', *Furniture History*, No. 22, 1986, pp. 81–105.

9. Brian Fagan, *The Little Ice Age: How Climate Made History 1300–1850*, Basic Books, New York, 2000.

10. See Asit K. Biswas, 'The Automatic Rain-gauge of Sir Christopher Wren', *Notes and Records of the Royal Society of London*, Vol. 22, 1967, pp. 94–104.

11. Lisa Jardine's studies of Wren and Hooke, *On a Grander Scale: The Outstanding Career of Sir Christopher Wren*, Harper Collins, London, 2002, and *The Curious Life of Robert Hooke: The Man Who Measured London*, Harper Collins, London, 2003, explore the complex working and personal relationship of the two men.

12. See Jankovic, *Reading the Skies*, cited in Note 4.

13. Margaret Harcourt Williams and John Stevenson (eds), *'Observations of Weather': The Weather Diary of Sir John Wittewronge of Rothamsted, 1684–1689*, Hertfordshire Record Publications, Hertford, 1999.

14. John Locke, 'A Register of the Weather for the Year 1692, Kept at Oates in Essex', *Philosophical Transactions of the Royal Society*, Vol. 24, 1704–1705, pp. 1917–1937. William Derham, 'The History of the Great Frost in the Last Winter 1703 and 1708/9', *Philosophical Transactions of the Royal Society*, Vol. 26, 1708–1709, pp. 454–478, and 'Concerning Frost in January 1730/1', *Philosophical Transactions of the Royal Society*, Vol. 37, 1731–1732, pp. 16–18.

15. Gilbert White, *The Natural History of Selborne*, first published 1788–1789, Penguin Classics edition, with Introduction by Richard Mabey, Penguin, Harmondsworth, 1987.

16. Gilbert White, *The Journals of Gilbert White* (ed. Walter Johnson), Futura, London, 1982.

17. Jankovic, *Reading the Skies*, cited in Note 4.

18. Luke Howard, *The Climate of London*, London, 2 vols, 1818; 2nd edition, 3 vols, 1833.

19. Luke Howard, 'On the classification of clouds', *Philosophical Magazine*, Vols 16 and 17, 1803–1804.

20. The Royal Meteorological Society has a collection of 51 pencil, ink and watercolour 'Cloud Studies' by Howard, dated 1808 and 1811.

21. A brief history of the Met Office, now its official title, is at www.metoffice.gov.uk/news/in-depth/overview.

22. *Weather and Climate Services for the Global Construction Industry*, The Met Office, Exeter, 2009.

23. None of these plants is a native of England, but in this combination they conjure a compelling image of the English countryside.

24. There is an extensive critical literature on the country house poem. See Alastair Fowler, *The Country House Poem: A Cabinet of Seventeenth-Century Estate Poems and Related Items*, Edinburgh University Press, Edinburgh, 1994.

25. John Evelyn, *Sylva, or a Discourse on Forest Trees*, London, 1664, Chapter 1: 'Of the Earth, Soil, Seed, Air, and Water'.

26. John Evelyn, *Fumifugum, or the Inconveniencie of the Aer and Smoak of London Dissipated. Together With some Remedies humbly Proposed*, London, 1661.

27. Jonathan Bate, *The Song of the Earth*, Picador, London, 2000.

28. James Thomson, *The Seasons*, first complete edition, London, 1730.

29. Martin Price, *The Renaissance and the Eighteenth Century*, The Oxford Anthology of English Literature, Oxford University Press, 1973, p. 637.

30. Bate, *The Song of the Earth*, cited in Note 7.

31. Jane Austen, *Emma*, John Murray, London, 1815.

32. Jan Golinski, *British Weather and the Climate of Enlightenment*, University of Chicago Press, Chicago, 2007.

33. Lord George Gordon Byron, *Don Juan*, cited in Peter Brimblecombe, *The Big Smoke: A History of Air Pollution in London since Medieval Times*, Methuen, London, 1987; paperback edition, Routledge, London, 1988.

34. Lord George Gordon Byron, 'Darkness', in *The Complete Poetical Works*, Clarendon Press, Oxford, 1986.

35. Bate, *The Song of the Earth*, cited in Note 7.

36. Charles Dickens, *Little Dorrit*, first published, 1855–1857; BBC Books edition, London, 2008.

37. E. M. Forster, *Howard's End*, first published Edward Arnold, London, 1910.

38. T. S. Eliot, *The Waste Land*, Faber and Faber, London, 1922.

39. Virginia Woolf, *Mrs Dalloway*, The Hogarth Press, London, 1925.

40. Evelyn Waugh, *Decline and Fall*, Chapman & Hall, London, 1928.

41. Ellis Waterhouse, *Painting in Britain, 1530–1790*, Pelican History of Art, 5th edition, with an introduction by Michael Kitson, Yale University Press, New Haven, CT, 1994.

42. *Ibid.*

43. Howard, *The Climate of London*, cited in Note 18.

44. Howard, 'On the classification of clouds', cited in Note 19.

45. See Thomas Werner, 'Cloud study and the Artists', in *The Cloud Watchers: Art and Meteorology, 1770–1830*, Exhibition Catalogue, Herbert Art Gallery and Museum, Coventry, 1975, and John E. Thornes, *The Accurate Dating of John Constable's Cloud Studies 1821–1822 Using Historical Weather Records*, Department of Geography, University College London, 1978 and *John Constable's Skies: A Fusion of Art and Science*, University of Birmingham Press, Birmingham, 1999.

46. Gustave Doré and Blanchard Jerrold, *London: A Pilgrimage*, Grant, London, 1872; facsimile edition, without Jerrold's extensive text, *Doré's London*, Dover Pictorial Archive Series, Dover, New York, 2004.

47. Brimblecombe, *The Big Smoke*, cited in Note 33.

48. Jacob Baker and John E. Thornes, 'Solar position within Monet's Houses of Parliament', *Proceedings of the Royal Society A*, Vol. 462, 2006, pp. 3775–3788.

49. Ebenezer Howard, *Tomorrow: A Peaceful Path to Real Reform*, London, 1898; reprinted as *Garden Cities of Tomorrow*, S. Sonnenschein, London, 1902.

50. Robert Upstone, *The Camden Town Group*, Exhibition Catalogue, Tate Britain, London, 2008.

51. Rosamond Allwood, *Spencer Gore in Letchworth*, Catalogue of Exhibition at Letchworth Museum and Art Gallery, Letchworth, 2006.

52. David Fraser Jenkins, *Paul Nash: The Elements*, Scala Publishers, London, 2010.

53. Paul Nash, 'Picture History', 1943 TGA 769.1.35 and 39. Tate Archive, cited in Jenkins, *Paul Nash: The Elements*.

54. See www.metoffice.gov.uk/construction for access to, for example, *Consultancy Construction Services Brochure* and *Operational Construction Services Brochure*.

55. James Turrell, quoted in *James Turrell Deer Shelter*, Yorkshire Sculpture Park, Breton, 2006.

56. Iain Sinclair, *Edge of the Orison: In the Traces of John Clare's 'Journey out of Essex'*, Penguin, Harmondsworth, 2006.

57. W. G. Sebald, *Rings of Saturn*, Vintage Classics, London, new edition, 2011.

58. Roger Deakin, *Waterlog: A Swimmer's Journey Through Britain*, Vintage, London, new edition, 2009a; *Wildwood: A Journey Through Trees*, Penguin, Harmondsworth, 2008; and *Notes from Walnut Tree Farm*, Penguin, Harmondsworth, 2009b.

Essay 2
Robert Smythson and the environment of the Elizabethan country house

The fashion for the tall and glassy we tend in England to attribute to a celebration by architects of the 'new' fuel . . . coal. Certainly the Elizabethan house plan is a remarkably climate-conscious machine: sit in the window-bays when the sun shines, retreat behind screens to fires on the spine walls deep in the interior with all one's clothes on when it is cold. Acts of inhabiting full of movement and drama matching the lives of their remarkable owners.

Inside the house not so different from outside . . . keep sheltered when the weather is cold and windy; walk, ride and lie in the open when it is sunny; clothing worn inside being suitable for both indoors and outdoors . . .

(1)

Peter Smithson (1923–2003), the notable twentieth-century British architect made this observation in 1987, at a conference in Munich. He was speaking of the buildings of his namesake, Robert Smythson (1536–1614). Here began a train of thought that has led, over twenty years later, to the present essay, in which Smithson's insight into the relation of architecture and climate in Elizabethan England is explored in depth.

On 4 October 1597, Elizabeth, Countess of Shrewsbury, moved, to the sound of music, into her new house at Hardwick in Derbyshire (see Plate 1). This remarkable building was the product of her collaboration with the 'Architector and Survayor', Robert Smythson (2). It has been surmised that this day was Bess's seventieth birthday and that she chose to mark her anniversary by occupying the house, even though it was in many respects incomplete (3). The house, with its tall, window-filled towers, is dramatically situated at the top of a steep hill to the east of the valley of the little river Doe Lea. From there it commands views for many miles over the surrounding countryside and, a matter of some significance, is itself seen.

Meteorology, in anything like its modern definition, was unknown in Elizabethan England, although, as we shall see, its origins were not far away.

We do have, however, an insight into the climate as experienced at precisely this time in William Harrison's *The Description of England*, published in 1587 (4). Chapter 18 is entitled 'Of the Air, Soil and Commodities of this Island' and here Harrison provides us with a vivid description of, respectively the air and the winds:

> The air (for the most part) throughout the island is such as, by reason in the manner of continual clouds, is reported to be gross and nothing so pleasant as that is of the main (i.e. the continent). Howbeit, as they which affirm these things have only respect to the impediment or hindrance of the clouds and oft engrossed air, so experience teaches us that it is no less pure, wholesome and commodious than that of other countries and much more temperate in summer than that of the Gauls.
>
> In this island likewise the winds are commonly more strong and fierce than in any other places of the main. . . . That grievous inconvenience also enforceth our nobility, gentry and commonality to build their houses in the valleys, leaving the high grounds unto their corn and cattle, lest the cold and stormy blasts of winter should breed them greater annoyance; whereas in other regions each one desireth to set his house aloft on the hill, not only to be seen afar off and cast forth his beams of stately and curious workmanship into every quarter of the country, but also (in hot habitations) for coldness' sake of the air, sith the heat is never so vehement on the hilltop as in the valley, because the reverberation of the sunbeams either reacheth not so far as the highest or else becometh not so strong as when it is reflected upon the lower soil.

At the end of the sixteenth century Britain had been in the grip of the so-called Little Ice Age for around two hundred years. In his comprehensive meteorological history of the period, Fagan notes that this last decade of the century was the coldest (5). More detailed accounts record that the period 1580–1620, embracing the final part of the reign of Elizabeth I and almost the whole of that of James I, suffered from frequent extremely cold winters, with extensive frosts and deep snowfall, but these were often compensated by warm summers and periods of drought (6).

These facts set the scene from which to begin an inquiry into the relationship of architecture and climate in renaissance England. We have an exposed site in an often-inhospitable climate in which a seemingly inappropriate 'house of glass' is to be inhabited by an elderly woman and her household. This all seems to contradict the conventional logic of environmental design in architecture, where, in uncongenial landscapes and climates, we seek sheltered locations, fashion our buildings to offer protection from the elements, and take care to ensure that we make interiors that are protective and comfortable. As we saw earlier, this is precisely the prescription offered by William Harrison in his description of the choice of a site for a house in the English climate. At first sight Hardwick seems to attend to none of these. But architecture is, at its best, never merely the product of mechanical logic. Closer study of Hardwick reveals how matters of personal expression, courtly ritual and domestic custom come together with concerns of architectural formalism and detail and the implicit facts of building tradition to achieve a deeply satisfying synthesis that is both a response to and an expression of the climate of its place and time. Bess of Hardwick and certain of her contemporaries set out to defy the implications of climate and, in almost exactly William Harrison's words,

> . . . to be seen afar off and cast forth her (his) beams of stately
> and curious workmanship into every quarter of the country.

To explore this theme I have chosen to consider three houses from Smythson's *oeuvre*: Wollaton Hall in Nottinghamshire (1580–1588) (Fig. 2.1), Hardwick New Hall, Derbyshire (1590–1597) (Fig. 2.2) and Bolsover Castle, also in Derbyshire (1612–1642) (Fig. 2.3) (7). As Girouard reveals, the Smythson/Smithson dynasty contributed to numerous other houses in the English Midlands and further afield, but this small group will, I suggest, bring particular focus to the central theme of the present studies. All three are set in the English Midlands, in a rolling landscape of low hills

2.1
Wollaton Hall, Nottingham:
view from south-east.

2.2
Hardwick Hall, Derbyshire:
view from south-west.

2.3
Bolsover Castle, Derbyshire:
view from west.

and shallow valleys, patterned by woods and fields (8), around the latitude of 53° north. The modern journey from Wollaton to Hardwick is a distance of just 24 miles, which may be covered comfortably by car in less than one hour. Bolsover, also sited above the Doe Lea valley, is a mere five miles to the north from Hardwick, an easy distance in both sixteenth and twenty-first centuries, and the two buildings may be seen one from the other. Robert Smythson lived in the village of Wollaton from 1580, when the construction of that house began, until his death in 1614 and his memorial may be seen in the south aisle of the village church of St Leonard's. At the end of the fifteenth century a journey of 24 miles across country to Hardwick or Bolsover was not unusual and we may imagine that over this period of 34 years Smythson became deeply familiar with this landscape and the character and rigours of its climate.

When Smythson died, at the age of 79, on 15 October 1614, his work as master mason, become architect, had left a sequence of buildings that remain some of the most distinctive in England. Mark Girouard has comprehensively explored Smythson's life and work in his monumental study, *Robert Smythson and the English Country House* (9). This places Smythson's works and those of his son John and grandson Huntingdon in the rich context of Elizabethan, and later of Jacobean, culture and society. From Robert's work as chief mason at Longleat, begun in 1568, to the experiments of Wollaton, the splendour of Hardwick and the lyrical conclusion of Bolsover, Girouard traces the emergence of a practice that becomes progressively recognizable as that of an architect in almost the modern meaning of the term (10).

Wollaton Hall 1580–1588

In 1568 Francis Willoughby inherited a fifteenth-century manor house in the village of Wollaton near Nottingham. Alice T. Friedman has described the complexities of the Willoughby household in the years during which it lived at the Old Hall (11). That was essentially a large farmhouse and gave little expression to the social pretensions of an ambitious gentleman. Planning for a new house began in the 1570s and construction began in 1580. The site is a hilltop to the south of the village with extensive views over the landscape. Surrounded by a park, this offered the opportunity to make a powerful social statement. Willoughby and Smythson seized this and together they fashioned a house whose appearance astonishes to the present day.

Smythson's plan drawing of Wollaton Hall (Fig. 2.4) shows the house set at the centre of a strictly organized geometrical scheme with distinct territories for all of the functions of the household and the estate. It is uncertain whether this plan was ever fully realized and the house today is in a very different setting (12). A century later the immediate context of the

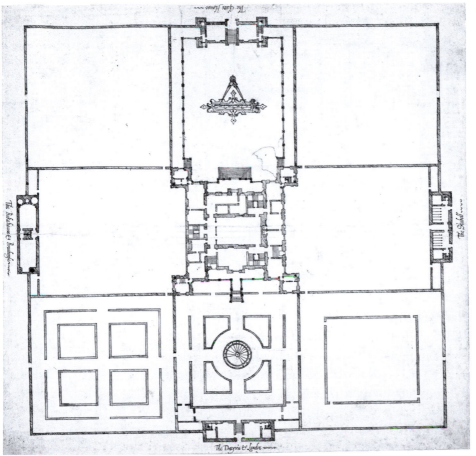

house was very different, as is depicted in Jan Siberechts' painting, dated 1695 (Plate 9). Smythson's plan does not show a north point and for our present purposes, as in all discourse regarding the architectural environment, orientation is an essential fact. The entrance of the house is often referred to as the north front, but examination of modern sources shows that the house is oriented 41° to the west of due north, in other words to the north-west. The 'south' front is correspondingly oriented to the south-east (13). The reasons for this orientation are hard to identify. In the setting of open parkland this could, apparently, have been a matter of free choice. It may be that specific aspects of the topography were the reason. Pamela Marshall's detailed archaeological investigations of the house show that it is served by an extensive system of underground works, of sewers and caves. The earliest of these are contemporary with the construction of the house and it is probable that they might have influenced the orientation.

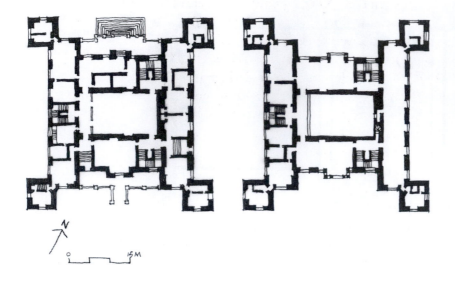

In the climate of the British Isles the orientation of a building has a
profound effect on the conditions that may be enjoyed within. Even though
we speak of our climate as 'temperate', a southerly orientation is always
more benign than a northern. This is explicitly reflected in the planning of
Wollaton. If we adopt the loose annotation of 'north' and 'south' fronts
to make the case, a study of the plans (Fig. 2.5) shows that this distinction
is acknowledged in the disposition of rooms, their uses and their detail. The
principal entrance is from the north and in its original arrangement the
approach was through a complex sequence that wound its way to arrive at a
screens passage to the west of the central great hall, the first destination of
ceremonial entry (14). If we imagine this sequence on a cold winter's day
during the Little Ice Age, the visitor would be progressively sheltered from
the raw cold of the outside as the route turns first right, then ascends a flight
of steps, turns to the left and finally reaches the entrance to the double-height
great hall, lit from high clerestories and warmed by two fireplaces set in its
long side walls. If this winter's day were sunny, the upper part of the great
hall would be illuminated by low winter sun projected across the room,
transmitting a sense of the conditions outside and modelling the rich detail
of the elaborate hammer beams of the ceiling.

A ring of rooms surrounds the great hall, with views across the park.
On the ground floor the largest of these is the private dining room on the
south – actually south-east – front. In Smythson's plan this looked over
the formal garden. The room had a fireplace in the north wall that divides it
from the great hall. Nearby the garden was approached by the 'garden
door' at the foot of a flight of stairs that terminates the screens passage.

The dining room receives sunlight from early morning until mid-afternoon. This would probably have been the room where the women of the household spent much of their time, as is suggested by Pamela Marshall in her analysis of the household inventories (15). In her study of Wollaton, Alice T. Friedman describes how Elizabethan gentlewomen passed their days in reading, needlework, card games, and dance and musical performance (16). They were obliged to educate their daughters in these skills, and this bright room, with its prospect of the garden, would have been an agreeable place at all seasons of the year. In noble Elizabethan households the principal meal of the day was taken in the afternoon, this in itself partly a matter of the availability of daylight in houses that were dark after sunset. Sunny days would bring a welcome light and some useful warmth to supplement that of the fire. At each corner of the ground-floor plan we find similar arrangements of paired rooms, each with a daytime room with a fireplace that leads to an inner chamber in the corner tower, used for sleeping, each with a garderobe, but without a fireplace. It appears that the chambers at the north-eastern corner were Willoughby's personal apartments (17). The remainder of the east wing was devoted to chambers, while the west wing houses the staircase that provides the main route from the kitchens below, the pantry and the buttery.

On the first floor we find the great ceremonial rooms of the house: the north and south great chambers. The west wing housed the two state bedchambers, north and south, each with directly connected withdrawing chambers and inner chambers. The long gallery originally occupied the whole length of the east wing (18). The south great chamber was lavishly furnished, with tables, chairs and 'stooles' of many kinds and was clearly regarded as the best room in the house. The corresponding north great chamber was, however, sparsely furnished. This seems to reflect the importance of orientation in determining the significance of rooms, and this point is reinforced by the description of the south state bedchamber in the Inventory of 8 October 1601 as:

> The Chamber at the southend of the southe greate chamber alias the best chamber.
>
> (19)

On close inspection, we discover that the fenestration of the south and north great chambers is subtly differentiated, with larger areas of glass to south than north.

The distant view of Wollaton on its hilltop is crowned by the towering mass of the so-called 'Prospect Room'. This sits directly over the great hall and is glazed on all four elevations, amply justifying its name. The purpose

of the room is quite obscure, other than for the enjoyment of the views that it commands. It is approached from the first floor by two spiral staircases, which would have been difficult to negotiate in Elizabethan female attire. It is also without a fireplace, although flues from ground- and first-floor apartments are carried upwards through its walls and are strongly expressed in the houses' silhouette. None of the inventories contains any note of its contents.

Roy Strong has observed that Wollaton is unique amongst Elizabethan houses in having house and garden conceived as a unity (20) and this nicely leads us to consider the relationship between the internal and external realms of the house. This relation of house and garden implied in Smythson's plan suggests that the garden was an important extension of the social space of the house. In taking a detail from Siberechts' painting (Fig. 2.6), we see that the connection of house and garden is much altered, showing a terrace across the full width of the south front between the corner towers and a central staircase seemingly allowing direct access from the dining room. This is a reflection of changes in social convention, but the image still allows us to appreciate the relation of house and garden as it was conceived by Smythson and Willoughby. From the orientation of the shadows cast by the trees and the building, it appears that Siberechts' image depicts a time around noon on a summer's day. The sunlit façade and the warm colour of the footpaths suggest gentle warmth and comfort, nicely tempered by the quiet activity of the fountain.

Taking exercise was an important part of Elizabethans' courtly life, and this could as readily be taken in or upon the house as in the garden. Mark Girouard observes that:

> Sixteenth century doctors stressed the importance of daily walking to preserve health, and galleries made exercise possible when the weather would otherwise have prevented it. Closed galleries were especially useful in winter . . .
>
> (21)

The Wollaton long gallery, 37 metres in length, amply provided for this. Fine weather walking could take place on the 'leads' of the rooftop. These surround the high central block of the clerestory of the great hall and the Prospect Room, and each corner tower terminates in a banqueting room. These chambers were directly accessed from the leads and were used for banquets, which were the taking of dessert and wine following dinner. Dinner, the main and often ceremonial meal of the day, typically began in mid-afternoon, so the banquet would be taken early in the evening (22). All of the turret rooms were well furnished with beds, mattresses and small items such as stools. Musical entertainment was apparently on call, as the inventory for the south-east chamber lists:

> 2 luttes, 3 instrumentes with wyer stringes, 1 basse vyall.

The inventory for this chamber also lists a fire shovel and a fire iron grate, indicating that it might have been used after dark, if not in the depth of winter. A fire iron and shovel are also listed in the south-west tower.

Jonathan Bate has observed that the contrast of dark winter and light summer held particular significance for the Elizabethans. In his introduction to the text of Shakespeare's *A Midsummer Night's Dream*, he writes:

> In the age of candle and rush-light, nights were seriously dark. The night was accordingly imagined to be seriously different from the day. The very fact of long hours of light itself conferred a kind of magic upon midsummer night. This is the night of the year when magical thinking is given full rein.
>
> (23)

This suggests that the leads of Wollaton, with the comforts of the furnishings and fireplaces in the turrets, would have been the setting for wonderful entertainments long into its own midsummer nights. We may surmise that the Prospect Room, which is directly accessible via a short staircase from the leads, would also have played a part in these pleasures.

The 'seriously dark' nights were countered at Wollaton by slender means. In the Inventory dated 8 October 1601 only the great hall has any light source specifically itemized:

> 3 lattine candlestick plates.

These are probably a mark of the significance of the great hall in the life of the house, which required it to be continuously lit after dark. All other rooms would rely on one or more of the 27 candlesticks – 25 of pewter and 2 of 'latten' – that were listed among the contents of the 'wardrobe', the place where all moveable household items were kept to be taken for use where and when required (24). All of the principal rooms of the house had a fireplace, and analysis of the plans shows how carefully these were placed within the inner walls of the east and west wings and the side walls of the great hall, all arriving at the elegant chimneys that are proudly expressed in the roofscape. This allows warmth to be accumulated in the thermal mass of the structure. Coal had been mined on the estate from at least the fifteenth century and production was at its peak at the time when the new house was under construction (25). This was precisely the period when coal began to replace wood as the favoured fuel for domestic use. In *Home Fires Burning* Lawrence Wright describes this transition and illustrates examples of early coal grates (26). It is unclear whether coal was burned at Wollaton, but the 1601 Inventory refers to the presence of 'fire iron grates' in most of the rooms, including the great hall, the dining parlour, the south great chamber and the state bed-chambers. The term 'grate' suggests that coal was the fuel. It is only in the two small 'Painted Chambers', at the head of the hall, that reference is made to the 'endirons' (or andirons) that are an indication of a log fire.

In the years following its completion in 1587 the new house was only intermittently occupied. The complexities of the relationship between Sir Francis Willoughby and his wife, Lady Elizabeth, are explored in detail by Friedman (27); as a consequence of these, the house seems to have been used only for formal occasions from time to time until Willoughby's death in 1596. From then it lay in a state of some neglect until 1609, when it was, finally, permanently occupied by the household of Willoughby's nephew, Sir Percival Willoughby, who had married Sir Francis' daughter, Brigid, and the house could, perhaps, finally bloom into its intended splendour.

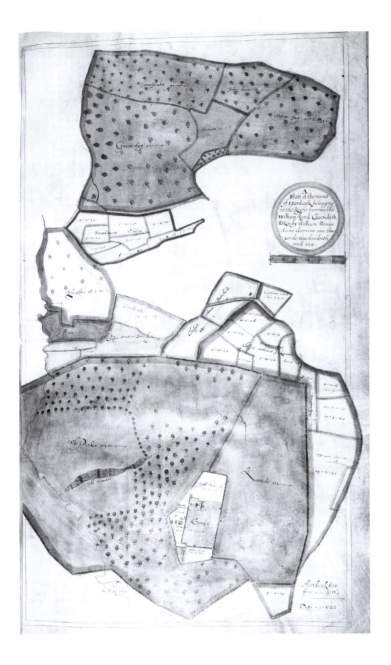

2.7
Hardwick Hall: estate
survey 1609–1610 by
William Senior. The house
and garden are at the
centre of the lower part of
the plan.

I hope that this analysis begins to reveal something of the environmental richness of the Elizabethan house in its relationship to the demanding climate, the Little Ice Age, of the time, and in the manner in which, alongside preoccupations with form, symmetry, iconography and ritual, one may glean a sense of practical needs effectively served and of grand events elaborately furnished. In particular we should note the precision with which the house provides settings for these events at all seasons of the year, from the lengthy days of summer to the dark, cold depths of winter and, perhaps of equal value, its capability to provide for the uncertainties of the English climate. Robert Smythson here reached a mastery of the art of architecture that enabled him to move on to new challenges and possibilities.

Hardwick Hall 'more glass than wall'

Girouard sketches the architectural transition from Wollaton to Hardwick (28). The key building in this is Worksop Manor, a hunting lodge in Nottinghamshire, where, in the 1580s, the Earl of Shrewsbury embarked on an elaborate reconstruction. Worksop, which was completed in 1586, has not survived, but Girouard is convinced that it was the work of Smythson (29). Shrewsbury's wife, Elizabeth, was soon afterwards to embark with Smythson on the construction of the new hall at Hardwick and it is certain that this project had its roots at Worksop. Surviving images of Worksop show that it was even bigger than Wollaton and, in Girouard's words, 'just as extraordinary', and in it lay the origins of some of the features that make Hardwick so remarkable.

From a previous marriage to Sir William Cavendish, Bess owned the great house at Chatsworth and, in 1583, purchased the nearby property at Hardwick where she had been born (30). In the same year the Shrewsburys separated and Bess first returned to Chatsworth and, the following year, moved on to the small manor house at Hardwick. By 1587 she had begun work to rebuild it in a manner that, Girouard suggests, owed much to Worksop, and this, Hardwick Old Hall, was completed in 1591. But, one year before, and at the time of Shrewsbury's death, she had embarked on building a new house just a stone's throw away, in which her collaborator was Robert Smythson.

The relationship of the new house and the landscape is contrived with great precision and, although it lacks the strictly arranged, gridded geometry of Smythson's plan of Wollaton, is in all respects a complete ensemble of house and garden. The plan of the house is an elaborated rectangle whose long axis is skewed just a few degrees to the east of due north. The original relationship of house and garden may be discerned from the survey of the estate undertaken by William Senior in 1609–1610, see Figure 2.7 (31). The approach is from the west, through a walled forecourt, and the east front overlooks a garden that extends to the south. The south garden contains a detached Banqueting House that survives to the present day. To the north lies an orchard. This plan underpins the present-day garden, in which the entrance court is intact, but the east lawn is terminated by a 'ha-ha' and the south garden is sub-divided into four distinct areas, both of which date from the eighteenth century. The orchard is now a car park.

The exterior of Hardwick is instantly striking, with six symmetrically disposed turrets rising above the three-storey body of the building.

The entire surface is articulated by arrays of gridded windows that give the impression that the building is 'more glass than wall', a 'phenomenal transparency' (32) that is out of all relationship to the actual proportion of solid to void. The silhouette is further elaborated by groups of tall chimneys, and strap-work balustrades, displaying Bess's initials 'ES' surmounted by her coronet, complete the six towers. In a chapter 'Of the Manner of Building and Furniture of our Houses', in *The Description of England*, published just at this time, William Harrison (33) made observations on the latest developments in building method that are directly pertinent to the appearance of Hardwick:

> . . . our lattices are grown into less use, because glass is come to be so plentiful and within a very little time so good cheap . . .
>
> there are old men . . . which have noted three things to be marvellously altered in England within their sound remembrance. . . . One is the multitude of chimneys lately erected . . .

The geometrical rigour, symmetry and simplicity of the exterior conceal the asymmetrical complexity of the internal organization. The plan (Fig. 2.8) rests on a simple *parti* in which a thick spine wall runs north–south

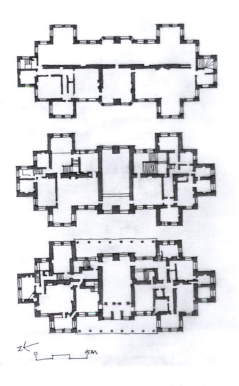

2.8
Hardwick Hall: plans.
Ground floor, bottom.
First floor, middle.
Second floor, top.

2.9
Hardwick Hall:
high great chamber.

and is slightly offset to the east, allowing the west-facing rooms to be wider. At ground and first floor of the plan the double-storey great hall cuts across the entire plan and is defined on each side by massive walls. In many ways this is reminiscent of the manner in which Smythson organized the plan of Wollaton. There we identified subtle inflections of arrangement and detail in relation to use and orientation, and at Hardwick these are taken to new limits. In the overall topography of the house the ground floor is dominated by the great hall, which is entered from the west through a screens passage. To its north, the cooler part of the house, lie the great kitchen and its associated buttery, larders and cellars and the lower level of the chapel. To the south a large pantry conveniently opens directly from the great hall. At the east end of the hall a turn to the south leads to the foot of the remarkable ceremonial staircase, which is one of the most striking features of the house. This proceeds, via a 'dogleg' with wide landings, to the first floor and continues on to terminate via a sweeping 'winder' at a landing in the south turret.

The southern end of the ground floor was devoted to chambers primarily for senior members of the household, including William Cavendish – Bess's second son – and a nursery. This reflects the priority for a southerly aspect that we saw at Wollaton and which becomes even more pronounced when we arrive at the first floor. There we find Bess's own apartments, her withdrawing chamber and bedchamber and that of her granddaughter Arbella. These all enjoy southerly and or westerly orientations. A direct route passes from Bess's withdrawing chamber, above the screens of the great hall, into the low great chamber. This extends into the north-east turret, through which it captures both south and west light. The remainder of this northern wing contains bedchambers and the upper chapel.

The high-ceilinged state apartments occupy the second floor. From the landing at the head of the great stair, one enters directly into the high great chamber (Fig. 2.9), the site of the grandest events of the household. This lies at the south-western corner of the house and consists of a rectangle that extends into a vast bay window to the west. As a conclusion of the ascent of

2.10
Hardwick Hall: long gallery.

the staircase, the room is flooded with daylight from windows that face south, west and, in one side of the bay window, north. A magnificent fireplace stands opposite the bay window. In the south–east corner a doorway leads to the long gallery (Fig. 2.10). This extends the full length of the house, 51 metres, and is longer than that at Wollaton. The primary orientation of the gallery is to the east, as at Wollaton, although the two bay windows and the short glazed return walls at either end bring in quantities of both north and south light that enliven the space. The west wall, covered in tapestries and portraits, contains two fireplaces. The entire upper floor was, as Girouard has observed (34), intended as the royal suite. In addition to the high great chamber and the long gallery, there is a west-facing withdrawing chamber and a suite of bedrooms: in their original nomenclature, the best bed chamber, the pearl bed-chamber and the little chamber. A significant detail of these grand apartments is the manner in which their ceiling heights are adjusted in relation to their plan dimensions and uses. Only the high great chamber and gallery extend the full height up to the underside of the roof. All the other rooms have lowered ceilings. This is almost certainly a matter of architectural proportion, but also produces benefits for the comfort and utility of the rooms by reducing the volume to be kept warm. As at Wollaton, the 'leads', reached by a staircase to the north, were an indispensible place for exercise and the turrets were again intended to be used for entertainment. The south turret, with the best views and orientation, has Bess's arms above the entrance and, although without a fireplace, was regarded as the most important of these (35).

Smythson's subtle management of sunlight and daylight is the most immediately striking feature of Hardwick's environment. The effect of this is seen in the sequence that leads from the great hall to the high great chamber by the wonderful complexity of the staircase. Following this on a bright summer's midday, we approach through the bright light of the forecourt and pass into the relatively dim light of the great hall, lit from high windows to east and west. The foot of the stair and the flight that leads to the first floor are well lit from the east, but, on reaching the second landing, a prospect opens of the final flight, where the brilliant light of the south turret above leads one towards the second floor and arrival at the high great chamber. In summer this is flooded with light that illuminates and animates the rich decoration of tapestry-covered walls surmounted by a coloured plaster relief frieze depicting the court of Diana set in a forest with hunting scenes. The allegorical figure of 'Summer' may be seen to the side of the window recess, perhaps a further mark of the Elizabethans' delight in the pleasures of that season and which this room captures to the full. The entire suite of state apartments enjoy similar qualities, but here tempered in keeping with their slightly less public functions. The long gallery would have played its part in the grand rituals. Its length and height and the great bay windows, opposite the long tapestry and portrait-covered internal wall with its two fireplaces, would invite its use on these occasions. But it would have been used at other times to allow the household to take exercise during the inclement weather that can occur at all seasons in Derbyshire.

In winter, and particularly the bitterly cold winters of the Little Ice Age, the house would take on an entirely different character. In the inventory of contents, compiled in 1601 (36), it is recorded that the Hall had:

> . . . too great Copper Candlestickes with severall places to set lightes in hanging in too ropes paynted, foure plate Candlestickes of brass to hand on the wales. . .

The adjacent pantry had 'foure brass Candlestickes' and the Buttery to the north of the hall had 'a plate Candlesticke'. These are the only rooms in the house that seemed to have light sources permanently allocated to them. At Hardwick the Porter's Lodge was where small items of household wares, amongst them numerous pots and pans and tableware, were kept. The inventory lists:

> . . . too long guilt Candlestickes waying threescore and too ounces, six Candlestickes wrought with stages and talbotes white waying twoo hundreth fortie ounces, six Candlestickes like gallies white waying Fourscore and too ounces, too wyer Candlestickes waying fifteen ounces, fowre white Candle-stickes waying one hundreth seaven ounces and a half, An other white Candlesticke waying twentie ounces three-quarters, an other whyte Candlesticke waying thirteen ounces, too other whyte Candlestickes waying twenty and foure ounces, a little whyte Candlesticke for waxe lightes waying three ounces. . .

This implies that, in addition to the fixed lights in the great hall and those few kept in the pantry and buttery, a total of 25 portable candlesticks, two fewer than at Wollaton, of various materials and sizes supplied the night-time illumination of this magnificent house. What a marked contrast to the luminosity of the house on a summer's day.

The arrangements for heating are similar to those at Wollaton and, like Willoughby, Bess owned extensive coal mines, which, in addition to their commercial benefits, may have supplied fuel to the house, although here the indication in the inventory of 'andirons' in the hearths of all the main rooms suggests that wood was the main fuel (37). Almost all the rooms have a fireplace, in total at least 28, and the inventory lists, in addition to the andirons, full details of the shovels, tongs and, in some cases, bellows that were needed to attend to these. The relationship of the glass-filled envelope enclosing the spine and transverse walls that are filled with fireplaces is almost modern and establishes a set of relationships of mass and void, light and dark, warm and cool that would eloquently serve the practical requirements of those dwelling here.

Girouard has proposed that Hardwick achieved 'magnificence before comfort' (38). By modern standards this would certainly have been the case and the great ceremonial apartments could never be considered cosy. But that was not their *raison d'être*. But if we take another perspective, a different interpretation emerges. There is ample evidence that the notion of comfort, as understood by an aristocratic Elizabethan household, would have been quite unlike ours. We have already noted Jonathan Bate's allusion to the enormous difference between summer and winter as they would have been registered by the Elizabethan psyche (39) and factors such as this must guide any analysis of the inhabitation of Hardwick during Bess's occupancy, from 1597 until her death in the house in 1608.

The location of Bess's apartments, and those of the closest members of the household, at the southern end of the first floor immediately confers some environmental benefit by admitting the warmth of the sun, which would have been present even on some winter's days. The first floor is also protected from the extremes of climate by its position in the middle of the mass of the house, sandwiched between the ground and second floors. The window-filled portion of the west-facing wall is the only part of the room that meets the external air. Otherwise the room is completely enclosed by other rooms. Bess's bedchamber at the south-west corner has its windows in the adjacent south and west-facing walls, and is, once more, otherwise surrounded by other spaces. The withdrawing chamber's fireplace is described in the 1602 Inventory as having '. . . a payre of Copper Andirons, an Iron Chymney, with a back of Iron. . .'. It is probable that the fire would be kept alight at all hours in winter. The room still contains the six tapestries that are recorded in the inventory, and, whilst these would be primarily decorative and symbolic, they would have the effect of, in the parlance of modern building science, improving the thermal response of the chamber, enhancing the sense of warmth. The inventory also mentions that the room contained three 'skreynes', or screens. These would be used to make smaller enclosures within the room and, if placed close to the fireplace, would have created a warmer microclimate within the general environment of the room. There is a sense that the inhabitation of the house became restricted as the winter drew in and the household retreated to the smaller, more confined apartments in their search of comfort. The great ceremonial spaces would be only intermittently used when climate and custom permitted.

A similar reading of Bess's bedchamber shows how the fabric of the building, when combined with a fireplace equipped with two andirons, one of copper the other of iron, and a pair of bellows, the wall hangings and the numerous items of furniture, a screen, rugs, carpets, curtains and a variety of pillows and cushions, would allow the inhabitants to resist the coldest days and nights of winter. The winter of 1607–1608 became known throughout Britain as the 'Great Winter'. Mary S. Lovell describes Bess's death, at the age of 80, late on the dark afternoon of 13 January 1608. Her closest family gathered, waiting for the end, by the fireplace in the small room between the bed-chamber and withdrawing chamber, as Elizabeth Digby, her gentle-woman, strove to keep the bed-chamber warm (40). Later Bess's embalmed body lay in state in the high great chamber awaiting the funeral, which did not take place until the beginning of May. It is likely that the high great chamber was draped in black cloth and David Durrant surmises that the great stair and the great hall would have been similarly enshrouded, utterly transforming the character of those luminous spaces (41). The funeral was held on 4 May at All Hallows in Derby and Bess was interred beneath a memorial designed by Robert Smythson.

If we bring together Robert Smythson's achievements at Wollaton and Hardwick, we may recognize the establishment of consistent principles of composition and planning in relation to the English climate. These houses provide a diversity of rooms and sequences of external spaces, both on the building itself – the 'leads' – and in the surrounding gardens, that meet the expectations of Elizabethan courtly life, both in its grand ceremonies and in the more modest events of everyday inhabitation. Many of these features may be found in other houses of the period, but Smythson gave them unique expression in his works, in which strict geometrical order of overall form is adapted to the particular circumstance of the climate, with its clear demarcation of the seasons, its contrast of day and night and its characteristic unpredictability.

Bolsover Castle, 1612–1642

Sir Charles Cavendish was Elizabeth Shrewsbury's youngest son and shared her enthusiasm for building. In 1607 he bought, from his brother-in-law, Gilbert Talbot, Welbeck Abbey in Nottinghamshire and Bolsover Castle, in Derbyshire just eight miles distant (42). Welbeck was to be his main residence, but it was at the much smaller Bolsover Castle that he made the more remarkable contribution to British architecture (43).

There had been a castle on the escarpment at Bolsover since the twelfth century and it is likely that the building that Cavendish began in 1612 stood, at least in part, on the foundations of this (44). The initial phase of building consisted of what is now referred to as the 'Little Castle' and it is this

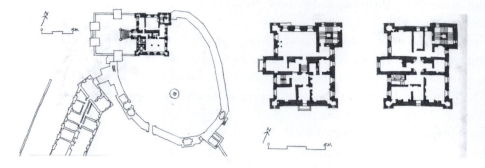

2.11
Bolsover Castle:
plan of the Little
Castle.

2.12
Bolsover Castle:
Little Castle, floor
plans.

that will be the focus of this analysis. The later works that continued to extend the house until 1642 will help to locate this in a broader context. In 1612 Robert Smythson was 77 years old and the surviving building accounts for Bolsover refer to payments to 'Smithson', who was almost certainly his son, John Smithson, who had adopted the alternative spelling. Girouard concludes that Robert had, if anything, a minor role in the project, but speculates that his son would have consulted him, going as far as to propose that,

> . . . the planning and possibly the main lines of the façades
> but not the ornament of Bolsover are one of the last products
> of his ingenious and experimental mind.

(45)

Nearly square in plan (Figs 2.11 and 2.12), the Little Castle rises three storeys above a basement that contains a lavish provision of kitchens. The remains of the earlier structure most probably determined its orientation. The diagonal of the plan lies almost on the cardinal points and the northernmost angle contains a stair that climbs around a hollow masonry core from ground to second floor. This releases the remainder of the external walls, at all orientations, to allow windows to be placed precisely in relation to the functions of the rooms within. It is necessary to consider this keep-like structure in relation to its surrounding open spaces. The house was designed to be approached by the south drive, high above the valley, before arriving at the grand double stair that leads into the entrance court (Fig. 2.13). Like the front court at Hardwick and the arrangement shown on Smythson's plan of Wollaton, this provides shelter from the exposure of this high hilltop. To the south and east lies a second enclosure, the Fountain Court, that may be on the foundations of the curtain wall of the medieval castle and is defined by a wide, curving stone wall, the Stone Walk, that is reached from the main staircase, and, at garden level, contains a sequence of hollowed-out garden rooms (Fig. 2.14).

2.14
Bolsover Castle:
Little Castle from the
Fountain Court.

Charles Cavendish died in 1617, three years after Robert Smythson, when the main fabric of the house was complete, but with much work required in its internal decoration incomplete, and this continued until 1621 (46). Charles's son, William, inherited Bolsover and Welbeck and, with John Smithson, carried the Little Castle through to completion. William also built the extensive terrace range to the south that today stands as a romantic ruin, and the fountain garden between 1627 and 1642. From 1635 to 1642 he built the riding house range that, with the terrace range, defines the present great court.

Bolsover was conceived as secondary to Welbeck. The Little Castle was, however, much loved by the Cavendishes and was used a great deal. Girouard explains the revival of the idea of chivalry during the late-Elizabethan and Jacobean years, and the consequent flurry of residential castle building, such as Lulworth in Dorset and Ruperra in Glamorgan (47). He locates Bolsover within this movement. Its strong, four-square form, with small, apparently carelessly positioned, windows, is quite unlike the transparency and geometrical discipline of Hardwick (48).

The ground floor, which has a Gothic structure of stone vaults, is devoted to reception rooms and in its decoration establishes a narrative that informs the entire building. The anteroom has wall paintings that depict

three of the four Humours: the *Choleric*, *Melancholic* and *Phlegmatic* (Fig. 2.15). Wall paintings in the vaulted and columned hall are on the theme of Hercules, who is paired to the side of the fireplace with Vulcan, god of fire. The final room is known as the Pillar Parlour and was originally referred to as the Lower Dining Room. Here the iconography is of the five senses, *Touch*, *Hearing*, *Taste*, *Scent* and *Sight*, all appropriate to the decoration of a dining room, but which equally suggest that the senses may be the key to interpreting the entire building. On the first floor the Gothic vaults give way to a simpler, more domestic timber construction. The largest room, and closest to the staircase, is the Star Chamber (Fig. 2.16) that was used for the grandest meals and entertainments. Off this lies the Marble Closet, taking its name from its non-structural marble-faced vault. This more intimate room was used for less grand occasions. Beyond these, and approached by a discreet stair in the inner core of the plan, lie a suite of rooms centred on Sir William's bedchamber, which is flanked by two 'closets', *Heaven* and *Elysium*. These have been the subject of much discussion and interpretation (49), but, in paraphrase, through their contrasted decoration, they offer a distinction between the sacred and the profane. The second floor contains the remaining family bedchambers ingeniously planned around an octagonal vestibule

(Fig. 2.17). The staircase continues to give generous access to the leads and their spectacular views.

On first encounter there seems to be little of the regard for orientation that is found at Wollaton and, most particularly, at Hardwick. But closer examination shows that the rotation of the plan, relative to the north point, allows all the major rooms to receive sunlight at some part of the day. The great hall is best lit in the morning and early afternoon, whereas the Star Chamber is best from early afternoon and into the evening. The high cills of the great hall's windows allow ample light, but provide privacy to the Fountain Court. In the Star Chamber the lower cills admit even more light and allow views over the valley and beyond. The whole arrangement may be interpreted as a response to the sun's diurnal progress.

The relationship between the building and the Fountain Court is precisely controlled. The high cills of the great hall deny any visual connection and only two openings are found in the upper part of the south-east façade; the principal of these, with a small, iron-railed balcony, is that of *Elysium* and offers a direct connection between this room of secular pleasures and the Venus Fountain from which the court takes its name (50). The second, smaller, window lights a small chamber on the floor above. The central vestibule at the second floor is brightly and surprisingly lit from the cupola that rises high above the roof to capture and transmit, to the precise centre of the building, the progress of the sun across the sky.

The building's fireplaces are some of its most striking features. These are remarkable in their varied designs, different in form and material in each room (51), but from our environmental viewpoint they indicate that the building was conceived to be made warm in winter rather than serving only as a summertime 'pleasure palace'. At the ground floor each of the three principal rooms has a fireplace that is related in size and position to the need for warmth, modest in the anteroom and grand in both the Pillar Parlour and the great hall. In the Star Chamber the fireplace is placed between the two windows of the west wall, directly opposite the entrance from the staircase, and in the Marble Closet a spectacular black-and-white surround is surrounded by wall hangings of 'red taffetie' (Fig. 2.18). Lucy Worsley explains that this was:

> an intimate room that could be kept warm and was usually used for playing cards or dressing.
>
> (52)

The soft fabric of the hangings would enhance the effect of the fire in keeping the room warm, compensating for the relative coolness of the marble floor and vault. Similarly, Worsley writes of the bedchamber that:

With a roaring fire this would have been a cosy room.

(53)

The tiny spaces of *Heaven* and *Elysium* are also furnished with striking fireplaces. That in *Elysium* is placed in the window corner and framed by a stone surround (Fig. 2.19).

The qualities of the fireplaces were celebrated in verse in a contemporary 'country house poem' by Mr Aglionby:

And then the chimneys give such heat,
And do the rest so well become,
'Tis strange they are so very neat,
And yet such servants to the room.
But these, like passions, if they can,
Must warm, they must not foul a man.

(54)

The Little Castle enjoys a carefully calculated relationship with the Fountain Court. On the exposed hilltop the high surrounding wall creates a microclimate that on summer's days would have encouraged all kinds of entertainments, both private and public. At three places the thick wall is hollowed to form little garden houses, two with fireplaces, which usefully extend the comforts of the garden, and elsewhere seats are placed in sheltered alcoves (Fig. 2.20).

The most important event in the early life of Bolsover was the visit, on 30 July 1634, of King James I and Queen Henrietta Maria. After a banquet, which was probably served in the state rooms of the terrace range, the party proceeded to the Fountain Court to witness a masque, *Love's Welcome at Bolsover*, specially written for the occasion by Ben Jonson (55). Jonson's script has survived, but, sadly, there is no record of the time of day at which the performance took place. It is reasonable, however, to surmise that this would have been in the afternoon and that the events would have concluded by sunset. In the English Midlands, in late July this would be around eight o'clock in the evening. In the absence of a contemporary account of the weather on the day, we must assume that it was relatively fine. This is where the garden houses might have played a part in providing temporary shelter. However, the general records of weather that have come down (56) show that a number of the summers of the 1630s were noticeably warm, even as the Little Ice Age continued to bring severe winters. On such a day the Fountain Court would have been a wonderful setting for this great pageant.

2.19
Bolsover Castle:
Elysium fireplace.

2.18
Bolsover Castle:
Marble Closet.

Conclusion

Built at the turn of the sixteenth and seventeenth centuries, and set in the rolling landscape of the north Midlands, the three remarkable houses at Wollaton, Hardwick and Bolsover are amongst the architectural wonders of England. Their architectural and social virtues and enigmas have properly been the focus of much scholarly discussion, but they additionally have a place in bringing a new perspective on the relationship between architecture and climate. In all three we find that the public and private rituals of aristocratic life, and the more mundane practicalities of domestic service that sustained them, are accommodated in an architecture that was simultaneously disciplined and experimental. Simple external forms and clear geometrical orders are combined with complex internal organizations, in both plan and cross-section. There is consistent attention to the benefits that careful orientation offers in the English climate, where south is always better than north and this is the basis of the rich environmental qualities of these remarkable buildings. These characteristics amply sustain the interpretation of these buildings by the Smythson's modern namesake, with which I began this essay.

Notes

1. Peter Smithson, 'Territorial imprint', in *Proceedings of 1987 European Conference on Architecture* (ed. W. Palz), H. A. Stephens & Associates, Bedford. The author was present at the conference and discussed Smithson's paper with him at length.

2. Smythson is described in these terms on his memorial stone in St Leonard's church at Wollaton near Nottingham.

3. Lady Shrewsbury is so strongly associated with the estate at Hardwick that she is almost invariably referred to as 'Bess of Hardwick'. Her precise date of birth is unproven, but the surmise is a reasonable inference. For accounts of her life, see Mary S. Lovell, *Bess of Hardwick: First Lady of Chatsworth*, Little Brown, London, 2005 (paperback edition, Abacus Books, London, 2007) and David N. Durant, *Bess of Hardwick: Portrait of an Elizabethan Dynast*, Peter Owen, London, 1977 (revised paperback edition, 1999).

4. William Harrison, *The Description of England*, 1587, reprint edition (ed. Georges Edelen), Dover, New York, 1994.

5. See Brian Fagan, *The Little Ice Age: How Climate Made History 1300–1850*, Basic Books, New York, 2000.

6. A useful annotated synopsis of climate events in England may be found at http://booty.org.uk/booty.weather/climate/histclimat.htm.

7. The standard references for the architecture of Robert Smythson and his heirs are Mark Girouard, *Robert Smythson and the Elizabethan Country House*, Yale University Press, New Haven, CT, 1983, and Girouard's monumental, *Elizabethan Architecture: Its Rise and Fall, 1540–1640*, Yale University Press, New Haven. CT, 2009. The former authoritatively establishes the part that Robert played in the conception and execution of Wollaton and Hardwick and sets out the more complex process by which Bolsover was created. This last owed most to Robert's son, John, who incidentally preferred the alternative spelling of *Smithson*, and at the conclusion of a lengthy construction process, the work was in the hands of John's son Huntingdon. Girouard's later book places Smythson's work in the wider context of its day. A further excellent source of analysis of all three of these houses is Timothy Mowl, *Elizabethan and Jacobean Taste*, Phaidon, London, 1993. See also John Summerson, *Architecture in Britain, 1530–1830*, Penguin, Harmondsworth, 1953; 9th revised edition, Yale University Press, New Haven, CT, 1993.

8. In *The Making of the English Landscape*, Hodder & Stoughton, London, 1953, Pelican, Harmondsworth, 1970, W. G. Hoskins establishes that the Midlands of Nottinghamshire and Derbyshire underwent the transformation from woodland to pasture and meadow that created their present-day appearance in precisely this period.

9. Girouard, *Robert Smythson and the Elizabethan Country House*, cited in Note 7.

10. Girouard, in *Robert Smythson and the Elizabethan Country House*, notes that the first mention of Smythson in the surviving building accounts for Wollaton is March 1583, but the existence of a plan of the ground floor of the house and its outbuildings in Smythson's hand at the British Architectural Library, RIBA, London, suggests that he was involved in the project from the outset.

11. For a detailed history of the Willoughby family and its role in the design of Wollaton Hall, see Alice T. Friedman, *House and Household in Elizabethan England: Wollaton Hall and the Willoughby Family*, University of Chicago Press, Chicago, 1989.

12. A geophysical survey was made in 1990 of the area of the main northern entrance as shown on Smythson's plan. This was inconclusive, but showed some evidence of dense material in the location of the gate piers and of debris distributed more widely in the area. See Appendix II by P. Strange in Pamela Marshall, *Wollaton Hall: An Archaeological Survey*, Nottingham Civic Society, Nottingham, 1996.

13. Reference to Ordnance Survey maps and to Google Earth images.

14. The house was much altered over the centuries and Wyatville made major changes at the beginning of the nineteenth century. These included a complete transformation of the entrance sequence to form an axial progression from the entrance directly to the hall.

15. Pamela Marshall's *Wollaton Hall: An Archaeological Survey*, cited in Note 12, contains an excellent review of the use of the principal rooms of the house in its first period of occupation. This is based on the surviving household inventories.

16. Friedman, *House and Household in Elizabethan England: Wollaton Hall and the Willoughby Family*, cited in Note 11.

17. *Ibid.*

18. The gallery was subdivided into three chambers, with lowered ceilings as part of Wyatville's early nineteenth-century alterations. For information regarding this, see Marshall, *Wollaton Hall: An Archaeological Survey*, cited in Note 12.

19. Household Inventory of 8 October 1601 reproduced in full in Appendix I of Marshall, *Wollaton Hall: An Archaeological Survey*.

20. Roy Strong, *The Renaissance Garden in England*, Thames and Hudson, London, 1979.

21. In Mark Girouard, *Life in the English Country House*, Yale University Press, New Haven and London, 1978; paperback edition, Penguin, Harmondsworth, 1980.

22. In *Life in the English Country House*, Girouard cites a mouthwatering list of typical banquet foods taken from Markham's *The English Housewife*, 1605.

23. Jonathan Bate, Introduction to 'A Midsummer Night's Dream', in *William Shakespeare: Complete Works* (ed. Jonathan Bate and Eric Rasmussen), The Royal Shakespeare Company/Macmillan, London, 2007.

24. Marshall, *Wollaton Hall: An Archaeological Survey*, cited in Note 12: 'lattine' or 'latten' was a description of a metal alloy that was neither brass nor bronze.

25. Friedman, *House and Household in Elizabethan England: Wollaton Hall and the Willoughby Family*, cited in Note 11.

26. Lawrence Wright, *Home Fires Burning: The History of Domestic Heating and Cooking*, Routledge & Kegan Paul, London, 1964.

27. Friedman, *House and Household in Elizabethan England: Wollaton Hall and the Willoughby Family*, cited in Note 11.

28. Girouard, *Robert Smythson and the Elizabethan Country House*, cited in Note 7.

29. *Ibid.*

30. See Lovell, *Bess of Hardwick: First Lady of Chatsworth* and Durant, *Bess of Hardwick: Portrait of an Elizabethan Dynast*, cited in Note 3.

31. Senior's plan is reproduced in the National Trust official guide to Hardwick, 2006. See also D. V. Fowkes and G. R. Potter (eds), *William Senior's survey of the estates of the first and second earls of Devonshire c.1600–28*, Derbyshire Record Society, Chesterfield, 1988.

32. This term was coined by Colin Rowe and Robert Slutzky in their essay 'Transparency: Literal and Phenomenal', in *The Mathematics of the Ideal Villa and Other Essays*, MIT Press, Cambridge, MA, 1976. The term 'transparent/transparency' came into English usage towards the end of the sixteenth century. Rowe and Slutzky cite the following definition of 1590: '*Transparent*: open, candid, ingenious', which beautifully captures the essence of Hardwick.

33. Harrison, *The Description of England*, cited in Note 4.

34. Mark Girouard in the National Trust official guide, cited in Note 31.

35. *Ibid.*

36. Lindsay Boynton (ed.), *The Hardwick Hall Inventories of 1601*, The Furniture History Society, London, 1971.

37. See Peter Thornton's commentary on the 1601 Inventory in *The Hardwick Hall Inventories of 1601*, in which he points out that andirons are a necessary accessory for a log-burning fireplace.

38. Mark Girouard in the National Trust official guide, cited in Note 31.

39. Jonathan Bate, Introduction to 'A Midsummer Night's Dream', cited in Note 23.

40. Lovell, *Bess of Hardwick: First Lady of Chatsworth*, cited in Note 3.

41. Durant, *Bess of Hardwick: Portrait of an Elizabethan Dynast*, cited in Note 3.

42. As before, the definitive source for the social and architectural background is Girouard, *Robert Smythson and the Elizabethan Country House*, cited in Note 7.

43. Cavendish's Welbeck has not survived, but see Girouard, *Robert Smythson and the Elizabethan Country House*, for an account of Cavendish's work there and, in particular, of Robert Smythson's role in the project.

44. Girouard, *Robert Smythson and the Elizabethan Country House*. See also, Lucy Worsley, *Bolsover Castle*, Guide Book, English Heritage, 2000.

45. *Ibid.*

46. Appendix II of Girouard, *Robert Smythson and the Elizabethan Country House*, presents a detailed chronology of the building of Bolsover.

47. Girouard, *Robert Smythson and the Elizabethan Country House*.

48. For a detailed description of the building see Lucy Worsley's text in the Guide Book, cited in Note 44.

49. See Girouard, *Robert Smythson and the Elizabethan Country House*; Worsley, Guide Book; and Mowl, *Elizabethan and Jacobean Taste*, cited in Note 7.

50. The significance of this connection is explored by a number of authors, including Girouard, Mowl and Worsley, and Paula Henderson, *The Tudor House and Garden*, Paul Mellon Centre for Studies in British Art/Yale University Press, New Haven, CT, 2005.

51. See Girouard's *Robert Smythson and the Elizabethan Country House* and Mowl's *Elizabethan and Jacobean Taste* for scholarly examinations of the stylistic development of the fireplaces from the precedents found in Book IV of Serlio's *Architecture* that was published in England in 1611.

52. Worsley, Guide Book.

53. *Ibid.*

54. Mr Aglionby (possibly George Aglionby), *On Bolsover Castle*; see Alistair Fowler, *The Country House Poem: A Cabinet of Seventeenth-Century Estate Poems and Related Items*, Edinburgh University Press, Edinburgh, 1994.

55. Girouard, *Robert Smythson and the Elizabethan Country House*, gives an account of this. See also Cedric C. Brown, 'Courtesies of place and arts of diplomacy in Ben Jonson's last two entertainments for royalty', in *The Seventeenth Century*, Vol. X, No.1, Spring 1994, which gives a detailed account of the events of the day, in addition to those one year earlier at Welbeck.

56. See http://booty.org.uk/booty.weather/climate/histclimat.htm.

Essay 3
Christopher Wren and the origins of building science

Christopher Wren (1632–1723) was a distinguished scientist who became by far the most important British architect of his day (1). By the date of his first completed building, the chapel at Pembroke College, Cambridge (1663–1665), Wren had made a number of important contributions to science – natural philosophy, in the terminology of the time – and had held significant academic positions. He was a fellow of All Souls at Oxford from 1653 to 1661 and became Professor of Astronomy at Gresham College, London between 1657 and 1661. In 1661 he was elected Oxford University's Savilian Professor of Astronomy, which position he held until 1673. On 28 November 1660, what was to become the Royal Society, Britain's premier scientific body, was founded at a meeting that followed a lecture by Wren at Gresham College in London. It was described as 'a Colledge for the Promoting of Physico-Mathematicall Experimentall Learning'.

The relationship between Wren's works as a scientist and as an architect has been widely discussed. John Summerson's essay 'The Mind of Wren' (2) is one of the earliest and most penetrating explorations. Writing of Wren's second building, the Sheldonian Theatre at Oxford (1663–1669), Summerson acknowledges its technical originality, 'especially as regards the roof, with its ingenious trusses whose composite bolted tie-beams suggest a background of research . . .' but is critical of its *architecture* as '. . . on the totally unimaginative plane of an academic Latin essay . . .'. We may recognize here a distinction drawn between technical expertise and the production of 'high' architecture that remains familiar in modern critical discourse. However, in considering Wren's much later design for the library at Trinity College, Cambridge (1676–1684) (Plate 2), Summerson observed, 'There we have the "essential Wren" in epitome; the adventurousness of the empirical approach, with a minimum of psychological inconsistency; and a loving appreciation of the Roman syntax, without artificiality or false compromise.' (3) Here is a hint that the empirical and theoretical may be effectively fused in a single design. In the years that separate these two buildings Wren's grasp of 'the Roman syntax' had become much more sophisticated, as had his ability to synthesize this with the practical requirements of building.

In a later study the historian of science J. A. Bennett offers an analysis in which he locates Wren's designs for buildings in relation to an extensive account of his work as a scientist, in, respectively, astronomy, longitude, cosmology, mechanics, microscopy, surveying, and medicine and meteorology, and, crucially, presents architecture as an equal amongst the 'mathematical sciences' (4). Bennett establishes the particular significance for Wren of *Convenience*, amongst the three Vitruvian virtues of 'Beauty, Firmness and Convenience', and asserts a closer connection between Wren's science and the architecture than had previously been claimed. Bennett refers to Wren's ideas on the 'function' of a church, as these were represented in his 'letter' on church design addressed to the Commissioners of the Building Act of 1708 (5). The 'functional' emphasis in the 'letter' is Wren's concern to ensure that congregations could both 'see and hear' in the large buildings demanded by the new, reformed church (6). Bennett's argument is illustrated by a review of a selection of the designs for City churches, in which attention is drawn to their 'functional' attributes in providing good light and acoustics.

From quite early in his career Wren was interested in meteorology. In *Parentalia*, the compilation of texts and other materials made by Wren's son, also Christopher, and published in 1750, there is an extended account of Wren's project for a *History of the Seasons*, which would be:

> ... of admirable Benefit to Mankind, if it shall be constantly pursued and deriv'd down to Posterity. His Proposal therefore was to comprehend a *Diary* of wind, weather and other Conditions of the Air, as to Heat. Cold and Weight; and also a *general Description* of the Year ... And because of the Difficulty of a constant *Observation of the Air*, by Night and Day, seem'd invincible he therefore devised a *Clock* to be annexed to a Weather-Cock which moved a Rundle cover'd with Paper, upon which the Clock mov'd a black Lead Pencil, so that the Observer by the Traces of the Pencil on the Paper, might certainly conclude what Winds had blown in his Absence for twelve Hours space: After like manner he contrived a *Thermometer* to be its own *Register* ...
>
> (7)

Wren made a number of demonstrations of the 'weather clocks' described here at meetings of the Royal Society (Fig. 3.1) (8).

Wren's aim in the invention of these devices was to provide the tools to collect information that might help understand the effects of climate on human health. There is no evidence that Wren made an explicit connection between the objective recording of elements of the English climate that his

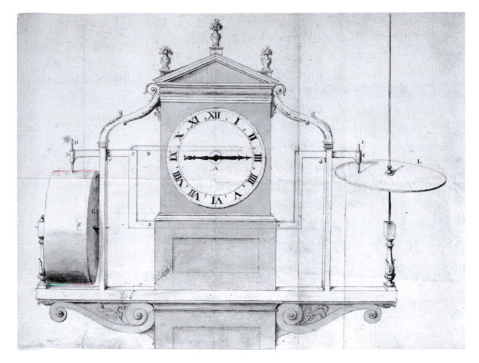

Weather clock.

weather clocks allowed and his architectural designs, but it would seem improbable that the two would be kept apart in his mind. It is equally improbable that his astronomical understanding of the geometry of the sun would not have filtered into his architectural thinking, even if unconsciously. This meeting of natural philosophy and architecture would certainly have provided a basis for architecture that was quite distinct from that from which Robert Smythson had worked less than a century earlier. My aim in this essay is to examine a number of Wren's buildings to show how they translate empirical understanding of the English climate into environmental form.

I have chosen to begin at the outset of Wren's work in architecture, with the Sheldonian Theatre at Oxford, because the building may be shown to resolve complex problems of what we now describe as the architectural environment that were to remain a consistent feature of Wren's architecture throughout his life. The study of the Sheldonian is followed by a survey of a selection of City churches. Here Wren's 1708 letter to the Commissioners provides a sound foundation for an environmental study. The buildings show how a consistent set of principles was adapted to different conditions of site and context. Finally, we will examine the library at Trinity College, Cambridge. The apparent simplicity of this structure conceals an original and sophisticated interpretation of the architectural problem of the academic library in which the conditions for readers and their books are resolved with breathtaking clarity.

The Sheldonian Theatre, Oxford, 1663–1669

Christopher Wren was 31 years old and was Professor of Astronomy at Oxford University when he was commissioned to design the Sheldonian Theatre (Figs 3.2 and 3.3). The primary purpose of the building was to house the university graduation ceremony – the Encaenia (9) – and other public events, plus dramatic and musical performances and even the 'dissection of bodies'. In addition, the building accommodated the university printing press (10). Previously the great ceremonies had taken place in St Mary's Church, but by this date their increasing secularism was considered inappropriate for a sacred building. On 29 April 1663 Wren presented a model of his design at a meeting of the Royal Society and construction began the following year. It is worth noting that, on 9 December of the same year, Wren demonstrated his design for a weather clock to the Society, a clear indication that his

3.2
Sheldonian Theatre, Oxford: exterior from the west.

interest in meteorological matters continued alongside his new activity as an architect (11).

The design of the Sheldonian is commonly taken to be based on the Roman Theatre of Marcellus, as represented by Vitruvius and Serlio (12). The D-shaped plan (Fig. 3.4) with tiered seating was appropriate, but the very different conditions of both function and climate found in Oxford dictated that the precedent would be no more than a point of departure. Most obvious was the need to provide a complete enclosure against the English climate. Wren's ingenious design for the 70-foot clear-span roof have been widely discussed (13), but little attention has been given to the equal ingenuity that he brought to bringing daylight into the interior of this large space. Twentieth-century building science has established that, under the English sky, good daylighting depends on having a clear view of the sky within a space (14). If we stand at the centre of the theatre and take in a 360° panorama, the impression is of an almost complete circumference of glazing. From all sides light floods the room from the clerestory above the gallery seating and this is reinforced by the lunettes that illuminate the seats beneath the gallery. The perimeter space that encloses the auditorium originally accommodated the compositors of the University Press and is well

3.3
Sheldonian Theatre, Oxford: interior.

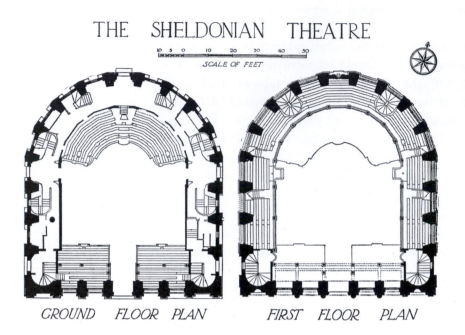

THE SHELDONIAN THEATRE

SCALE OF FEET

GROUND FLOOR PLAN   FIRST FLOOR PLAN

3.4
Sheldonian Theatre,
Oxford: plans.

3.5
Sheldonian Theatre,
Oxford: exterior.

lit by tall, narrow windows, and the basement, which was designed to house the printing presses, receives ample light from windows in the base of the façade. The roofspace above Wren's structure was used as a bookstore for the press and was copiously lit by the 11 dormer windows that may be seen in Loggan's engraving (Fig. 3.5) (15).

The Encaenia is customarily held on the Wednesday of the ninth week of the university's Trinity Term. This is the week in June during which the summer solstice occurs. At this brightest time of the year the interior is filled with light appropriate to this grandest of ceremonies. It is hard to think that Wren, at this date still the Professor of Astronomy, was not alert to this fact, nor that it did not have a direct bearing on his design. The building's opening ceremony was held some weeks after the solstice, on 19 July 1669, but would have enjoyed quite similar conditions. In his diary John Evelyn (16) gave an extensive account of the day's events, ' . . . all of which lasted from 11 in the morning till 7 at night . . .' (17), that is, well within the daylight hours of a summer's day and hence brightly illuminated within the building.

The organization of the façades of the Sheldonian has been widely and critically discussed. Summerson concluded that 'The result is a somewhat mechanical composition' (18). It is difficult to disagree with this judgement, but a different perspective emerges if we consider the design as an attempt to reconcile the principles of classical composition with a complex and demanding environmental programme. The key to an environmental analysis may be found in the cross-section of the building. This clearly reveals the way in which daylight is channelled into the principal space through the clerestory and the ring of lunettes. It equally illustrates the care given to lighting the compositor's accommodation and the spaces for the printing press in the basement. In view of this analysis, the secondary string course that links the arches of the arcade may, perhaps, be read as an expression of the building's internal volumetric organization in relation to light.

Images of the Encaenia ceremony depict the theatre packed to the rafters. One may easily imagine that, in the heat of midsummer, the building would become very warm, particularly for an assembly clad in heavy academic dress. There is ample evidence that Wren was alert to these other environmental needs. There is a detailed description of the building in Robert Plot's *The Natural History of Oxfordshire*, published in 1677 and, incidentally, printed in the building (19). Plot gives a very detailed description of the design of the window frames in the building:

The great *bivalve wooden windows* in the upper gallery of the *Theater* are so ingeniously contrived, that notwithstanding their great *weight*, yet can never sink so as to be brought out of *square*, as tis usual in such *windows*. . . Nor are the *round windows* below unworthy of consideration, being contrived to admit *air* in foul weather, yet not one drop of rain . . .

(20)

Plot's sketch of the upper windows does not indicate precisely how the opening mechanism operated, but that for the 'round windows' clearly shows what we call, in modern terminology, a horizontal centre pivot opening (Fig.3.6). The important point in the present discussion is the evidence here of Wren's concern for and understanding of the processes of natural ventilation in a building of this type, even of the need to achieve this in inclement weather.

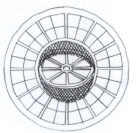

3.6
Sheldonian Theatre,
Oxford: window detail.

Acoustics is the branch of building science that is, generally, independent of the effects of climate. It is, however, one of the most important aspects of architecture in which principles of physics come into play. The programme for the Sheldonian required good acoustics to support the elaborate verbal ritual of the Encaenia and for the associated musical performances. Lisa Jardine reports that the acoustics of the theatre were greatly admired at the opening ceremonies in July 1669. A Pindaric Ode, *In Theatrum Sheldonianum, et eius Architectum*, recorded that there were no unwanted echoes and that both voice and music were heard with 'pleasing purity' (21).

If we view the Sheldonian as one of the first architectural works of a man schooled in the forefront of the science of his day we may begin to recognize it as a considerable achievement. The building combines antique precedent with the demands of a complex building programme. Wren's solution to the problem of the wide-span roof was a major innovation, and the hitherto little studied environmental qualities of the building may plausibly be seen to reflect his 'scientific' understanding of those elements of astronomy and meteorology that directly bear upon the building environment. This experience undoubtedly helped to prepare him for the other architectural challenges that were soon to come his way.

Although Summerson had good grounds for his critique of the Sheldonian's quality as architecture *per se*, he was fulsome in his recognition of its virtues as a symbol of the relation of the arts and sciences in Wren's day:

> . . . of all buildings (the Sheldonian) most exactly reflects the early image of (the Royal Society) and embodies its philosophy.
> . . . this Theatre is . . . the dispensation of a mode of thought most obviously manifested in the field which we

now call science but which can be seen, more rarely to have left its imprint on the arts and especially in architecture.

... everything in this building wears the livery of the Experimental Philosophy and of that Society with whose founding members it was so concerned.

It reflects, like no other I can think of, a crucial phase in our intellectual history – a phase of energy and optimism when the arts and sciences were conceived to be as symmetrically and devotedly disposed about Truth . . .

(22)

Fumifugium and ice fairs: the climate of seventeenth-century London

In 1661 John Evelyn published *Fumifugium*, a powerful tract in which he describes the foul atmospheric conditions of London (23). Evelyn provides a lyrical description of the natural qualities of the city's situation:

> ... the City of London is built upon a sweet and most agreeable Eminency of Ground, at the North-side of a goodly and well-condition'd River, towards which it hath an Aspect by a gentle and easie declivity, apt to be improv'd to all that may render her Palaces, Buildings and Avenues usefull, graceful and most magnificent: The Fumes which exhale from Waters and lower Grounds lying South-ward, by which means they are perpetually attracted, carried off or dissipated by the Sun, as soon as they are born and ascend.

Sadly this idyll was compromised by the effects of:

> ... that Hellish and dismall Cloud of SEA COAL . . . which is not onely perpetually imminent over her head, For as the Poet,
>
> *Conditur in tenebris altum caliine Coelum:*
>
> But so universally mixed with the otherwise wholsome and excellent Are, that her Inhabitants breathe nothing but an impure and thick Mist accompanied with a fulginous and filthy vapour, which renders them obnoxious to a thousand inconveniences . . .

Evelyn goes on to make ambitious, but unrealized, proposals for the replanning of London. The industrial processes that he identifies as the major sources of pollution would be moved to the periphery of the city and extensive gardens would be created at its centre to help cleanse the atmosphere.

Seasonal extremes of climate were commonplace during this phase of the Little Ice Age, with warm summers followed by the fiercest of winters. The winter of 1683–1684 was the most severe in living memory and notable for the freezing of the Thames. Fagan cites John Evelyn's diary entry for 24 January 1684:

> Frost . . . more & more severe, the Thames before London was planted with bothes (booths) in formal streets, as in a Citty . . .
>
> (24)

This condition is depicted in a celebrated engraving of the Ice Fair of 1683, captioned:

> An Exact and Lively Mapp or representation of Boothes and all the varieties of Showes and Humours upon the ICE on the River of THAMES by London During the memorable frost . . . MDCLXXXIII

Compare this description with Canaletto's benignly lyrical image of a 'Venetian' London in summer, painted in 1746 (Plate 10).

From these fragments we may construct a description of the physical climate of London in Wren's day in which the atmosphere was extremely polluted throughout the year and the winters were bitterly cold.

So extreme was the cold that year that the Royal Society requested Evelyn to present a paper to report on the extent of the damage in his celebrated garden at Deptford, to which he responded by letter giving a detailed account of the destruction. Robert Plot and Jacob Bobart also spoke to the Society on the subject of the 1683 frost (25).

The Great Fire

> dim reddish sunshine . . . Tis unusual colour of the Air without cloud made the Sunbeams of a strange red dim light, was very remarkable. We had then heard nothing of the Fire of *London*. But it appeared afterward to be the smoke of London then burning, which being driven this way by an Easterly wind, caused this odd Phenomenon.

This quotation from the diary of John Locke describes the effects of the Great Fire of London, as they were experienced in Oxford (26). Lisa Jardine provides convincing evidence that Wren was an eyewitness of the fire, which began on 2 September. He is recorded to have been with Evelyn in London on 27 August, with all probability that he had other commitments in the city during the following days (27). Nonetheless, the fact that the Great Fire had effects as far away as Oxford links Wren's fledgling project at the Sheldonian, which was still under construction at the time of the fire, to the great project that he was about to begin in reconstructing the City churches. The fire destroyed 86 churches, and Wren's role in replacing these was one of his greatest tasks and achievements (28).

Numerous proposals were made for dramatic replanning of London, not least by Wren, Evelyn and Robert Hooke, none of which was adopted, and the pragmatic prescriptions of the Rebuilding Acts of 1667 and 1670 were to have the most profound effect on the reconstruction that was swiftly underway. The Acts are principally concerned with defining new standards of construction of buildings, requiring the use of brick in place of timber and defining new relationships between the widths of streets and the heights of buildings (29), but make no significant attempt at radical replanning. It was in this context that the rebuilding of the churches took place. Many of them are on the sites of earlier structures and these primarily define their dimensions and conditions. Under the Rebuilding Act of 1670, Commissioners were appointed to direct the reconstruction of churches. A list of 51 was authorized by Parliament and a short-list of 15 identified for early rebuilding (30). Thus began a process that continued for half a century.

Spaces of light and sound: the City churches

The dire effects of the fire and the vivid descriptions of the extremes of the climate of London, at precisely the time that Wren was beginning his architectural work in the city, suggest that the project of rebuilding the City churches was undertaken in circumstances that were often dramatically different from those that are depicted in Canaletto's paintings of summer scenes.

We have the great good fortune to have Wren's own words on the key questions concerning the design of churches. These are to be found in the *Letter to a Friend on the Commission for Building Fifty New City Churches* that he wrote following the Act of 1708 that established a new Commission (31). Towards the end of his life Wren presumed to offer the benefit of his experience to his successors. The letter is an objectively prescriptive statement on all practical matters in relation to the design of churches for '. . . the reformed religion'. He proposes that the aim should be to house a congregation of two thousand and that the priority should be to ensure that:

. . . all who are present can both hear and see. The *Romanists*, indeed, may build larger churches, it is enough if they hear the Murmur of the Mass, and see the Elevation of the Host, but ours are to be fitted as Auditories.

Here Wren declares the importance of seeing and hearing in the design of a church, hence of daylight and acoustics – exactly the concerns that underlay the design of the Sheldonian Theatre. The matter of acoustics – Wren uses the term 'auditory' to describe this function of a church – is resolved by a practical formula, 'Concerning the placement of the Pulpit':

A moderate voice may be heard 50 feet distant before the preacher, 30 feet on each side and 20 behind the Pulpit . . .

From this analysis he advises that a church '. . . should be at least 60 Feet broad and 90 Feet long . . .'.

3.7
St James's, Piccadilly, London: exterior from south-east.

As an illustration of these principles translated into form, Wren refers in the letter to his design for St James's, Piccadilly (1676–1684) (Fig. 3.7), not strictly a city church, but, probably because its site was free from many of the limitations found in the city, the most clear-cut exemplar. The plan of St James's (Fig. 3.8) is a rectangular box, with galleried aisles either side of a five-bay, barrel-vaulted nave. It stands on a relatively open site that permits ample light to enter from large windows to both north and south, as is clearly shown on John Strype's map of the parish in the 1720 edition of Stow's *Survey of London* (32) (Fig. 3.9). The interior is flooded with light from the high, arched windows above the galleries on either side of the nave. These were filled with clear glass in leaded lights. The walls were originally painted a bright, pale stone colour, which reinforced the direct light. Even in the more densely built surroundings of today, the interior is amply lit and the aisles are also bright from the openings beneath the galleries. As so often in environmental analysis, the cross-section is the key to the effectiveness of the design. A large proportion of sky is visible from all points

3.8
St James's, Piccadilly, London: plan and section.

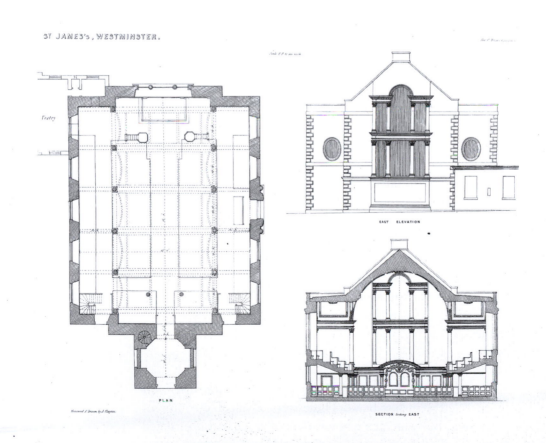

ST JAMES's, WESTMINSTER.

PLAN

EAST ELEVATION

SECTION looking EAST

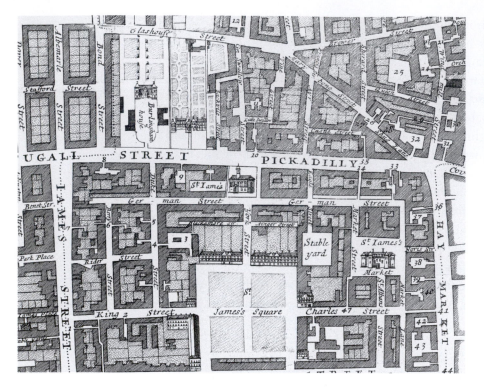

3.9
St James's, Piccadilly,
London: site plan from
Strype's *Survey of London*,
1720 edition (Motco
Enterprises).

of the interior. Under the English sky this is the guarantor of good light. The Sunday services were held in the morning and afternoon to take advantage of this daylight. Artificial light, when necessary for wintertime evensong, was provided by candles mounted in free-standing metal candelabra. Jeffrey suggests that a typical church would have just four or six of these (33). Wren's prescription for good acoustics is observed almost to the letter (34).

The Commissioners required the new churches to be unadorned, plain boxes. The provision of furniture and fittings was the responsibility of the parish. Wren expresses his opinion on the subject in the 'Letter', where he urges:

> A Church should not be so fill'd with Pews, but that the Poor may have room enough to stand and sit in the Alleys, for to them equally is the Gospel preach'd. It were to be no Pews, but Benches . . .

(35)

This seems to be a strong reaction to the extent to which the first-built churches had been filled with box pews. These were a valuable source of income for the parishes, but were extravagant users of space and obstructed the view of the service. But there was, almost certainly, another reason for

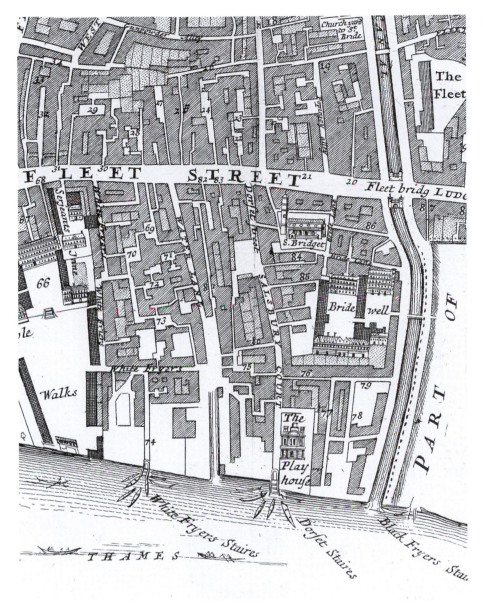

3.10
St Bride, Fleet Street,
London: site plan from
Strype's *Survey of London*,
1720 edition (Motco
Enterprises).

their popularity. This was to provide a modicum of thermal comfort for their occupants. As built, the churches were unheated and, bearing in mind the extreme cold of late-seventeenth-century winters, attendance at service would have been a thermal ordeal. The enclosure of a box pew protects against draughts and, by conserving the heat of closely and presumably well-clad bodies, provides a slightly more comfortable microclimate.

Of the city churches proper, St Bride, Fleet Street (1671–1675) closely resembles the principles that Wren set out in the 'Letter'. Strype's 1720 map (Fig 3.10) shows the churchyard closely bounded by buildings, as

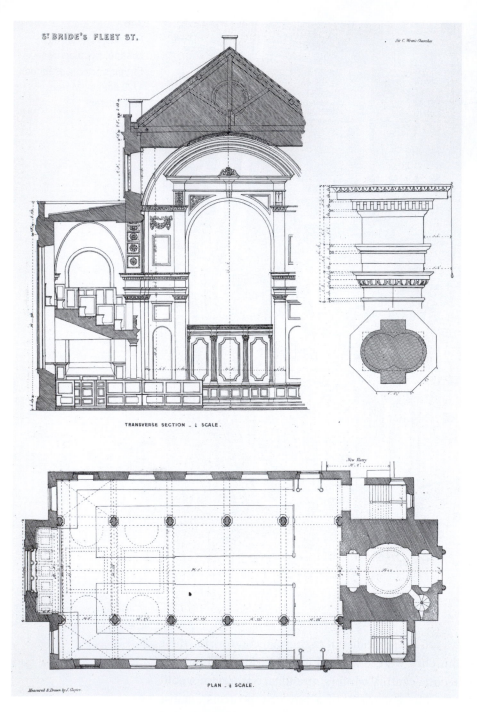

ST BRIDE'S FLEET ST.

Sir C. Wren's Churches

TRANSVERSE SECTION _ ⅛ SCALE.

Measured & Drawn by J. Clayton.

PLAN _ ⅛ SCALE.

3.11
St Bride, Fleet Street,
London: plan and section.

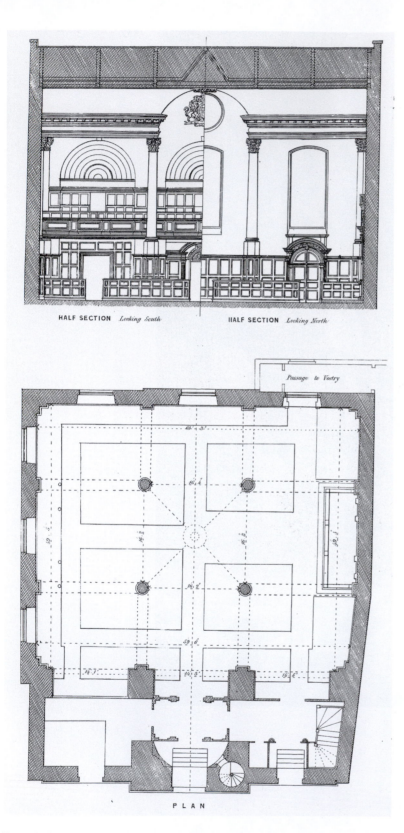

HALF SECTION *Looking South*   HALF SECTION *Looking North*

Passage to Vestry

P L A N

it remains today, but adequate space is left to north and south to ensure that the interior is not unduly obstructed. The five-bay nave is, in plan, similar to that of St James's, but the cross-section is quite different (Fig.3.11). Here, however, there are no galleries and the light of the barrel-vaulted nave is substantially provided from clerestory windows. These are free from any obstruction by neighbouring buildings and we may surmise that this was Wren's response to the density of the surrounding city (36) to ensure that the interior was illuminated by a clear view of the sky (Fig. 3.12).

From these studies of St James's and St Bride, we may suggest that Wren and his collaborators in the reconstruction of the churches established a set of underlying principles that would guide the design of spaces that met

the needs of the church, whatever the specific conditions of their sites. At the heart of these lies a deep, 'scientific' understanding of the relationship between form and light. Studies of other churches help to support this hypothesis.

The situation of St Martin, Ludgate (1676–1686) is one of the most restricted of all. It occupies more or less the same site as the earlier structure and stands hard against the pavement in Ludgate. To east and west are party walls with adjoining buildings and the garden of Stationer's Hall lies to the north. Wren's design makes the most of this compressed space. The church is entered from the south through an ingenious spatial layering that creates a deep porch within the simple enclosure. This leads into the nave that juxtaposes a cross-in-square upon an east–west axis. Once more it is the cross-section that reveals the subtlety of the arrangement (Figs 3.13 and 3.14). Three large arched windows project south light across the deep space above the low enclosure of the porch, and corresponding segmental headed openings and a high circular opening provide balancing north light from over the garden that miraculously survives in the much-transformed modern city. The present, near-white decoration renders the interior wonderfully bright, even allowing for the effects of stained glass that has replaced in part the original clear glazing. The original box pews survived until 1894, when the present pews were made from their timber (37).

St James Garlickhythe (or Garlic Hill) (1676–1684) stands to the north of Thames Street close to the river (Fig. 3.15). The church is unusual in having a distinctly defined chancel and is a further variant on the nave-and-aisle plan, with clerestory lights to the nave. At the central of the five bays the clerestory is interrupted, to both north and south, by cross vaults terminated by large circular windows (38). An intriguing asymmetry is introduced by the omission of low-level windows to the south aisle, in contrast to the north wall, which has large windows in all but the central bay. We may surmise that this was in response to the noise and clamour of Thames Street, which, in Wren's day, was a major thoroughfare giving access to the wharves that lined the river just to the south (39). The interior (Fig. 3.16) is, nonetheless, light-filled, even in its denser modern surroundings. The luminosity of the interior soon earned St James the appellation of 'Wren's Lantern'.

St Stephen Walbrook (1672–1680) is one of the earliest of the new churches and is, perhaps, one of the most spatially complex. John Summerson described it as 'a magnificent new departure', and Pevsner referred to its 'spatial polyphony' as 'architecture of Purcell's age' (40). The church is entered from Walbrook to the west, and the area to the north was, at the time of construction, the open space of the Stocks Market, but soon occupied by George Dance Senior's Mansion House (1739–1751) (Fig. 3.17). Buildings pressed close from the south, and to the east was an open churchyard, still

3.15
(facing page)
St James Garlickhythe, London: exterior from south.

surviving in part. The plan of the body of the church is a simple rectangle, but its complexity is the result of Wren's play between an aisled and a centralized plan and the development of this in cross-section. The space is dominated by the dome, which is supported on eight arches springing from eight columns (Fig. 3.18). Triangular vaults span the spaces behind the diagonal arches. The complexity of the roof form that follows from this arrangement produces a distribution and intensity of daylight that exceeds that of all the other city churches. The arched windows of the clerestory admit light from all orientations and this is reinforced by the elliptical windows that occupy the upper walls of the aisles. Some light also creeps around the tower and other obstructions to the west and the group of large

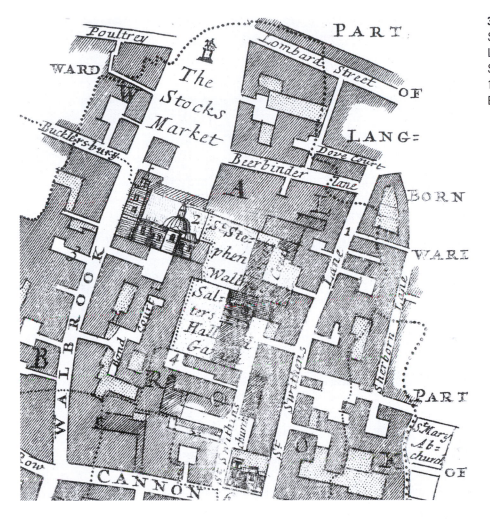

3.17
St Stephen Walbrook,
London: site plan from
Strype's *Survey of London*,
1720 edition (Motco
Enterprises).

windows to the east are largely unobstructed. The lantern light of the dome
completes the ensemble (Fig. 3.19). The effect is to invest the interior with
ever-changing light that, as the sun moves on its daily course and clouds
come and go, plays upon walls, floor and structure with 'polyluminous' effects
that entirely support Pevsner's analogy with the polyphonic music of Henry
Purcell, a far cry from the 'functional' prescriptions of the 'Letter'. Kerry
Downes has written:

> Wren considered geometry to be the basis of the whole
> world and the manifestation of its Creator, while light not
> only made that geometry visible, but also represented the
> gift of Reason, of which geometry was for him the highest
> expression.

(41)

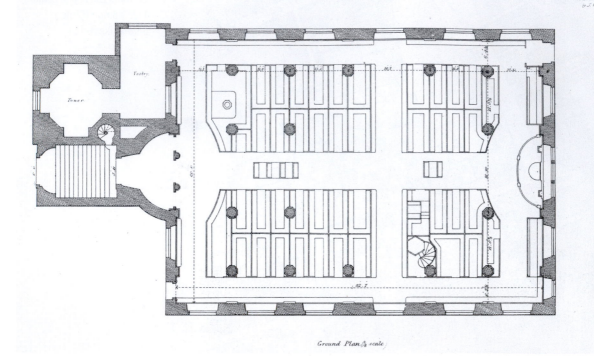

Ground Plan (⅛ scale)

The light at St Stephen is ample for all practical purposes. But the alternating patterns of light and shade, the sudden and brief illumination of the shaft of a column, that reshape the space from hour to hour and from season to season show that Wren's scientific understanding of light was fused with a remarkable environmental imagination. The liturgical requirement for an east–west orientation in the Christian church has the consequence of investing the dominant spatial symmetry of the church buildings with an asymmetry of light. This is the case in all churches, but the effect is emphasized in all Wren's designs and is most powerfully revealed at St Stephen's.

Although it is the daylight that dominates any discussion of the environmental quality of St Stephen, we should pay attention to the other elements. Samuel Wale's 1746 engraving of the interior looking west shows it without pews, but Downes states that these were installed in 1678 (42). Thomas Malton's engraving, dated 1792, shows the high box pews, which would have brought their familiar thermal benefits (Fig. 3.20). This image shows no indication of any source of artificial light. This is an omission from architectural rendering that persists to the present day, but confirms that such arrangements, unlike those of most modern buildings, were regarded as

3.18
St Stephen Walbrook, London: plan.

secondary to daylight, both in their utility and certainly in their architectural significance. The image also omits the magnificent pulpit by William Newman that was installed in 1679. This commands the space and, with its imposing sound-reflecting canopy, ensures that the spoken word is heard throughout the interior.

In progressing from his adaptation of models from antiquity in his design for the Sheldonian Theatre to the diversity and invention shown in the City churches, it is possible to identify the significance of Wren's scientific knowledge of the 'mathematical sciences' and, in particular, his grasp of aspects of astronomy and meteorology in defining the 'functional' and

1
Robert Smythson, Hardwick Hall: west front.

2
Sir Christopher Wren, Library, Trinity College, Cambridge: west front.

3
Lord Burlington,
Chiswick House:
entrance front.

4
Sir Charles Barry,
The Reform Club, London:
view from Pall Mall.

5
Charles Rennie
Mackintosh, The Hill
House, Helensburgh.

6
George Checkley, Willow
House, Cambridge:
south front.

7
Alison and Peter Smithson, Upper Lawn Pavilion, Wiltshire.

8
Jan Siberechts, 'Henley on Thames', 1698.

9
Jan Siberechts, 'Wollaton Hall and Park', 1695.

10
Antonio Canaletto, 'View of London
from Richmond House', 1746.

11
Thomas Gainsborough, 'Mr and Mrs Andrews', 1749.

12
Luke Howard, 'Cloud Study'.

13
Claude Monet, 'The Houses of Parliament, sunlight in the fog', 1904.

14
Spencer Gore, 'Harold Gilman's House
at Letchworth', 1912.

15
Paul Nash, 'Landscape of the summer
solstice', 1943.

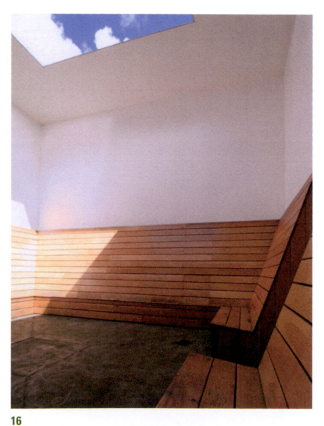

16
James Turrell, 'Skyspace', Houghton Hall,
Norfolk, 2005–2006.

17
Le Corbusier, *Le Poème de l'Angle Droit*.

expressive qualities of these buildings. To conclude this exploration of Wren as a master of the architectural environment we now turn to the library of Trinity College, Cambridge.

Complete, Magnanimous Serenity

My title here is John Summerson's description of the library at Trinity College, Cambridge (43) (Plate 2). This judgement is supported by Kerry Downes, who wrote, 'No single Wren building is more masterly, or exemplifies better the qualities of his style . . .' (44). These observations provide the basis for the present examination of the building from an environmental viewpoint.

David McKitterick explains the background to the conception of the library and its subsequent history, explaining its significance within the life of college and university (45). Let us establish the facts of the building. It stands at the western edge of the college, close to the bank of the River Cam and overlooking the sweep of college gardens known as the 'Backs' (Fig. 3.21). The building consists of a single, large, rectangular room at first-floor level, standing above an open cloister. The long axis of the rectangular plan is oriented almost exactly north–south. The approach is from the north up a simple, but elegant staircase within a brightly lit enclosure (46). From the entrance the entire library is revealed in a perspective that is reinforced by the black-and-white chequered pattern of the marble floor (Fig. 3.22). The interior is some 200 feet (60 metres) long and 45 feet (13.5 metres) wide and is horizontally divided between the dark hardwood of the book presses and the bright upper realm of windows and white-painted plaster. Construction began in 1676 and the books were moved from the old library into the new building in 1695.

From these simple elements Wren wrought a radical transformation of the architecture of the library. Before this, libraries, certainly in Britain, had followed the mediaeval model derived from the monastery. At Cambridge the library at St John's College followed this precedent just half a century before Trinity, in 1623–1624 (47). There the book presses are placed at right angles to the piers of outer walls to form well-lit aedicules. This arrangement has the disadvantage of limiting the number of books that may be kept in the space. Wren's design raised the windows above the top of the book presses and this allowed him to combine the mediaeval arrangement with wall shelving, thereby increasing the book capacity of the building, and to greatly enlarge the area of windows, which now occupy most of the upper walls (Fig. 3.23).

The remarkable luminosity of the building follows directly from this arrangement. Wren's experience in the management daylight at the Sheldonian, completed seven years before work began at Trinity, and the concurrent

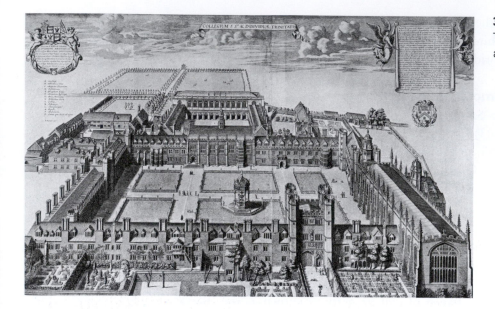

3.21
Trinity College, Cambridge,
after Loggan.

work on City churches is brought to bear on this new problem. The east–west orientation of the site was determined by the existing structures of the college, but Wren would certainly have understood the effects of this for lighting the building. The sun directly enters from the east in the early morning and the west late in the afternoon, but is excluded as it moves through the southerly quarter of the sky for the hours astride noon. This excludes the greatest heat of the day in the summer months, but provides agreeable light and warmth at other times. In the summer, morning and evening sunlight reaches into the lower part of the room, but in winter it is contained just to the upper part. Its presence, moving diurnally and seasonally, animates the interior and provides a quiet and constant reminder of the otherwise invisible world outside. Even under the frequently overcast skies of England the large areas of glass provide ample light that is reinforced by the reflectance of the brightly painted walls and ceiling. In the terminology of modern building science the room has high values for both the 'sky component' and the 'internally reflected component' of the 'daylight factor' (48). Wren designed tables and stools to be placed in the aedicules formed by the book presses. These are still in place today and the modern scholar continues to enjoy ample light for study. More than any of the other buildings discussed here, Trinity Library offers an anticipatory sense of its light from the exterior. This is most potently seen when the building is viewed from the east on a bright afternoon and the sun penetrates through the clerestories and into Whewell's Court.

3.22
(facing page)
Library, Trinity College,
Cambridge: interior.

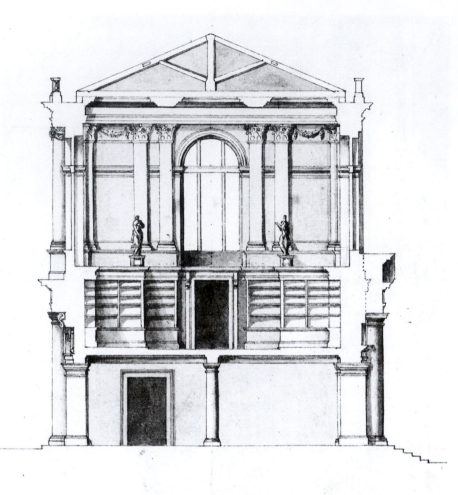

Artificial lighting would, if available at all, have been furnished by simple, portable candlesticks, but it is unlikely that the library would have been much used after dark, particularly in the winter months, when the inside temperature would have been very low. The Fellows of the college would have been able to retire with books to their nearby rooms to enjoy their firesides and to work, if they did, by candlelight. An insight into this condition may be found from John Evelyn, who had a 'little Cell and Cabinet' in which to work at his house at Deptford. From there he wrote, in a letter to Pepys, that 'tis now neere Three in the morning' (49), suggesting that, with the primitive means at his disposal, he had sufficient light to work through the night. Gaskell and Robson (50) note that, from the outset, the library was open at defined times, under the supervision of the undergraduate Sub-Librarian. The library was open to Fellow-Commoners in addition to Fellows, but 'no one would choose to stay for long during cold weather'.

In the seventeenth century the climate of the Fens (51) would have suffered the same general effects of the Little Ice Age as we noted in Oxford and London. The winters might have been even more severe because the region is particularly exposed to chill continental airflow at this season. A useful, detailed source is the weather diary kept from 1684 to 1689 by Sir John Wittewronge at Rothamsted in Hertfordshire (52). Rothamsted is just over forty miles to the south-west of Cambridge and it is reasonable to assume that the weather recorded by Wittewronge was broadly similar to that at Cambridge, during the construction of the library. Wittewronge possessed a 'weather glass', a barometer, to which he makes frequent reference in the diary, but his reports of thermal conditions are entirely subjective. They are, however, vividly descriptive. The overall picture confirms the temperature pattern of the late Little Ice Age as this is described in the Central England Temperature (CET) records (53), with very cold and lengthy winters, but also with frequently warm summer periods. There were, as one would expect in Britain, departures from the rule. For example, the months of December in 1685 and 1686 are both recorded as being 'calm and warm', as is corroborated in the CET records. But, in 1684, 1687 and 1688, December was very cold and snow either fell or lay on the ground on Christmas Day at Rothamsted. Perhaps the most relevant lesson of Witte-wronge's diary is that it reveals the manner in which the weather was an ever-present factor in everyday life at this period and would affect perceptions of the utility of buildings for all purposes, including so grand an enterprise as a college library. On a point of detail, James Campbell has revealed that there was a particularly long gap in the construction of the library, as revealed by the building accounts, during the winter of 1683–1684, the year of the Great Frost (54).

There is some speculation that there may have been a hearth or stove at the north end of the library, where evidence of a chimney was found during a major restoration of the building in the 1970s. Gaskell and Robson correctly observe that this would have provided little heat in this large room, but it would have offered a degree of comfort to readers who might have gathered close by. The same authors provide a further clue to the thermal experience of the building:

> when the Master and Seniors required a new catalogue in 1739, they ordered the Librarian to undertake it 'as soon as the weather permits'.
>
> (55)

Seventeenth-century users of public and institutional buildings would not expect them to provide the comforts to which we are accustomed. They would accept a range of temperatures higher and lower than those proposed in modern design codes, and the building would be quite intensively used, within these limits. It may be that Wren was seeking to achieve a little more comfort by raising the timber floors of the aedicules above the marble paving of the open centre. As with the box pews of the churches, the timber floor and book presses create tiny microclimates for study. Ever alert to acoustic matters, Wren's intention in using marble paving in the body of the library was to quieten the sound of footsteps (56).

Conclusion

Life in seventeenth-century England was made eventful by the oscillations of political and religious events, from monarchy to republic, on to restoration, and the tensions between Catholicism and Protestantism. It was also the time when the foundations of modern science were being laid, most notably with the creation in 1660 of the Royal Society. Climate history tells us that these events were enacted against the background of a physical climate that was more extreme even than that of previous decades. The Little Ice Age was characterized by frequent extreme winters, although there are records of benign summers (57). The metropolis suffered from atmospheric pollution to the point that this provoked statements of the power of Evelyn's *Fumifugium* and was responsible for high mortality rates and damage to buildings (58). Christopher Wren's long life spanned almost all the significant years of the century and on into the next. He was affected by these events in many ways (59). This essay explores a neglected aspect of the influence of this context by proposing a connection between his early experience in the emerging sciences with his architectural work and the manner in which this demonstrates a response to both the generalities and specifics of the natural and artificial climate of the time. From this Wren emerges, in addition to all of his familiar achievements, as a precursor of the science-based architect of later centuries.

Notes

1. For the most comprehensive scholarly review of Wren's life and work see, Lisa Jardine, *On a Grander Scale: The Outstanding Career of Sir Christopher Wren*, Harper Collins, London, 2002.

2. John Summerson, 'The Mind of Wren', in *Heavenly Mansions and Other Essays on Architecture*, Cresset Press, London, 1949. The essay was written in 1936, when it was awarded the RIBA Essay Prize and printed in the *RIBA Journal*.

3. *Ibid.*

4. J. A. Bennett, *The Mathematical Science of Christopher Wren*, Cambridge University Press, Cambridge, 1982.

5. *Ibid.*

6. The letter is in Christopher Wren, Junior, *Parentalia: or, memoirs of the family of the Wren; viz Of Mathew Bishop of Ely, Christopher Dean of Windsor, etc. but chiefly of Sir Christopher*

Wren, Late Surveyor-General of the Royal Buildings, President of the Royal Society, etc. etc., T. Osborn and R. Dodsley, London, 1750, reprinted Gregg Press, London, 1965 (the 'heirloom' copy). Wren's churches were amongst the first to be designed specifically to meet the needs of the reformed church, following the destruction of the earlier Gothic churches in the Great Fire.

7. Wren, Junior, *Parentalia*, pp. 207–208.

8. Bennett, cited in Note 4, effectively reviews Wren's work on the development of meteorological instruments. A design for a weather-clock is illustrated on page 209 of *Parentalia*. See also Asit J. Biswas, 'The Automatic Rain-Gauge of Sir Christopher Wren, FRS', *Notes and Records of the Royal Society*, Vol. 22, 1967, pp. 94–104.

9. The Encaenia is today the annual ceremony at which honorary degrees are awarded. In Wren's day it included extensive musical performances and satirical speeches.

10. The most succinct account of the architecture of the Sheldonian Theatre may be found in Howard Colvin, *The Sheldonian Theatre and the Divinity School*, Oxford University Press, Oxford, 1981, reprinted 1996.

11. John Summerson illustrates both the building and the instrument in 'Sir Christopher Wren, PRS (1632–1723)', *Notes and Records of the Royal Society*, Vol. 15, 1960, pp. 99–105.

12. Kerry Downes, *Christopher Wren*, Allen Lane, The Penguin Press, London, 1971, asserts this connection. John Summerson, *Architecture in Britain: 1530–1830*, Penguin, Harmondsworth, 1953; 9th revised edition, Yale University Press, New Haven, CT, 1993. Margaret Whinney, *Wren*, Thames and Hudson, London, 1971.

13. See Downes, *Christopher Wren*, and Whinney, *Wren*.

14. The fundamentals of daylighting, in which the importance of the 'sky component' is demonstrated, are clearly set out in R. G. Hopkinson, *Architectural Physics: Daylighting*, HMSO, London, 1963.

15. The dormers were removed when the roof was reconstructed in the nineteenth century by George Saunders.

16. Evelyn was a founding fellow of the Royal Society and a friend of Wren. See Gillian Darley, *John Evelyn: Living for Ingenuity*, Yale University Press, New Haven, CT, 2006.

17. E. S. de Beer (ed.), *The Diary of John Evelyn*, Clarendon Press, Oxford, 1955, Vol. III.

18. Summerson, *Architecture in Britain*, cited in Note 12.

19. Robert Plot, *The Natural History of Oxfordshire*, Printed at the Theatre, Oxford, 1677.

20. Plot, *The Natural History of Oxfordshire*, paragraph 147. The original gallery window frames no longer exist. The present frames lack the diagonal arrangement of the leaded lights of the originals. The existing lunettes, Plot's 'round windows', appear similar to those described.

21. See Jardine, *On a Grander Scale*, cited in Note 1. The Ode is in Wren, Junior, *Parentalia* (cited in Note 6), pp. 339–342.

22. John Summerson, *The Sheldonian in its Time*, Clarendon Press, Oxford, 1964.

23. John Evelyn, *Fumifugium, or The Inconveniencie of the Aer and Smoak of London Dissipated. Together With some Remedies humbly Proposed*, London, 1661.

24. John Evelyn, *Diaries*, cited in Brian Fagan, *The Little Ice Age: How Climate made History 1300–1850*, Basic Books, New York, 2000.

25. John Evelyn, 'An Abstract of a Letter from the Worshipful John Evelyn Esq.; Sent to One of the Secretaries of the R. Society concerning the Dammage Done to His Gardens by the Preceding Winter', *Philosophical Transactions of the Royal Society*, Vol. 14, 1684, pp. 559–563. Robert Plot and Jacob Bobart, 'A Discourse Concerning the Effects of the Great Frost, on Trees and Other Plants Anno 1683', *Philosophical Transactions of the Royal Society*, Vol. 14, 1684, pp. 766–779.

26. John Locke, cited in Peter Brimblecombe, *The Big Smoke: A History of Air Pollution in London since Medieval Times*, Methuen, London, 1987; paperback edition, Routledge, London, 1988.

27. Jardine, *On a Grander Scale*, cited in Note 1. Jardine also points out that Wren would have no obligation to be in Oxford in connection with his duties as Professor of Astronomy at that date, because it was the university vacation. She also suggests that the supervision of the construction of the Sheldonian Theatre was in the hands of others.

28. See Paul Jeffrey, *The City Churches of Sir Christopher Wren*, Hambledon Continuum, London, 1996, for a comprehensive account of Wren's work in connection with the churches. Most valuably this presents a gazetteer of 59 churches that were built 'under the care and conduct of Sir Christopher Wren'. These include churches, such as St James's, Piccadilly, that were without the City of London, as well as St Paul's itself. Invaluable earlier sources are J. Clayton, *The Works of Christopher Wren: The Dimensions, Plans, Elevations and Sections of the Parochial Churches of Sir Christopher Wren. Erected in the Cities of London and Westminster*, Longman, Brown, Green & Longman, London, 1848–1849, and A. H. Mackmurdo, *Wren's City Churches*, G. Allen, Orpington, 1883.

29. C. C. Knowles and P. H. Pitt, *The History of Building Regulations in London, 1189–1972*, The Architectural Press, London, 1972, summarizes the provisions of the Acts.

30. Jeffrey, *The City Churches of Sir Christopher Wren*, cited in Note 28.

31. 'Letter to a Friend on the Commission for Building Fifty New City Churches', in Wren, Junior, *Parentalia* (cited in Note 6), Part 2, Section 9, pp. 318–321. The letter is reproduced in full in Lydia Soo, *Wren's Tracts on Architecture and Other Writings*, Cambridge University Press, Cambridge, 1998.

32. John Strype, *Survey of the Cities of London and Westminster*, 1720.

33. Jeffrey, *The City Churches of Sir Christopher Wren*, cited in Note 28.

34. It is worth observing that these acoustics, which are preserved relatively unchanged, not only serve modern liturgical needs, but are also appreciated at the numerous musical performances that are nowadays held in the church.

35. Wren, '*Letter to a Friend . . .*', in Wren, Junior, *Parentalia*, cited in Note 6.

36. Galleries were inserted over the aisles in the eighteenth century and these are shown in the cross-section published in Clayton, *The Works of Christopher Wren*, cited in Note 26. They were destroyed by bombing during the Second World War and were not reinstated in the rebuilding.

37. Jeffrey, *The City Churches of Sir Christopher Wren*, cited in Note 28.

38. Paul Jeffrey records that these circular windows replace the original large, round-headed openings.

39. The asymmetry continues to be an effective barrier against the hostile, modern, dual-carriageway motorway that Thames Street has become. A perhaps incidental benefit of the asymmetry is that the interior receives less direct sunlight on summer's days and therefore remains cool in hot weather. The custodian confirmed this experience to the author during a research visit on an unusually warm day in May 2009.

40. Summerson, *Architecture in Britain*, cited in Note 12. Nikolaus Pevsner, *An Outline of European Architecture*, 7th edition, Pelican, Harmondsworth, 1963.

41. Kerry Downes, *A Thousand Years of the Church of St Stephen Walbrook*, pamphlet, St Stephen Walbrook, London, undated.

42. Downes, *A Thousand Years of the Church of St Stephen Walbrook*.

43. Summerson, *Architecture in Britain*, cited in Note 12.

44. Downes, *A Thousand Years of the Church of St Stephen Walbrook*.

45. David McKitterick (ed.), *The Making of the Wren Library*, Cambridge University Press, Cambridge, 1995. This contains an extended essay by Howard Colvin describing the building.

46. Wren's original design showed staircases at both north and south ends, but the latter was not built.

47. See Howard Colvin in David McKitterick, *The Making of the Wren Library*.

48. The *daylight factor* is defined as the illumination at a point within a building expressed as a ratio of the simultaneous exterior illumination from the unobstructed sky. For computational purposes it is often expressed as the sum of three components: the *sky component*, the *external reflected component* and the *internal reflected component*.

49. Cited in Darley, *John Evelyn: Living for Ingenuity*, cited in Note 16.

50. Philip Gaskell and Robert Robson, *The Library of Trinity College, Cambridge: A Short History*, Trinity College, Cambridge, 1971.

51. The Fens is the region of England extending northwards from Cambridge to meet the North Sea some forty miles away at The Wash. Much of the terrain lies at or below sea level and the landscape is criss-crossed by drainage ditches. The region has low rainfall, although the ground waters lead to high humidity. It enjoys one of the highest incidences of sunshine in Britain. The winters are, however, colder than the average for the south of Britain.

52. Margaret Harcourt Williams and John Stevenson (eds), *'Observations of Weather': The Weather Diary of Sir John Wittewronge of Rothamsted 1684–1689*, Hertfordshire Record Publications, Vol. 15, Hertfordshire Record Society, Hertford, 1999.

53. This comparison is made by Williams and Stevenson, *'Observations of Weather'*.

54. James Campbell tabulates winter gaps in the building accounts of the library in *Constructing the Trinity Library: An Investigation of the Role of Constructional Technology in the Work of Sir Christopher Wren*, Diploma in Architecture dissertation, Department of Architecture, University of Cambridge, 1993 (unpublished).

55. Gaskell and Robson, *The Library of Trinity College, Cambridge*, cited in Note 50.

56. Colvin in McKitterick, *The Making of the Wren Library*, cited in Note 45.

57. Fagan, *The Little Ice Age*, cited in Note 24.

58. Brimblecombe, *The Big Smoke*, cited in Note 26.

59. See Jardine, *On a Grander Scale*, cited in Note 1.

Essay 4
Palladianism and the climate of England

In the second decade of the eighteenth century a profound change took place in English architecture. John Summerson ascribes the beginnings and the essence of 'the Palladian movement' to the publication of two books, both of which first appeared in 1715 (1). The first was *Vitruvius Britannicus* by Colen Campbell, which presented one hundred engravings of classical buildings in Britain and was followed, in 1717 and 1725, by two additional volumes illustrating further buildings (2). The second book was the English translation of Andrea Palladio's *I quattro libri dell'architettura*, with the illustrations redrawn by Giacomo Leoni and the text translated by Nicholas Dubois (3).

In Summerson's analysis *Vitruvius Britannicus* is 'a conspectus of English country houses considered as architecture' (4). In the first volume these include works by Christopher Wren, Thomas Archer, Inigo Jones, Thomas Talman, John Vanbrugh and Campbell himself. Campbell's texts that accompany the engravings are predominantly descriptive, being concerned with establishing, in some cases, the overall dimensions of the buildings and, in others, discussing the materials used and aspects of the classical style. This pattern continues in the second and third volumes. Throughout the three volumes no mention is made of the means by which all of these architects carefully adapted their Italianate designs to the English climate, so different from that of the European and mainly Italian precedents that they follow. In *I quattro libri*, however, Palladio provides detailed prescriptions for the calibration of a building to the characteristics of the Italian climate, specifically to that of the Veneto. In the First Book, in Chapter 25, we find a formula by which windows may be given dimensions in relation to the rooms that they serve:

> Make sure when making windows that they do not let in too much or too little light and that they are not more spread out or closer together than necessary. One should, therefore, take great care over the size of the rooms which will receive light from them, because it is obvious that a larger room needs much more light to make it luminous and bright than a small one; and if the windows are made smaller and less

numerous than necessary, they will be made gloomy; and if
they are made too large the rooms are practically uninhabit-
able because, since cold and hot air can get in, they will be
extremely hot or cold depending on the season of the year,
at least if the region of the sky to which they are oriented
does not afford some relief. For this reason windows should
not be made broader than a quarter of the length of the
rooms nor narrower than a fifth and their height should be
made two squares and a sixth of their breadth.

In Chapter 2 of the Second Book Palladio expands on the orientation of
rooms:

It would ... contribute to comfort if the summer rooms
were large and spacious and oriented to the north, and those
for the winter to the south and west and were small rather
than otherwise, because in the summer we seek the shade
and breezes, and in the winter the sun, and smaller rooms
get warmer more readily than larger ones.

(5)

Chapter 27 moves on to the question of winter comfort and addresses the
design of chimneys and, following a brief account of the heating methods of
'the antients' and a quite detailed description of the means by which the
'TRENTI' sought to provide cool air in the heat of the Veneto summer,
Palladio presents a precise prescription for the sizing of chimneys in order to
ensure that they provide effective combustion.

The construction of the first significant examples of Palladian
architecture in Britain coincided with the publication of these two texts. In
the first volume of *Vitruvius Britannicus* Campbell illustrated his design for
Wanstead House, which was constructed between 1715 and 1720 (demolished
in 1822), placed, according to Summerson, 'Right at its (the book's)
psychological summit . . .' (6). Inspection of the design, as represented in the
engravings, suggests that, in matters of response to climate, Campbell followed
British precedents, rather than the unmodified Italian formulae of Palladio.
The windows are larger than would follow from Palladio, allowing more
light from the duller English skies, without suffering the excesses of heat that
would arise under the Italian sun. The plan of the principal floor (Fig. 4.1)
shows fireplaces consistently located on internal walls, either parallel with or
perpendicular to the façades, rather than placed on the outer walls as
prescribed by Palladio. In this respect the plan may be read as a transformation
of that of Hardwick Hall (see Essay 2), although the adoption of the

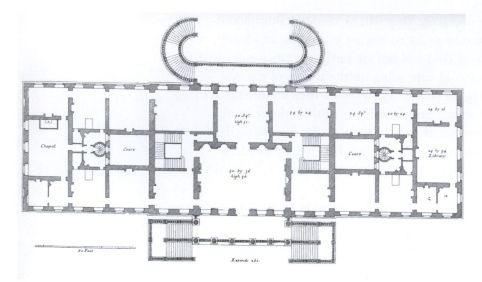

conventions of classical composition permits neither the fantasy nor the environmental complexity of Robert Smythson's glass-filled bays.

The relation of theory and practice in architecture is frequently complex. The conventional supposition might be that theory precedes and thereby informs practice, but, as in many applied fields, this is not always so. As Igor Stravinsky insisted in the case of music, theory may often be shown to derive from practice (7). It was inevitable that English treatises, derived from the model of *I quattro libri*, would appear in due course, providing guidelines for practical design in relation to all manner of concerns, including adaptation to the climate. One of the earliest of these was Robert Morris's *Lectures on Architecture* (1734) and a later and significant example was William Chamber's *A Treatise on the Decorative Part of Civil Architecture* (1759). Summerson considered that with the latter, '. . . architectural literature enters a new phase' (8). These texts were influential in shaping British architecture, not least through their observations on how to design for the British climate and will be studied here, but this translation had already been achieved in designs for buildings of the utmost significance in the new Palladian style some years before – a vivid instance of practice leading theory.

Robert Morris and William Chambers:
theorizing architecture and climate

Amongst the flood of books on architecture that appeared in England in the first part of the eighteenth century, Summerson identified the writings of Robert Morris as being uniquely concerned with theoretical matters (9). Morris described himself as a 'Surveyor' and published a number of books between 1728 and 1757. In the present context the most important of these is *Lectures on Architecture*, published in 1734 (10). The lectures were read, over a period of months, to a society that Morris himself founded (11). Their content included a general historical background, a discourse on proportion and illustrations of Morris's own designs. In the present context, the most significant parts of the *Lectures* are those where Morris, on the model of Palladio, presents detailed guidance on questions of climate and environment.

In Lecture II, and almost certainly influenced by Isaac Newton's great work published in 1704, Morris emphasises the significance of 'Opticks' in providing the knowledge from which to ensure sufficient daylight in a building:

> OPTICKS will be requisite to be understood, as far as they relate to Proportions of Light in large or small Rooms, or as the Situation is as to the four Cardinal Points . . .

Lecture VI addresses the subject of determining the 'Situation' of a house. Strictures on the problems of building in deep valleys are followed by detailed prescriptions on the design of country seats in relation to elements of climate that closely mimic those offered by Vitruvius, in Book VI of *De architectura*, and by Palladio in his First Book (12):

> The South Aspect is most preferable for the principal Front, if it can be conveniently had, in which should be the Rooms of State and Grandeur. The East is the most proper for a Library, because in the Morning Sun gives an enlivening Warmth to Nature, and then the Spirits are more open, more active and free in the Choice of beautiful Ideas . . .
>
> In Hunting Seats . . . as the Seasons for Hunting are in that Part of the Year which is generally cold, and require a temperate Warmth . . . preserve the Lodgings as warm as can be, by making as few Doors and Windows into those Rooms as Conveniency will permit . . . All Winter Houses should be so contriv'd, while those for Summer should be more open, to cool and make the Dwellings comfortable and agreeable.

The same lecture follows the example of Palladio in presenting precise formulae by which to calculate appropriate sizes of 'Chiminies', which, more precisely, is a reference to fireplaces and hearths, and for windows, in relation to the dimensions of specific rooms:

By these Rules the Breadth of the Chimney, its Height, Depth and Square of the Funnel for Conveyance of Smoke, are demonstrated, and in so easy a Manner, that none of you can mistake their Application and Use.

Typical results of the calculation are presented in a table.

There follows the formula for calculating the dimensions of windows:

... by which any room may be illuminated more or less, according to the Uses of them ...
Let the Magnitude of the Room be given, and one of those Proportions I have propos'd to be made use of, or any other; multiply the Length and Breath of the Room together, and that Product multiply by the Height, and the Square Root of that Sum will be the Area or superficial Content in Feet, etc. of Light requir'd.

A number of 'worked examples' demonstrate the application of the formula to rooms of various dimensions. Comparisons between the Italian formula of Palladio and Morris's English variant show that, for England, windows are consistently larger, in proportion to the rooms they serve, than the Italian examples, all in keeping with the implications of the different climates.

A quarter of a century after the publication of Morris's 'Lectures', William Chambers' *A Treatise on the Decorative Part of Civil Architecture* was published (13). Unsurprisingly this also follows the models of Vitruvius and Palladio but, as with Morris, adapts prescriptions that originated in warm climates to the cooler conditions of England. An extended chapter on 'Windows' addresses the now familiar themes of the design of windows and chimney pieces:

The first considerations with respect to windows, are, their number, and their size; which must be such as, neither to admit more, nor less light than is required ...
In determination of this object, regard must be had to the climate, the aspect, the extent and elevation of the place to be lit ... In hot countries, where the sun is seldom clouded, and where the rays dart more intensely upon the earth, the light is stronger than in those which are temperate or cold; therefore a smaller quantity of it will suffice: and more than sufficient should not be admitted, as the consequence is the admission of heat likewise.

Chambers makes an explicit comparison between design for the Italian climate and that of cooler places:

> In Italy, and some other hot countries, although the windows be less in general than ours, their apartments cannot be made habitable, but by keeping the window shutters almost closed, while the sun appears above the horizon. But in regions where gloom and clouds prevail eight months of the year, it will always be right to admit a sufficiency of light for these melancholy seasons; and have recourse to blinds, or shutters, whenever the appearance of the sun renders it too abundant.

Chambers describes Palladio's formula for determining the size of windows as 'surely too vague' and proceeds to refer to the authority 'of my own practice' to propose the following formula:

> . . . I have generally added the depth and the height of the rooms on the principal floor together, and taken one eighth part thereof, for the width of the window; a rule to which there are but few objections; admitting somewhat more light than Palladio's, it is, I apprehend, fitter for our climate than his rule would be . . .

When discussing the design of chimney pieces Chambers is equally clear about the necessary differences between continental and English practice:

> The Italians frequently put their chimnies in the front walls, between the windows; for the benefit of looking out while sitting by the fire: but this must be avoided; for by so doing that side of the room becomes crouded with ornaments and the other sides are left too bare . . . and the chimney shafts at the top of the building, which must necessarily be carried higher than the ridges of the roofs, have from their great length, a very disagreeable effect . . .

The size of the chimney, for which here read fireplace, should be related to the dimensions of the room that it is to warm. Chambers gives simple rules of thumb for this, with a reminder that 'should the room be extremely large', for example in halls, galleries and ballrooms, ' . . . it will be more convenient, and far handsomer; to have two chimney pieces of a moderate size . . .'.

He continues to offer guidance on the location of fireplaces in relation to the use of the room, demanding that 'The chimney should always be situated so, as to be immediately seen by those who enter; that they may not have the persons already in the room, who are generally seated about the fire, to search for. In bedchambers the chimney is always placed in the middle of one of the side partition walls.'

Tanis Hinchcliffe has proposed that Robert Morris's writings were influenced by the Newtonian scientific spirit that was a strong influence on English thought in the first half of the eighteenth century (14). In support of the argument, she draws particular attention to Morris's use of 'scientific' tabular presentation of his principles of mathematical proportion. She makes no reference to Morris's *environmental* prescriptions, but these would seem to offer additional support for the hypothesis. One may go further to propose that the origins of this 'scientific' perspective in architecture, may reasonably be extended to include William Chambers' related text, and, furthermore, be traced back to Wren and the application of his 'scientific cast of mind' to his architectural works (see Essay 3).

The climate of Palladian Britain

Throughout the eighteenth century it became almost commonplace in England to make systematic records of the weather. The keeping of a 'weather diary' was a popular pastime amongst both city and country dwellers (15). Some of these restricted their observations to simple, but often detailed, written notes, but others, in acknowledgement of the growing availability of instruments of measurement – thermometers, barometers and rain gauges – kept quantitative records. From these it is possible to construct a comprehensive, 'scientific' description of the climate of these times and thus establish a framework by which to examine the relation of climate to the design of buildings. But, at the same time, climate and weather remained a significant subject of other modes of description and representation, not least in literature and the fine arts. These are of immense value in helping to define and understand the widest cultural context in which architecture was conceived.

The Central England Temperature (CET) record (16) shows that the eighteenth century experienced wide variations of temperature. Statistically the first two decades had few extremes, with the dramatic exception of the 'Great Storm', which occurred on the night of 26–27 November 1703 and resulted in widespread damage to buildings and trees across much of the south of the country. But within the overall pattern, severe winters occurred in 1708–1709 and 1715–1716, when frost fairs were again held on the Thames. Overall the 1730s were uncharacteristically mild except for a severe frost in January 1731 (17). This relative calm was followed by the shock of an extremely cold winter in 1740, after which lower winter temperatures continued to be experienced for much of the second half of the century. On the other hand, the summer mean temperatures were generally quite warm, at or above 15° Celsius throughout the entire century. In both 1718 and 1719 good crops of grapes were harvested at Richmond on Thames and, throughout England, 1719 was one of the hottest summers for some years. But the unpredictability of the English climate produced a summer so cold in 1725 that, this time, the Richmond grape crop was a complete failure (18).

In spite of its frequent vagaries and relative lack of extremes, the British climate engenders in the observer a clear sense of the distinctions between the four seasons and of their annual progression. At exactly the time at which Palladianism began to dominate architectural taste, James Thomson (1700–1748) wrote his long and influential poem, *The Seasons* (19). 'Winter' was published in 1726 and the complete work in 1730. It passed through a number of revisions over the years and received wide attention and acclaim.

Jonathan Bate identifies the influence of Enlightenment thought on *The Seasons* by observing that:

> Thomson celebrated the variety of the seasons, but the thrust of his argument was that the weather itself had a fundamental order, a concord in its discord, disorder resided in the morality of the observer and was accordingly a matter of human agency. The constancy of nature was something against which to measure the vicissitudes of culture.
>
> (20)

At the outset of each poem, the text of *The Seasons* draws out the essence of each of the stages of the English year (21):

> Come, gentle SPRING ethereal mildness, come,
> And from the bosom of yon dropping cloud,
> While music wakes around, veiled in a shower
> Of shadowing roses, our plains descend.
>
> From brightening fields of ether fair disclose,
> Child of the Sun, refulgent SUMMER comes,
> In pride of youth, and felt through Nature's depth:
> He comes accompanied by the sultry Hours,
> And ever fanning Breezes on his way;
>
> CROWNED with the sickle and the wheaten sheaf,
> While Autumn, nodding o'er the yellow plain,

Comes jovial on; the Doric reed once more,
Well pleased, I tune.

SEE WINTER comes, to rule the varied year,
Sullen and sad, with all his rising train –
Vapours and Clouds, and Storms. Be these my theme,
These! that exalt the soul to solemn thought.
And heavenly musing.

It is particularly apt in the present discussion that William Kent (1685–1748), who played a major part in the interior decoration of both Houghton Hall and Chiswick House, made a series of four paintings, which, in engravings by Nicholas Tardieu, were published as frontispieces to the first complete edition of Thomson's poem of 1730. These depict pastoral scenes, attuned to each season, beneath allegorical representations of the weather. It has been observed that the representation of 'Winter' shows the potential discomfort of Nature, in contrast to the more conventional 'smiling mode' that was common during this period (22). Perhaps this is a response to the greater impression of this season on the English psyche. In all the engravings, except 'Summer', when much of life would be conducted out of doors, there is a glimpse of architecture with its implication of shelter, explicitly Palladian in 'Spring' and 'Autumn', more obviously a primitive vernacular in 'Winter'.

Three buildings will be the focus of this study, built within three years of each other and a decade before the publication of Robert Morris's treatise. These are Houghton Hall in Norfolk, begun by Campbell in 1722 and continued by James Gibbs; Campbell's Mereworth Castle, in Kent, begun in 1723; and Lord Burlington's Chiswick House of 1725.

Houghton Hall, Norfolk, 1722–1735

Summerson describes Houghton Hall (Fig. 4.2) as 'no less consequential than Wanstead' (23). The demolition of Wanstead deprives us of direct experience of that pioneering building, but Houghton is a more than adequate substitute. The client for the house was Sir Robert Walpole, later to become Prime Minister, who inherited the family estate at Houghton in 1700. In the first two decades of the new century he carried out a series of alterations and 'improvements' to the existing house and began the expansion and redevelopment of the park. The authorship of the new house, whose foundation stone was laid in 1722, is complex. John Harris refers to '. . . a real compote of architects on the job: (Thomas) Ripley, James Gibbs, William Kent, (Colen) Campbell and (Isaac) Ware' (24). Whatever the reality of the design process, in which it is clear that the client also played a major part, the outcome is a house of the greatest quality and significance. In view of the different

personalities involved, it is unsurprising that the design underwent a number of changes. The most striking was the series of proposals for the termination of the four corner turrets, from Campbell's first design, dated 1723, to the pedimented attics shown in *Vitruvius Britannicus III* (1725) and, finally, the cupolas, by Gibbs, which we see today. William Kent's contribution began in 1727, when he produced the design for the entrance portico to the east front. Thereafter he undertook the decoration and much of the furnishing of the principal apartments.

Turning to the facts of the building as completed, the plan is of a principal block with side pavilions connected to the main house by curved links (Fig. 4.3). The principal entrance was from the east, with the *piano nobile* approached externally by Kent's grand portico and staircase, sadly no longer in existence. Internally the route is by the equally impressive Great Staircase, elaborately decorated by Kent. The plan of Houghton may only loosely be described as 'Palladian', in the strict sense of the term, but follows the precedent of Wanstead and, in what we might dare to call its 'environmental strategy', refers back, albeit probably unconsciously, to the houses of Robert Smythson. The long axis of the plan is oriented north–south and, as Morris and Chambers were later to recommend, the fireplaces are almost all located on internal walls, just as at Hardwick. The windows are larger than would follow from Palladio's formula and bring ample English light to the main apartments, without suffering the disadvantages of winter chill or summer heat. On close inspection we discover that the allocation of

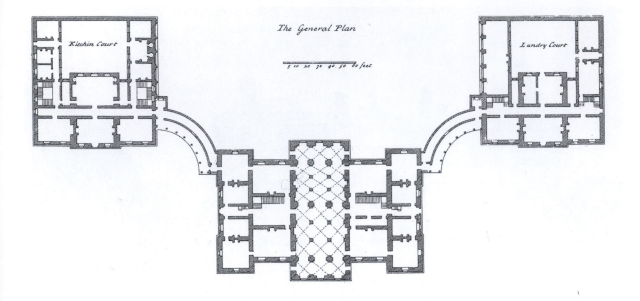

The General Plan

Kitchin Court

Landry Court

rooms to occupants and uses was quite profoundly influenced by orientation, just as at Hardwick.

     The ground floor, referred to in the eighteenth century as 'the Rustic' (25), provided rooms for informal, and often boisterous, living. A suite of rooms included a breakfast room, a family dining room, a drawing room and a study, all simply decorated and furnished. At the heart of the plan is the 'Arcade', a columned hall, running through from east to west, that was, in the manner of earlier long galleries, used for indoor exercise. All the rooms had fireplaces, no fewer than four in the Arcade, to ensure that they would be warm on the cold autumn days of the hunting season. The dining room, also referred to as the hunting hall, was the principal eating place for family use and even for grander occasions. During Walpole's years as Prime Minister, Britain was frequently governed for lengthy periods from Houghton. Walpole would summon ministers and other dignitaries to the house for what became known as the 'Norfolk Congresses'. The activities of these, both governmental and social, took place in the Rustic, the family dining room becoming a dining hall with the introduction of trestle tables. At this date the main meal of dinner was still served in the afternoon to take advantage of the daylight (26). It is important to realize that even a house as grand as Houghton would be extremely dark after sundown. One of the best descriptions of this condition is that by Peter Thornton (27), who emphasizes the cost and poor quality of the available sources of light. He describes how:

    . . . lights were conserved and life was lived as far as possible
    in the daylight hours.

4.3
Houghton Hall:
general plan showing
lower floor of the house.

Thornton additionally stresses the value of the illumination provided by the fire:

> It was an exceptional occasion when the candles were so numerous that they equalled the fire in brightness.

At the first floor, above the hurly burly of the 'Rustic', we find the great formal apartments of the house, which are centred on the 40-foot cube of the Stone Hall and the adjacent saloon (Fig. 4.4). Originally each of these had direct access from the exterior: the Stone Hall to the east by Kent's great portico and double staircase, now demolished, and the saloon, as in the present day, with its somewhat simpler double stair leading down to the park to the west. To the south of these, grouped around the rooflit great staircase, are the private apartments for the senior members of the Walpole family: the Common Parlour, for everyday uses; the corresponding, slightly more formal, Yellow Drawing Room; and the private apartments, respectively, of Sir Robert and Lady Walpole. The southerly location is reminiscent of the disposition of the Countess of Shrewsbury's apartments at Hardwick, where they similarly enjoy the benefits of direct sunlight that are so helpful in the English climate. One may imagine the east-facing Common Parlour, where family meals were taken, being enjoyed during the morning and early afternoon and the Yellow Drawing Room on the west front providing an ideal environment in late afternoon and evening, its colour scheme enhancing the evening light. Sir Robert's study, in fact his Library, has a prime position on the south-east corner, where it receives sun from early morning to mid-afternoon. His south-facing bedroom next door is quite modest and is in contrast to the splendour of Lady Walpole's accommodation in the Blue Damask Chamber at the south-west corner.

In the north wing we find the state apartments. These are magnificently furnished and decorated in keeping with their purpose, providing the best of comforts for the most distinguished guests. The daytime rooms are the Velvet, now the White, Drawing Room at the west front and the Marble Parlour, or Great Dining Room, to the east. The bedchambers, Green Velvet and Embroidered for male and female respectively, have fine enclosed beds and warm wall and floor finishes, which would in some measure compensate for their location to the north. The Cabinet that completes the enfilade of rooms at the north range was originally also planned to be a bedchamber, but became the closet for the display of the smaller pictures in Walpole's fine collection. When the house was completed the walls were lined in the same green velvet as the principal bedchamber, but, by the end of the eighteenth century, this was replaced by the blue Chinese wallpaper that survives to the present day. It may be surmised that the cool, stable environment of the

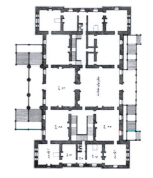

4.4
Houghton Hall: principal-floor plan.

north-east corner was considered to be appropriate for the care of the paintings.

On great occasions the Stone Hall (Fig. 4.5) and saloon (Fig. 4.6) would come fully into play as the centre of events. The Stone Hall is a 40-foot cube with an upper gallery on three sides and a geometrical patterned stone floor. The decoration is austere, with elaborate statuary on display in, as John Cornforth proposes, 'celebration of Walpole's triumph as a new Roman' (28).

4.6
Houghton Hall:
the saloon.

The original nighttime light was provided by a much discussed, extravagant lantern that held 18 candles. However, special occasions were even more brightly lit. It is recorded that a grand dinner held in 1731 was illuminated by 130 wax lights and that the adjacent saloon had 50. The cost is estimated to have been £15 for one night's lighting (29). The thermal image of these two grand rooms could hardly be more contrasted. To step from the Stone Hall to the saloon is to enter a different world. The hard, cool surfaces of the

Stone Hall would not be out of place in Italy, where the issue is to keep cool in summer, but the west-facing saloon, with its crimson wool and silk velvet wall hangings, and timber floor, almost certainly in part carpet-covered, is more attuned to the cool Norfolk climate. At all seasons the room would be welcoming, particularly on bright afternoons, when the heat of the fire would be supplemented by warm sunlight. Kent's elaborate decorative scheme for the room includes the *Four Seasons* painted in the lunettes of the attic storey. These are almost exactly contemporary with his designs that accompany Thomson's poem on the same theme, hinting at a symbolic acknowledgement of the relationship between the seasons and architecture.

The second floor contains additional bedrooms neatly planned on either side of the double-height volumes of the Stone Hall and saloon. With their steeply pitched roofs concealed behind the parapets, these are well insulated against the more extreme effects of winter cold and summer heat. This is in contrast to the model of the Veneto villas, where the top floor would be used for storage, or probably as servants' quarters, to act as a climate buffer for the grand rooms of the *piano nobile*.

Before moving on it is worth noting that, even though we have suggested some similarity of organization and use of rooms between Houghton and Hardwick, a profound shift had occurred in the environmental expectations and social practices of the country house in the century or more that divides these two great buildings. In all its magnificence, Hardwick is, at heart, still a product of mediaeval thought and custom. There is a sense that its wintertime occupation would at times be closer to a matter of survival rather than expansive, uninhibited inhabitation. One the other hand, Houghton uses a similar repertoire of materials and constructional methods to fashion spaces that are more refined in their ability to provide comfort at all seasons of the year. Rooms are generally better proportioned in relation to their use and the dimensions of windows are better calibrated to meet needs for good daylight whilst avoiding undue heat loss. The shift from large windows of leaded lights to carefully proportioned, timber-framed, sliding sashes would bring great benefits. New designs of furniture also enhance the effect, with upholstered chairs placed in relation to the circle of radiant heat emitted by a well-designed fireplace.

Mereworth Castle, Kent, 1723

Burlington's design for Mereworth Castle is the building in England that most closely resembles Palladio's Villa Rotonda at Vicenza (1565). The house was built for Colonel John Fane, who conceived it as a place for entertainments rather than as a permanent residence. Like its model, the house is a square pavilion, here 90 feet rather than the original's 80 feet, with porticoes on all four fronts (Fig. 4.7). The house is oriented almost exactly on the cardinal points, with the main entrance from the north, thus giving very different characters to the four faces. This is more likely to be a response to topography rather than environmental intention, although the site is sufficiently extensive and the contours relatively flat to have permitted the choice of almost any aspect. At Vicenza the Rotonda is oriented with the diagonal of the square on the cardinals, and this modifies the extreme contrast that would have occurred between north and south. The magnificent circular 'Vestibule' dominates the interior and exterior of Mereworth, as Campbell described it in *Vitruvius Britannicus* (30), 34 feet in diameter and crowned by an enormous lead-covered dome.

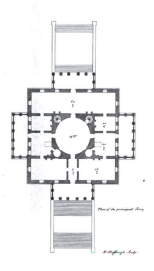

4.7
Mereworth Castle, Kent: principal floor plan.

The entrance from the north portico leads into a passage from which open two fine north-facing rooms. Ahead lies the Vestibule, and the axis continues to the long gallery, which occupies the entire south front. To east and west are pairs of chambers, each with a bedroom and dressing room. These have access directly onto the east and west porticoes. The basement houses extensive service and storage spaces, and the attic contains bedrooms. Unlike Villa Rotonda, which has just four fireplaces, serving the four large *sale* of the *piano nobile*, Mereworth has no less than 24, eight at each of the three levels. Palladio's fireplaces are on the outside walls and the flues are carried up to appear just above the eaves on the north-west and south-east fronts. It is of some interest that the chimneys are omitted from most drawings of the villa, suggesting that they were regarded as perhaps an embarrassing necessity, rather than an architectural opportunity. Campbell is equally coy about directly expressing his large collection of flues, but expends many words in describing his clever design in *Vitruvius Britannicus*. The fireplaces are placed on internal walls of the rooms. In effect they are built into the masonry mass that supports the dome. This has advantages in ensuring that the flues will be quickly warmed, which promotes a good draught from the fire, and that the heat will be retained in the thermal mass. It does, however, present a constructional problem in finding an unrestricted route for each flue up to and beyond roof level. This is particularly so if the overall formal expression of the building would be compromised by the appearance of a forest of chimneys. What was an expressive advantage for Robert Smythson has become a problem for Campbell, who omitted the highly visible chimneys at Houghton from the engravings of the house. The complex construction of the dome is illustrated in the published cross-section (Fig. 4.8) and clearly shows the curved flues that run within the fireproof construction of the internal brick dome to discharge through the lantern:

> which is finished with a Copper Callot, without any Injury to the Smoke, which was not the least difficult Part of the Design.

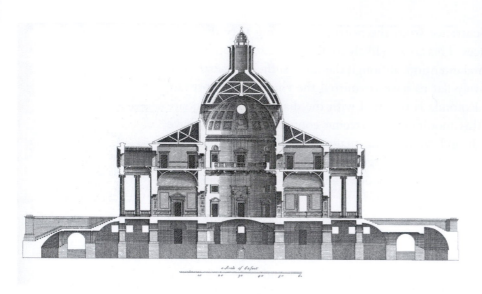

The house must have presented a remarkable sight when a number of fires were simultaneously in use.

The daylighting of the house is beautifully contrived. The two north-facing rooms each have three windows, including one in the end wall, to achieve excellent distribution. The long gallery has five south-facing openings and one in each of the east and west walls. In the bedrooms and dressing rooms, the overshadowing of the porticoes, which become, in effect, private loggias for these suites of rooms, is subtly compensated by increasing the ratio of window to wall in comparison with that of the principal apartments. Light enters the central Vestibule from four large circular windows in the dome with splayed cills set within the plaster coffers of the ceiling. These ensure that the upper region of the sky is visible from the floor of the space. As we have noted before, in the English climate a direct view of the sky and, particularly its brightest, higher regions, is a crucial requirement for giving good daylight.

Chiswick House, London, 1725–1729

Chiswick House (Plate 3) was designed, for his own use, by Richard, Lord Burlington (1694–1753). There has been much discussion regarding its specific purpose, including a hypothesis that it was intended for use as a Masonic temple (31). Whatever the case, it is almost certain that the house was never a fully self-sufficient dwelling. When first built it was adjacent to an existing, much larger, Jacobean house that housed all the usual domestic service apartments. As with Mereworth there is a quite clear reference to the Villa Rotonda, but Vincenzo Scamozzi's Rocca Pisani at Lonigo (1576) is likely to have been equally influential. The square plan measures 68 feet, but,

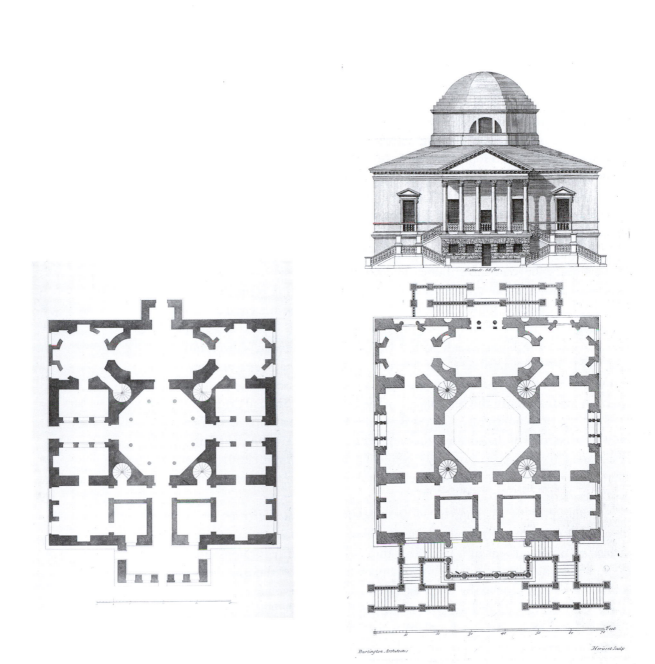

unlike the Rotonda and exactly like Rocca Pisani, there is just one portico at the main entrance. A further similarity with Palladio's villa, although probably coincidental, is that the plan is placed diagonally on the cardinal points. This means that the entrance front faces south-east (Figs 4.9 and 4.10).

    At the centre of the lower floor of the house we find the columned lower tribune or hall, which may be directly approached from the entrance front by a short passageway. This receives only borrowed light from the

4.9
Chiswick House: lower-floor plan.

4.10
Chiswick House: principal-floor plan and entrance front.

rooms to either side, but Rosoman suggests, on the evidence of the 1770 inventory of the house's contents, that it served as daily living quarters and as an eating room (32). There is evidence, again from the 1770 inventory, that the rooms to the south-west were originally used as bedrooms, although it is uncertain whether Burlington and his close family used them. Their furnishing included two four-post beds, with ample blankets and quilts, and there were two stoves and a brazier for winter heating. The inventory also lists just a single candlestick to provide minimal light after dark. The corresponding rooms to the north-east were service rooms, one the butler's pantry, the other a linen room.

The principal apartments at this level are the three linked spaces to the north-west beyond the tribune. These housed Burlington's library in bookcases designed by William Kent. The larger central room has no fireplace, but these are found in the two smaller end rooms, one circular and one octagonal. The 1770 inventory mysteriously refers to the existence of *three* stoves in the library, each with a complement of fender, shovel and tongs. This may be a simple error of description, although that seems unlikely. It may, on the other hand, suggest that some improvised arrangement had been made to warm the central part of the library. If there had originally been just the two end fireplaces, it is easy to imagine the reader retreating to the warmth of one of the smaller rooms on winter's days. That to the south-west would have been particularly congenial when the sun shone. The reference to just 'two Gilt Candlesticks' implies that the rooms were little used after dark.

The first floor is approached from below by spiral staircases set in the *poché* of the central Tribune on the model of the Villa Rotonda. In view of their small dimensions, it is likely that these were primarily for household use and that the main approach to the upper level was by the grand stair leading to the entrance on the south-east front. The plan revolves around the central saloon (Fig. 4.11), which is octagonal, unlike the precedents of Palladio and Scamozzi and Mereworth, all of which are circular. The dome was painted white and the walls, probably, a light stone colour, which would have reflected the large quantity of daylight entering from the four large lunette windows located on the axes of the plan (and therefore on the quarters of the cardinal points). This is thus a brighter space in comparison with Mereworth. It is unheated and its exposed stone floor reinforces its literal and metaphorical coolness. In 1770 artificial light was provided by a 'Cut-Glass Lustre' – a chandelier, presumably with candles. The gallery lies above the library on the central axis, directly beyond the tribune on the central axis. This sequence of tall spaces, with white plastered walls and stone floor, is brightly lit, with a tripartite Venetian window in the central room. The light from this is reflected in a pair of large mirrors on the opposite wall. As on the ground

floor, only the end rooms have fireplaces, each with a large mirror above. These were fitted with 'Steel Stove Grates'. For nighttime here were 'Two Six Light Brass Shandeliers Ballance Weights and Lines'. The balances and lines would allow the chandeliers to be lowered for lighting and then raised to a suitable height more effectively to distribute their light. The location of these is not given, but whether in the central space or in each end room, their light would have been wonderfully reflected in the many large mirrors, whose function was as much a matter of light as of vanity. There were, in addition two gilt candlesticks, whose location is not specified.

The principal rooms to either side of the central axis are, respectively, the Red Velvet Room (Fig. 4.12) on the south-west front and the Green Velvet Room (Fig. 4.13) to the south-east. These are identical in size and are strikingly different from the Tribune and gallery. The former served as the antechamber to Burlington's quarters and the latter was the principal apartment of Lady Burlington's quarters. In both, the rich, deep-coloured wall surfaces absorb the light from the Venetian windows and convey a great sense of warmth, albeit quite different in nature. Carpets cover much of the

stone floors and each room has two fireplaces, in the outer wall in the manner of the Italian precedents and all with the usual implements. Each also had 'an Eight light brass Shandelier'. The theme of decorative warmth is maintained in the Blue Velvet Room, which is entered through the Red Velvet Room and served as Burlington's study. With its rich decoration, fireplace and location at the southern tip of the house, this is a glowingly comfortable place, which one may imagine Burlington savouring as his own. The 1770 Inventory refers to the presence of 'Spring Window Blinds' in all of Burlington's personal apartments, including the small closet. These, identical in most respects to modern roller blinds, would have allowed him to modify the amount of sunlight – and heat – entering these south-facing rooms. We may wonder if they were original fittings or, as in some modern buildings, were fitted later when the problem of excessive sunlight became apparent, but

4.13
Chiswick House:
the Green Velvet Room.

whatever the case these are the only rooms in the house to have these devices. The Blue Velvet Room was lit by two gilt candlestands with brass mouldings. Each would almost certainly have held at least two candles. The corresponding room to the Blue Velvet Room on the eastern corner is assumed to have been Lady Burlington's bedchamber, and has a similar arrangement of windows and fireplace, but has less decorative splendour. The inventory refers to 'two Needlework pole screens', whose purpose was to protect ladies' made-up faces from the heat of the fire

A number of features at Chiswick are directly relevant in interpreting its environmental qualities. The orientation may be entirely pragmatic, but it may be that it consciously follows the precedent of the Villa Rotonda. The effect is to avoid the more extreme differences between different aspects that follow in the English climate from having exact north and south orientations as at Mereworth. The windows are of English, not Italian, dimensions and the 'Venetian' windows that light the principal rooms at the *piano nobile* have, in the layering and decoration of their internal frames and architraves, the effect of conveying the impression of light entering the room, as it is reflected from white paint and gilded columns.

Comment should also be made about the thermal qualities of the house. First we should note that it was not designed to provide winter heating in all the principal apartments. This may be a consequence of the intention to use it as a place for entertainment or ritual, rather than full domestic inhabitation. In the cold winters of the first decades of the eighteenth century, the tribune, the central spaces of the gallery and the library would have been inhospitable, although, in compensation, all the other principal rooms, with their fireplaces and luxurious furnishings, would have offered a high degree of warmth. In summer these very spaces would, however, have become quite cool, with cross breezes flowing through the house.

A final remark should be made about the design of the chimneys at Chiswick. As noted above, the fireplaces are placed on the outside walls, in the Italian manner. The positive effect of this in the rooms is to bring sources of warmth and light together on the same wall. The disadvantage is more pragmatic. External flues take longer to become warm and thus to promote efficient combustion and there is little retention of heat in the fabric of the building. The other problem is that of the appearance of the chimneys on the exterior of the building. Palladio avoided the issue in part by omitting the chimneys from the drawings of his villas and by trying to make them as inconspicuous as possible in the buildings themselves. We have seen and enjoyed Campbell's ingenious solution at Mereworth. At Chiswick we now see the arrays of obelisk-like flues that adorn the side elevations. But there is quite a story to be told about these. No chimneys are shown in the engravings of the elevations made by Henry Flitcroft for publication in 1727 (33).

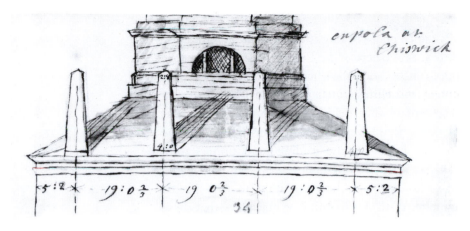

4.14
Chiswick House: the
obelisk chimneys.

But an undated sketch of the cupola, in Burlington's hand, proudly shows the obelisks (Fig. 4.14). As John Harris observes (34), these derive from Scamozzi, not Palladio, and similar chimneys may be seen in an engraving of Rocca Pisani. The obelisks are visible in early engravings of Chiswick, including that by Rigaud of 1733–1734, which shows plumes of smoke issuing from them (Fig. 4.15). Later images show more conventional chimneys, which were probably constructed to remedy problems with the fire-draught in the obelisk form. The present obelisks are the result of restorations carried out in 1956–1957.

4.15
Chiswick House:
view showing smoking
chimneys.

Conclusion

Summerson identified the Palladian phase of English architecture, in the first part of the seventeenth century, as subject to 'the Rule of Taste' (35). There is, however, a further dimension to both the theory and practice of this period. This is, as suggested by Hinchcliffe (36), the influence of the emerging sciences in the form and content of the treatises of theoreticians such as Robert Morris, and the evidence that, even as Morris was delivering the lectures that came to constitute his book, the leading practitioners were carefully modifying the quantitative environmental prescriptions of Palladio and his contemporaries in order to adapt their buildings to the specific conditions of the English climate. With this in mind we may show that these important buildings, here Houghton Hall, Mereworth Castle and Chiswick House, mark a great forward step in bringing architecture into a new and more precise relationship with the British climate.

Notes

1. John Summerson, *Architecture in Britain: 1530–1830*, Penguin, Harmondsworth, 1953; 9th revised edition, Yale University Press, New Haven, CT, 1993. See Chapter 20, 'The Palladian Movement: Campbell, Burlington, and Kent.'

2. Colen Campbell, *Vitruvius Britannicus, or The British Architect*, 1715, 1717 and 1725, London. The three volumes have been published in unabridged facsimile by Dover, New York, 2006.

3. The original text of *I quattro libri* appeared in England in instalments over several years. Other editions were published in 1736, by Edward Hoppus, and in 1737, by Isaac Ware. The Ware edition is published in facsimile, with an introduction by Adolf. K. Placzek, by Dover, New York, 1965. An excellent modern edition is *The Four Books of Architecture* (eds Robert Tavernor and Richard Schofield), MIT Press, Cambridge, MA, 2002.

4. Summerson, *Architecture in Britain: 1530–1830*, cited in Note 1.

5. This translation is from the Tavernor and Schofield edition cited in Note 3.

6. Summerson, *Architecture in Britain: 1530–1830*, cited in Note 1.

7. In the introduction to *The Environmental Tradition: Studies in the Architecture of Environment*, E. & F. N. Spon, London, 1996, the present author cited Igor Stravinsky's observations on the relation of theory and practice in music as an appropriate analogy to the case of architecture. In response to the question 'what is theory in relation to composition', Stravinsky replied, with splendid contradiction, 'Hindsight. It doesn't exist. There are compositions from which it is deduced. Or, if this isn't true, it has a by-product existence that is powerless to create or even to justify. Nevertheless, composition involves a deep intuition of theory.' The original quote may be found in Igor Stravinsky and Robert Craft, *Conversations with Igor Stravinsky*, Faber Music, London, 1959.

8. Robert Morris, *Lectures on Architecture: Consisting of Rules Founded upon Harmonic and Arithmetical Proportions in Building*, London, 1734; facsimile edition, Kessinger, Whitefish, MT, 2009. William Chambers, *A Treatise on the Decorative Part of Civil Architecture*, London, 1759; facsimile edition, Dover, New York, 2003. Summerson, *Architecture in Britain: 1530–1830*, cited in Note 1.

9. Summerson, *Architecture in Britain: 1530–1830*, cited in Note 1.

10. Morris, *Lectures on Architecture*, cited in Note 8.

11. The precise location at which the lectures were delivered has been widely discussed. Joseph Rykwert has suggested that they were presented at a meeting of a Masonic Lodge. See Joseph Rykwert, *The First Moderns: Architects of the Eighteenth Century*, MIT Press, Cambridge, MA, 1984.

12. Marcus Vitruvius Pollio, *De architectura*, 1st century BC); English translation by Morris H.J. Morgan, *Ten Books on Architecture*, 1914, Dover, New York, 1960. Palladio, *I quattro libri*, cited in Note 3.

13. Chambers, *A Treatise on the Decorative Part of Civil Architecture*, cited in Note 8.

14. Tanis Hinchcliffe, 'Robert Morris: architecture and the scientific cast of mind in early eighteenth-century England', *Architectural History: the Journal of the Society of Architectural Historians, Great Britain*, Vol. 47, 2004, pp. 127–138.

15. See Jan Golinski, 'Putting the Weather in Order: Narrative and Discipline in Eighteenth-Century Weather Diaries', Paper given at UCLA, Los Angeles, 1998 and 'The weather in eighteenth century Britain', in *Weather, Climate, Culture* (ed. Sarah Strauss and Benjamin S. Orlove), Berg, Oxford, 2003.

16. G. Manley, 'Central England Temperatures: monthly means 1659 to 1973', *Quarterly Journal of the Royal Meteorological Society*, Vol. 100, 1974, pp. 389–405. D. E. Parker, T. P. Legg and C. K. Folland, 'A new daily Central England Temperature series, 1772–1991', *International Journal of Climatology*, Vol. 12, 1992, pp. 317–342.

17. William Derham submitted many important records of extreme climate events to the Royal Society. See 'The History of the Great Frost in the Last Winter 1703 and 1708/9 By the Reverend Mr. W. Derham, Rector of Upminster, F.R.S.,' *Philosophical Transactions of the Royal Society*, Vol. 26, 1708–1709, pp. 454–478, and 'Concerning the Frost in January 1730/1', *Philosophical Transactions of the Royal Society*, Vol. 37, 1731–1732, pp. 16–18.

18. These events are from the compilation of data from a selection of authoritative sources to be found at the website, *Climate History in the British Isles*, http://booty.org.uk/booty.weather/climate/histclimat.htm.

19. James Thomson, *The Seasons*, first complete edition, London, 1730.

20. Jonathan Bate, *The Song of the Earth*, Picador, London, 2000.

21. The text here is from the edition published by Clark, Austin & Co., New York, 1854, available at Google Book Search.

22. Michael I. Wilson, *William Kent: Architect, Designer, Painter, Gardener, 1685–1748*, Routledge & Kegan Paul, London, 1984.

23. Summerson, *Architecture in Britain: 1530–1830*, cited in Note 1

24. John Harris, 'The Architecture of the House', in *Houghton Hall: The Prime Minister, the Empress and the Heritage* (ed. Andrew Moore), Philip Wilson, London, 1996.

25. Mark Girouard, *Life in the English Country House: A Social and Architectural History*, Yale University Press, New Haven, CT, 1978; Penguin, Harmondsworth, 1980.

26. See the catalogue description of individual rooms in *Houghton Hall* (ed. Andrew Moore), cited in Note 24. The introductions to the individual rooms and the architectural comments are by Sebastian Edwards.

27. Peter Thornton, *Seventeenth-Century Interior Decoration in England, France and Holland*, Yale University Press, New Haven, CT, 1981.

28. John Cornforth, 'The genesis and creation of a great interior', in *Houghton Hall* (ed. Andrew Moore), cited in Note 24.

29. *Ibid.*

30. Colen Campbell, *Vitruvius Britannicus or The British Architect*, three volumes published in London in 1715, 1717 and 1725.

31. The house is discussed in numerous sources. Amongst the most important of these are John Harris, *The Palladian Revival: Lord Burlington, His Villa and Garden at Chiswick*, Yale

University Press, New Haven, CT, 1994; T. C. Barnard and Jane Clark (eds), *Lord Burlington: Architecture, Art and Life*, Hambledon Continuum, Harrisburg, PA, 1994; Richard Hewlings, *Chiswick House and Gardens*, Official Guidebook, English Heritage, London, 1st edition, 1989, 2nd edition, 1991; and Roger White, *Chiswick House and Gardens*, Official Guidebook, English Heritage, London, 2001.

32. T. S. Rosoman, 'The Chiswick House Inventory of 1770', *Furniture History*, No. 22, 1986, pp. 81–105. Although this itemises the contents of the house some 40 years after its completion, it offers a good indication of the environmental amenities that were typical of the Palladian house.

33. See Harris, *The Palladian Revival*, cited in Note 31.

34. *Ibid*.

35. Summerson. *Architecture in Britain: 1530–1830*, cited in Note 1.

36. Hinchcliffe, 'Robert Morris', cited in Note 14.

Essay 5
Building in the climate of the nineteenth-century city

It must be admitted that architecture in the nineteenth-century city is a somewhat abstruse agency of emotional effect. In any age, the 'language' of architecture is an almost exclusively professional affair; in the nineteenth-century. When many architectural languages came to be spoken simultaneously, often in archaic dialects, with broken accents and much rhetorical improvisation, the situation is the equivalent of an exclusive babel, architects making speeches to each other or mumbling to themselves.

(1)

John Summerson beautifully captures the stylistic complexity of nineteenth-century architecture in Britain, but, behind this 'emotional effect', other forces were stirring that were to have a profound effect on the buildings of the century and also influence the development of the architecture of the future. In this century the emphasis in architectural practice moved emphatically towards meeting the building needs of the ever-growing cities. In 1801, 20 per cent of the British population lived in cities and towns with more than 10,000 inhabitants. By mid-century this proportion had increased to 38 per cent. For the first time, the urban population of Britain was greater than that in the country (2). The population of London grew from around 1 million in 1800 to over 6.5 million in 1900. With this growth there came not only a corresponding increase in the volume of building, but also the emergence of new building types to accommodate the emerging needs of the urban population. At the same time the new technologies of construction and building services that were the products of the Industrial Revolution were being brought into use in buildings for all purposes.

Henry-Russell Hitchcock's *Architecture: Nineteenth and Twentieth Centuries*, presents a useful outline of nineteenth century architecture in Britain (3). Although the emphasis is upon stylistic matters, Hitchcock offers a good idea of the immense variety of building types that came to constitute such a significant part of the fabric of these ever-expanding cities. New theatres, law courts, banks, museums, gentlemen's clubs and town halls are all found in the centres of cities and towns alongside more utilitarian types such as office buildings and warehouses. In his essay, 'London, the artifact', Summerson constructs a more detailed architectural image of nineteenth-century London from descriptions of individual buildings of many types (4). Hitchcock writes a chapter on 'Building with iron and glass, 1790–1855' (5). This focuses on the new methods of construction that emerged out of the Industrial Revolution and illustrates their application in bridges, gallerias, railway stations and, of course most spectacularly, in the construction of the Crystal Palace in London in 1851. He omits to mention, however, the parallel developments that took place in the production of devices for the warming, ventilating and lighting of buildings in this period. These matters are also largely absent from the two most significant early attempts to introduce a technological narrative into the history of architecture: Siegfried Giedion's *Mechanization Takes Command* and Lewis Mumford's *Technics and Civilization* (6). This omission has been redressed in more recent work in the wake of Reyner Banham's pioneering, *The Architecture of the Well-Tempered Environment* (7), but it remains one of the most curious facts of the historiography of architecture in the nineteenth century that this quite fundamental aspect of so many significant buildings remained so long unremarked. This is particularly so when one considers the environmental conditions of the nineteenth-century city.

A foggy century

As Peter Brimblecombe has chronicled (8), the climate of London had been notoriously polluted for many centuries before the nineteenth. In spite of frequent attempts to address the matter, not least in John Evelyn's appeal to Charles II in *Fumifugium*, conditions had not improved and the newly arrived city dwellers found that, in their search for better employment, they had to sacrifice the clean air of the countryside. The new industrial cities of the north of England were no better, although their condition was of more recent origin and more directly the product of the recent industrialisation. From the early years of the century efforts were made to address the problem of pollution and a sequence of bills were placed before Parliament as the problem became more acute and public support for action grew (9).

By this date meteorology was assuming the status of a properly organized science. One of the most significant contributors to its development was Luke Howard (1772–1864). Howard, who was elected a fellow of the Royal Society in 1821 (10), was a pharmacist by trade, but devoted much of his time to making systematic studies of the climate. He made extensive meteorological observations in London from 1801 to 1831, which were published in his major study, *The Climate of London* (11). This presents in detail all of the variables of climate – temperature, atmospheric pressure, wind direction and rainfall – during a period of rapid urban growth. Howard's observations were made in the first years to the east of the city at Plaistow and then at Tottenham Green. At that time these locations were relatively rural and Howard's measurements therefore present a somewhat different impression of the climate from that experienced in the urban core of the city. He was alert to this, however, and made a number of correlations between his data and those collected at the same period by the Royal Society. These consistently showed a difference in temperature between the centre of the city and its suburbs and are one of the first representations of the phenomenon of the urban heat island. Howard is also remembered for establishing the classification of clouds that is still in use today (12). He illustrated his classification in a series of watercolour renderings (Plate 12). These attracted the attention of many, including John Constable (whose own cloud studies were influenced by Howard's work) and Johann Wolfgang von Goethe, with whom Howard conducted a lengthy correspondence during which Goethe sent poems written in celebration of Howard's work (13).

Brimblecombe makes an important observation in relation to the notorious London fogs:

> There have always been fogs along the Thames, but somehow they had become particularly notable in the nineteenth century. At this time people began to sense that the fogs were related to air pollution. . . . The fogs of the nineteenth century were thicker, more frequent and of a different colour from those of the past.
>
> (14)

This sense of a foggy century affected numerous perceptions and representations of London. As was noted in Essay 1, Byron, in *Don Juan*, and Dickens, in the 'London' novels, are amongst those who wonderfully captured this condition (15).

The fogs of nineteenth-century London became an irresistible subject for painters. J. M. W. Turner is probably the first to be attracted by the expressive potential of this literal atmosphere. Later, Gustave Doré casts a veil of murk over many of the scenes in his sequence of engravings, *London, A Pilgrimage*, published in 1872 (Fig. 5.1) (16). In many of these the atmospheric gloom is in accord with the depiction of social squalor. At almost exactly the same date James McNeil Whistler produced his painting of *Old Battersea Bridge* in which the structure rises from the mists that swirl above the Thames. At the end of the century the most celebrated and extensive representation of the fog is found in the series of no less than 95 paintings of London made by Claude Monet (1840–1926) between 1899 and 1904. Monet

deliberately timed his visits to London to the winter months to ensure that he would experience the atmospheric fogs, writing in his letters:

> I so love London! But I love it only in the winter. It's nice in the summer with the parks, but nothing like it is in the winter with the fog, for without the fog London wouldn't be a beautiful city . . .
>
> (17)

Like Whistler, Monet also chose to paint at riverside locations. The 'London Series' focuses on three specific views over the Thames: of Waterloo Bridge painted in the morning, Charing Cross Bridge at midday and the Houses of Parliament in the afternoon. This sequence allowed him to capture each scene with the sun filtering through the fog. The Houses of Parliament paintings are all taken from a single vantage point within St Thomas's hospital on the south bank (Plate 13) (18). Although the paintings were most probably completed in the studio at Giverny, they do, in fact, as Monet's diaries record (19), depict precise moments on identifiable days during his visits to London. They thus become documents of meteorological record in addition to their immense value as unique works of art.

Building *against* the urban climate: warming and ventilating – Soane the pioneer

By the beginning of the nineteenth century, a number of alternatives to traditional means of heating and ventilating buildings were already in use in a range of building types. The early decades of the century also saw the publication of numerous texts and treatises on the theory and practice of heating – or warming – and ventilation (20). Sir John Soane (1753–1837) was a pioneer in this endeavour. He began experiments with these systems early in his practice and continued to explore their development and application throughout his life. The sequence of installations for heating and ventilating at his own house at Lincoln's Inn Fields and at the Dulwich Picture Gallery have been widely discussed (21). The final installation at Lincoln's Inn Fields was one of the principal subjects of *A Popular Treatise on the Warming and Ventilation of Buildings*, written by Charles James Richardson, who was Soane's last pupil and later worked in the office, housed at the rear of the house (22). Richardson's *Treatise* is illustrated entirely with examples of the Perkins system of hot-water-borne heating. The frontispiece of the book is a representation of the installation in the Picture Room, Monk's Room and Gallery at the rear of the house at Lincoln's Inn Fields. With its location close to the centre of the metropolis Lincoln's Inn Fields would have endured the worst effects of London's pollution and fog, and it is probable that Soane's series of experiments with heating systems and his elaborate arrangements to fill the interior with daylight, particularly from rooflighting, were in some measure a reaction to his daily, first-hand experience of the disagreeable urban microclimate. By the use of a variety of coloured glasses in the rooflights and by a masterly juxtaposition of warmly coloured reflective surfaces in relation to light sources, Soane was able to create the illusion of a benign, idealized climate quite unrelated to the often-grim reality of the city without (23). This was to become a recurrent theme in many of his other urban projects.

In his London buildings Soane consistently brought his expertise in environmental management to bear on designs whose purposes depended on good air quality and ample illumination. Between 1788 and 1833 he carried out a series of projects for the enlargement and improvement of the Bank of England. Particularly relevant to the present discussion is the group of rooflit offices at the south-east corner of the building. Immense ingenuity was applied to the design of rooflights and clerestories to light these large volumes, and the contemporary illustrations show heating devices similar to those used at the Dulwich Picture Gallery (24). Although security would have been an important factor in the design of the bank, it is possible that these wholly internalized spaces were also a reaction to the disagreeable condition of the city without. From the beginning of his work at the Bank Soane was concerned

to find effective means of warming these large spaces. In the Stock Office (1792–1793) (Fig. 5.2) he first proposed the use of a central stove, with a 'column-flue' rising to support the vaulted roof. This was superseded by a design for a hypocaust system, in which a labyrinth of hot air and smoke ducts fuelled by an external furnace were to circulate beneath the floor. In the event Soane's heating installations at the Bank were limited to the strategic positioning of stoves. In 1831, towards the end of his involvement with the building, he presented a scheme proposed by an engineer, William Stark, for the installation of a hot-water system in the Court Room and other offices (Fig. 5.3). This drawing is accompanied by a detailed written specification:

AA Five large square coppers to be fixed to the Basement floor each to hold about150 gallons of water with a tube through the body of the water to bring the external air through the tubes BB to be rarefied by passing between a column of steam as shown by the red lines CC.

DDDD Four brass Ventilators fixed flush in the floor of the Accountants Office to discharge the Warm Air after it has passed through the tubes BB.

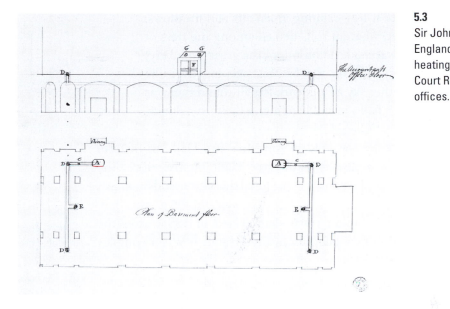

5.3
Sir John Soane, Bank of England: William Stark's heating installation in the Court Room and other offices.

EE   Two Ventilators for the discharge of Warm Air in the Basement Story, but more of them may be introduced if required.

In 1833, the year Soane retired as the Bank's architect, a Perkins hot-water system was finally installed in the Court Room. A drawing showing 'Plan and Elevation of building erected to contain the Furnace for the Hot water Apparatus for warming the Court Room by Mr A. M. Perkins' is in the archive at the Soane Museum. Ironically, after Soane's death the Bank was, seemingly, quick to accept the new means of warming (25).

A similar emphasis on the creation of an idealized interior world, as a reaction to the imperfections of the atmosphere of the city, may be seen in Soane's designs for the Law Courts built in the 1820s adjacent to the mediaeval Westminster Hall. Here a specific and potent connection may be drawn between the condition of London's climate and the architectural project. Charles Dickens' *Bleak House*, published in 1853 (26), begins with the most graphic description of the London fog in the entire literature and specifically locates this description at Lincoln's Inn:

> London. Michaelmas term lately over, and the Lord Chancellor sitting in Lincoln's Inn Hall. Implacable November weather. ... Smoke lowering down from chimney-pots, making a soft black drizzle with flakes of soot in it as big as full-grown snowflakes – gone into mourning, one might imagine, for the death of the sun. ... Fog everywhere. Fog

up the river, where it flows among green aits and meadows; fog down the river, where it rolls defiled among the tiers of shipping and the waterside pollutions of the great (and dirty) city. . . . Chance people on the bridges peeping over the parapets into a nether sky of fog, with fog all round them, as if they were up in a balloon and hanging in the misty clouds.

The Lord Chancellor's Court was held in Lincoln's Inn Hall out of term time and, during term, it met at Westminster Hall, in, therefore, the courtroom designed by Soane. It should be imagined that this was also subject to this gloomy atmosphere.

Soane's Law Courts building was demolished in 1883, after the completion of G. E. Street's new building in the Strand. It was a complex

5.4
Sir John Soane, Law Courts, Westminster: model of ground plan.

MODEL PLAN OF THE LAW COURTS, WESTMINSTER, 1821–1826.

organization of top-lit courtrooms placed between the west side of Westminster Hall and Parliament Square. The principal circulation route of the building was in a top-lit passage, an internal street, running north–south along the flank of Westminster Hall (Fig. 5.4). The courtrooms themselves displayed a virtuosic variety of rooflight and clerestory types in which Soane's domestic experiments with top lighting at Lincoln's Inn Fields were translated to the grander scale of the public institution. These remarkably inventive designs provoked one observer to protest that the courtrooms 'have more the air of fairy halls than of seats of justice' (27). The building had at least a partial central-heating installation. In the Appendix to his *Treatise* Richardson (28) lists the Vice-Chancellor's Court as having a Perkins system. A drawing, dated 1823, in the collection at the Soane Museum, shows '. . . the method proposed to be adopted to warm the Court of Chancery and the Vice

5.5
Sir John Soane, Law Courts, Westminster: heating installation for the Court of Chancery and Vice-Chancellor's Court.

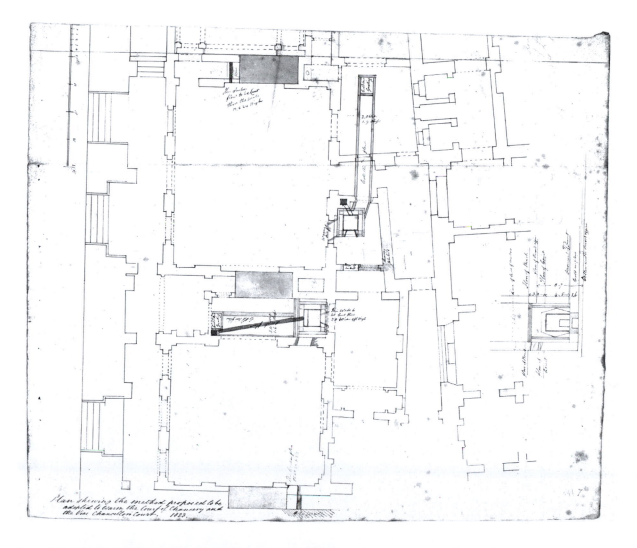

Chancellors Court'. This shows separate systems for each of the courts consisting of incoming cold-air ducts leading to heat exchangers, which were probably coal-fired as is suggested by the flues shown nearby. These then directed warm air directly into the adjacent courtrooms (Fig. 5.5) and there is clear indication of a floor grille in the foreground of one of Joseph Michael Gandy's renderings of the Court of King's Bench (Fig. 5.6).

Westminster is the setting for the conclusion of Dickens' drama, in *Bleak House*, of the trial of Jarndyce and Jarndyce, but now we are in summer and the gloomy description of the novel's opening is replaced by reference to 'the lively streets'. There is, however, a passing, but significant, reference to the atmosphere of the building when we read:

> . . . a break-up soon took place in the crowd and the people came streaming out looking flushed and hot, and bringing a quantity of bad air with them.

Here is a suggestion that even Soane's careful arrangements for the ventilation of the courts were unable to cope with the crowd attracted to the conclusion of a long-running and controversial trial on a summer's day in the city.

The Palace of Westminster

In October 1834 the historic Palace of Westminster was destroyed by fire, the event captured in a dramatic image by J. M. W. Turner, who was an eyewitness. In December of the following year 97 entries were received in the architectural competition for the design of a new building to be built on the site of the original palace on the banks of the Thames (Fig. 5.7). The successful design was that submitted by Charles Barry (1795–1860) (29). The question of ventilation had long been a problem in the earlier building and was to be in the forefront of the brief for the new one. This was, in part, a function of the need to supply quite high and controllable levels of ventilation to densely inhabited chambers like the respective houses of Lords and Commons. The problem was exacerbated by the pollution of the atmosphere of the metropolis and – in particular relation to the Palace of Westminster – by the unhygienic condition of the waters of the Thames flowing by the site and thereby compromising the quality of the air that might be drawn into the building. A useful description of the unfortunate experiences with the heating and ventilating of the old chambers is given by Soane's former assistant, Charles James Richardson in his *Treatise* (30). There he describes in detail the complicated recent history of this aspect of the Palace:

> The Commons appear to have given greater attention than their Lordships to the warming of their house, having had

5.7
Sir Charles Barry, Palace
of Westminster: view
across river Thames.

several different systems introduced from time to time for that purpose. The Upper House had been warmed almost from time immemorial on the ancient and classical system of smoke or hot air flues placed immediately beneath the floors, which system at last caused the destruction of the whole building.

In June 1835 a select committee of Members concluded that 'special provision should be made for the due ventilation of all the rooms in the new House'. And in August of the same year an expert committee, which included among its members Robert Smirke, Michael Faraday and David Boswell Reid, an Edinburgh chemist who had carried out some experiments in heating systems, was commissioned to investigate the 'Ventilating and Warming of the New Houses'. Reid, who was to be the author of one of the important nineteenth-century texts, *Illustrations of the Theory and Practice of Ventilation* (31), played an important and eventually controversial role in the development of Charles Barry's design. Reid had been responsible for the heating and ventilating installation in the temporary chamber for the House of Commons, formed by Smirke soon after the fire within the shell of the old House of Lords, whilst the Lords were lodged in the mediaeval Painted Chamber. Reid's installation, which Richardson described as 'excellent', although later judgements were less flattering (32), used what he described as an 'upcast' system of combined warming and ventilation in which incoming air was drawn down a vertical shaft before being warmed, if required, and delivered to the chamber through floor vents. The air was removed through ceiling vents and returned to an extraction chimney, 120 feet high, where, it is recorded, a steam engine of '25 horses power' gave momentum to the

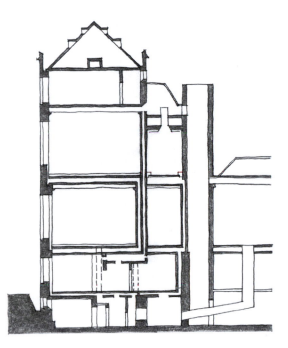

5.8
Sir Charles Barry, Palace of Westminster: cross-section showing river-front heating and ventilating system.

exhausted air (33). An illustration of this installation was given in Reid's book.

Upon Barry's appointment as architect for the new building he requested technical assistance in connection with the heating and ventilation design. Reid was appointed in this role, presumably on the strength of his apparent success with the temporary House of Commons. From the outset it was established that the effective heating and ventilation of the building would require elaborate and extensive physical provisions within the fabric of the building (Fig. 5.8). The intake and exhaust of air would be via tall shafts that would be placed at strategic positions around the building. It was as a result of the need to accommodate these that the magnificent lantern above the central lobby and other vertical elements were added to the silhouette of Barry's design. In addition, voids were required both below and above the principal spaces, in particular the debating chambers themselves, and the whole building had to be interpenetrated by a network of ducts and flues. In comparison with all previous buildings with such mechanical systems, this was a tour de force of the integration of practical necessity with high style.

Very soon the relationship between Barry and Reid broke down and, in 1846, their responsibilities were divided, with Barry taking over the job of ventilating the Lords, leaving Reid in charge of the Commons. In his design for the Lords Barry adopted the 'downcast' system of ventilation, in which air is admitted to the space at high level and extracted through the floor. Reid persisted with the 'upcast' system that he had used in the temporary Commons. This characteristically British compromise was short-lived and, after many controversies, Reid was dismissed from the project in 1852. This was not the end of the story, however, and satisfactory heating and ventilation was not fully achieved until well after the final completion of the architectural body of the building in 1870 under the direction of Edward Barry, who had succeeded his father upon his death in 1860. The later development of electrically assisted systems eventually provided the key to achieving a workable solution to this complex problem (34).

In spite of the technical and personal complexities of the project, the story of the design and construction of the new Palace of Westminster is one of the most powerful demonstrations of the importance given to designing with an explicit regard for the problem of creating healthy internal environments in response to the foul atmosphere of the ever-growing city. Not all building projects suffered the trials of the new parliament. No other was as large in scale, or as complex in its spatial and technical programme, and there are significant cases in which architectural ambition and technical expertise were comprehensively realized.

Charles Barry and the Reform Club

Following the peace with France in 1815 a fashion arose in London for the establishment of clubs for professional men. These clustered around Trafalgar Square and its extension westwards into Pall Mall. Their function was to provide comfortable, even luxurious, rooms for meeting, dining, recreation and overnight accommodation for out-of-town members. Most of the important architects of the time received club commissions, including Robert Smirke, William Wilkins, Decimus Burton and Charles Barry. Barry designed the Traveller's Club in Pall Mall (1829–1831), but his masterwork of the *genre* is the Reform Club on an adjacent site to the west (Plate 4). John Olley's study of this building provides the most comprehensive investigation into its conception and execution (35). Barry won the competition for the building in 1837 and construction took place in 1838–1840. The model was the Palazzo Farnese in Rome, and the competition design followed the original by proposing an open courtyard, *cortile* in the original, at its centre, albeit surrounded by a glazed colonnade to offer protection against the English climate. But, as Olley reports, it was decided, in discussion with the club's building committee, that the best translation of the precedent to the English climate and, in particular, to the microclimate of nineteenth-century London would be to roof over the courtyard. This instantly transforms the relation between interior and exterior and brings the courtyard into year-round use. The principal rooms are grouped on two floors around

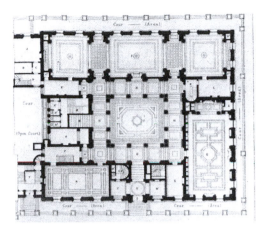

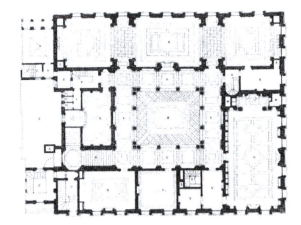

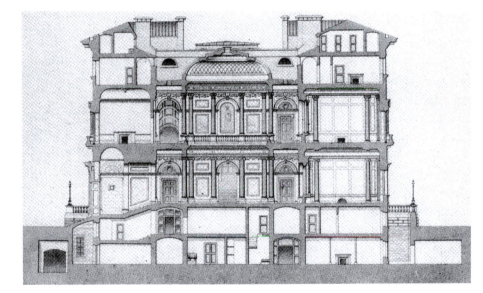

the courtyard and receive daylight through generously proportioned windows in the three open faces of the plan: north, west and south (Figs 5.9 and 5.10). The cross-section (Fig 5.11) shows the sequence of rooms from north to south, with the great rooms to the south, overlooking the gardens towards Carlton House Terrace, raised above the extensive service basements and beneath two floors of bedrooms and staff quarters.

The exact relationship between the design of the Reform Club and Barry's work at the Palace of Westminster is difficult to trace, but it is likely that the work at the Reform benefited from the early stages of the work at Westminster – although this time Barry scrupulously avoided any engagement with Reid. To provide the necessary specialist knowledge Barry was authorized by the building committee 'to confer with Mr Oldham in conjunction with Messrs. Manby and Price' (36). Dublin-born John Oldham (1779–1840) was an artist and inventor who had worked at the Bank of Ireland, where, amongst many activities, both artistic and technical, he installed a mechanical system of warming and ventilation. A similar system was also installed at the Bank of England (37). The warming and ventilation of the Reform Club, in accordance with Oldham's principles, was achieved by a steam-driven system in which a five-horsepower steam engine, located under the vaults beneath the pavement of Pall Mall, provided steam to a heat exchanger and then drove a ventilating fan that propelled warmed air through a system of ducts to all the principal rooms. Olley describes how the installation conforms to Tredgold's recommendation, in his treatise, that, to avoid draughts, the warmed air was best delivered to the rooms at ceiling level.

From the outset the building was conceived to enjoy the benefits of gas lighting, using the gas mains supply that had been piped along Pall Mall in 1820. This was quite an innovation and it is likely that the decision was made in response to the fogs that frequently made day into night. The unwanted products of combustion from the light fittings were vented away by a number of routes. The so-called 'sun burner' at the centre of the saloon roof was mounted below a ventilator that led the waste gases directly away to the atmosphere and, incidentally, provided some motive power for the ventilation of the space. Elsewhere the gases were conducted through a system of ducts and vents threaded through the building fabric. Barry exercised great ingenuity in contriving ducts and outlets in the cornices of these sumptuously decorated rooms. The exhaust air passed through the ducts associated with the gaslights and up the fireplace chimneys. In such a quintessentially English institution as the Reform Club, the open fire remained an important symbol and producer of comfort.

> I do not know of anything more grateful to the senses, or more essential to health, than pure and wholesome air . . .

Thomas Tredgold made this observation in his *Principles of Warming and Ventilating* of 1825 (38). The statement may be read as a direct reaction to the fetid state of London's atmosphere. In translating theory into design at the Reform Club, Charles Barry and his engineer collaborators strove to bring satisfaction to the senses of the members of the Reform Club, as they enjoyed their Roman palazzo in the heart of the nineteenth-century metropolis, in an environment that, if not quite Roman, was one of the most successful attempts to that date to create a consistent and reliable standard of comfort comprehensively integrated into the sumptuous architectural detail.

The British Museum Reading Room (1852–1857)

The British Museum has a long architectural history. Following its foundation in 1753 a search began to find a suitable building, and Montagu House, a mansion in Bloomsbury, was selected (39). The original Montagu House has been attributed to Robert Hooke and works were carried out to make it suitable to house the museum and its library in readiness for its opening in January 1759. The pressure for space to house the expanding collections of artefacts and books led to the appointment as architect of Robert Smirke, who worked at the museum from 1823 until 1838. Smirke's design, which progressively replaced Montagu House, was complete by 1838. Behind the grand Ionic colonnade of the south façade, the building consisted of a central quadrangle enclosed by wings of relatively narrow cross-section, which would be amply daylit. The entire east wing contained the King's Library, facing the courtyard, with reading rooms to the south. The northern wing was devoted to printed books and, within this, further reading rooms were provided at the north-east corner. Smirke, who had been briefly articled to Soane (40), had an interest in the new methods of heating and ventilation that, we may surmise, derived in some measure from the explorations in this field of his former master (41). From the outset he brought this interest to bear on the museum project and, as with many other pioneering installations, problems ensued (42). Mordaunt Crook summarizes the fluctuating opinions of these early installations:

> In 1836 a Parliamentary committee was told how well the British Museum's central heating was operating: Bloomsbury readers seldom shivered, unlike scholars in the Royal Library in Paris, who 'must keep themselves warm as well as they can'. Two years later *The Times* praised not only the function of the reading room's heaters but also their appearance: four 'great sort of chests of hot water pipes' covered with marble slabs to appear 'exceedingly classical and ornamental'. But in the long run Smirke's heating of the British Museum can hardly be called successful. The 'Museum Headache' and 'Museum Megrims' . . . were all signs of the inadequacy of these ephemeral processes.
>
> (43)

By the date of its completion Smirke's building was already too small to accommodate the growing collections and the public demand for access. This was particularly so in regard to the needs of the library. Sir Henry Ellis was principal Librarian at the museum from 1827 to 1856. At the beginning of his tenure the library had fewer than 150,000 printed books, but on his retirement the number was more than 520,000 (44). Ellis was succeeded by Anthony Panizzi (1797–1879), who had been appointed Keeper of Printed Books in 1837. It is generally agreed that Panizzi was responsible for one of the most dynamic periods in the history of the British Museum. The focus of Panizzi's attention was Smirke's underused quadrangle and in 1852 he made the first sketch for a new, circular reading room to occupy this space, which the Trustees quickly approved in principle.

Robert Smirke had formally resigned from the Museum project in 1846 and had been succeeded by his younger brother Sydney. It was he who carried out the hugely difficult technical task of translating Panizzi's sketch into a buildable structure, a task minimized by Panizzi, who stated that 'He will have nothing to do but carry into execution my ideas . . .' (Figs 5.12 and 5.13). The structure of the building used the new constructional method of the iron frame that had received so much attention in the wake of the construction of Paxton's Crystal Palace at the Great Exhibition in 1851. Work began on site in May 1854 and the first readers were admitted in May 1857.

In 1867 a detailed description of the New Reading Room (Fig. 5.14) was published by John Murray. This describes the arrangements for heating and ventilation, which were installed by the firm of George Haden of Trowbridge, and merits extensive quotation:

> The framework of each table is of iron, forming air-distributing channels, which are contrived so that the air may be delivered at the top of the longitudinal screen division, above the heads of the readers, or, if desired, only at each end pedestal of the tables, all the outlets being under the control of valves. A tubular footrail also passes from end to end of each table, which may have a current of hot water through it at pleasure, and be used as a footwarmer if required.
>
> The Catalogue tables, with shelves under, and air-distributing tubes between, are ranged in two concentric circles around the central superintendant's enclosure, or raised platform . . . The pedestals of the tables form tubes communicating with the air chamber below, which is 6 feet high, and occupies the whole area of the Reading-room. It is fitted with hot-water pipes, arranged in radiating lines. The supply of fresh air is obtained from a shaft 60 feet high, built on the north side of the north wing, about 300 feet distant, communicating with a tunnel or sub-way, which has branches or 'loop-lines' fitted with valves for diverting the current either wholly through the heating apparatus, or

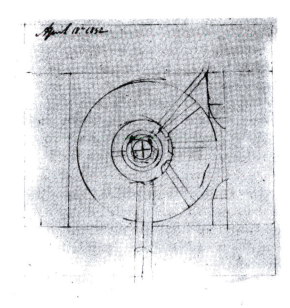

5.12
British Museum, London:
Anthony Panizzi's sketch
(1852).

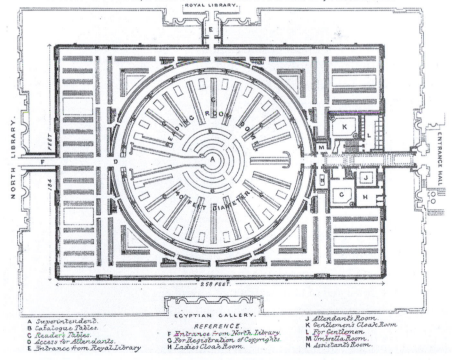

BRITISH MUSEUM, PLAN OF NEW READING ROOM IN QUADRANGLE.

REFERENCE.
A Superintendent.
B Catalogue Tables.
C Reader's Tables.
D Access for Attendants.
E Entrance from Royal Library.
F Entrance from North Library.
G For Registration of Copyrights.
H Ladies Cloak Room.
J Attendant's Room.
K Gentlemen's Cloak Room.
L For Gentlemen.
M Umbrella Room.
N Assistant's Room.

5.13
British Museum:
plan showing Reading
Room (1857).

through the cold-air flues, or partly through either, as occasion may require. The air-channels are of sufficient capacity to admit a supply of fresh air for 500 persons at the rate of 10 cubic feet per second. For summer ventilation steam-pipes, placed at the summit of the roofs and dome, will be heated, and extract the foul air when the external and internal temperature is unfavourable for the purpose.

(45)

The New Reading Room was surrounded by bookstacks in a rectangular structure set back from the façades of Smirke's quadrangle. These were also of iron construction and became known as the 'Iron Library'. The stacks were top-lit with the intermediate gallery floors of perforated iron grilles, to allow daylight to percolate to the lower levels.

The account in John Murray's pamphlet omits a detailed description of the way in which the ventilation system was integrated into the construction of the dome. This important structure consisted of two separate air chambers that extended over the whole hemisphere. One was between the brick lining and the outer copper covering of the dome, and its function was to act as a thermal buffer between inside and outside. The other, internal, chamber was between the brick lining and the suspended ceiling, and served as a plenum through which vitiated air was evacuated. Ventilation grilles were placed in the soffits of the window openings and at the top of the dome.

When the Reading Room first opened it was regarded by most as an unqualified success, particularly by readers who had endured the overcrowding and poor environment of the older reading rooms. Some claimed that the space conveyed the sense of being out of doors. But these impressions were soon contradicted by growing dissatisfaction with the atmosphere of the room, an important part of which followed from the absence of any source of artificial lighting, which limited the hours during which the room could be used. Smirke had provisionally proposed that the room might be lit by gaslights placed outside the lantern of the dome. The Trustees quickly rejected the idea, and the room was entirely dependent on natural light. Barwick reports that in 1862 there was agitation for the introduction of gas lighting to allow evening opening, but this was again rejected until an electric lighting system of 'Yablochkov candles', which used a spluttering carbon arc to produce illumination, was installed in 1879 (46). Even in so-called daytime, the absence of effective artificial lighting was a serious problem in the fogs of nineteenth-century London. In July 1865, for example, London suffered extremely dense fogs – these were not solely a winter phenomenon – and the *Builder* magazine complained:

> The book-worms who haunt the reading-rooms of the Museum are on these occasions left without the means of pursuing their various avocations. Many of this industrious and useful community leave the beautiful dome, which in this light has a dim, lurid and somewhat ghastly appearance, and grope their way homeward . . . But no candlelight, lamplight or gas light can, under present arrangements, be allowed to the student of the national library, although the plan has been tried with so much success at Kensington and Elsewhere.
>
> (47)

A relevant comparison may be drawn between the Reading Room and the great contemporary libraries that were constructed in Paris by Henri Labrouste (1801–1875): the Bibliotèque Ste-Geneviève (1838–1851) and the Bibliotèque Nationale (1859–1868) (48). Both of these were artificially lit by gas from the outset and this highlights the conservatism of the London authorities with regard to the potential of this aspect of the new technologies and to the social function of the library in relation to the growing urban population. On the other hand, the attention paid to the thermal comfort of the reader demonstrated by the design of the reading desks in the Bloomsbury building, with their integrated heating elements, must surely have influenced the similar arrangement found at the Bibliotèque Nationale. It must also be observed that the essentially pragmatic approach of Panizzi and Wilkins to the design of the Reading Room displays none of the sophistication of tectonic expression and iconography of Labrouste's designs.

The significance of the Reading Room in the present discussion, however, is the thoroughness with which the latest technologies of construction and environmental management were brought together in the service of the nation's principal cultural institution. Even allowing for the problems that were later experienced with these systems, the project represented a major ambition and achievement. The perseverance of the officers and Trustees of the Museum in the application of the new technologies, in spite of many setbacks, was of course necessitated by the new demands for wider access to public institutions and, in all probability, by the need to protect readers and collections from the aggressive atmosphere of the city without.

The Natural History Museum

The idea of creating a Natural History Museum in London was first ventured in 1856 by Richard Owen, who had recently become superintendant of the Department of Natural History at the British Museum (49). Owen, who had strong views on the organization of such a museum, produced a sketch layout of a building in 1859 (Fig. 5.15), and a schematic design based on this, made by Henry Hunt, who was surveyor to the Office of Works, was published in 1862. Owen had been centrally involved in the debate that followed the publication of Charles Darwin's *On the Origin of Species* in 1859, the year of Owen's sketch, and had been one of the principal opponents of Darwin's theory. In 1864 a competition was held for the design of a new museum building on a site in South Kensington. The winning design was by Captain Francis Fowke, but following his death in December 1865, Alfred Waterhouse (1830–1905) was appointed to realize Fowke's design. In the event, the building that eventually rose on Cromwell Road, completed after a protracted process in 1881, was an elaborate development of Fowke's design.

Owen's sketch, whilst hardly a developed architectural proposition, showed a series of adjacent exhibition galleries disposed on either side of a central circular space. This implied that the galleries would be rooflit, which remained a consistent principle in the sequence of designs that followed. This almost certainly derived from Owen's ideas about the display of botanical and zoological exhibits, in which the layout was to represent a divine view of the essence of nature as a critique of Darwin's new ideas. A more pragmatic aspect of Owen's intervention was his clear and perceptive notion of the benefits of controlled toplighting. These offered a quantity and quality of daylight that was not available in the side-lit galleries of the British Museum, where the collections were previously housed and proved to have an influence throughout the development of the design.

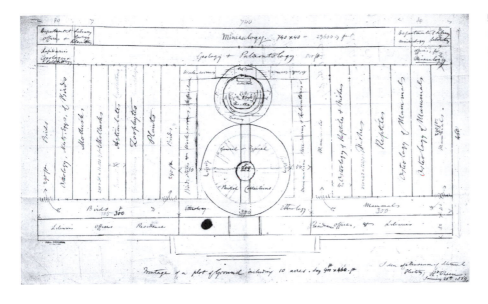

Alfred Waterhouse began his architectural practice in Manchester, where he was responsible for many of the rapidly growing industrial city's significant public buildings, including the Assize Courts (1859), Strangeways Gaol (1861), the Town Hall (1868) and Owens College, later to become the University (1870). In all of these he made extensive use of the latest and best systems for heating, ventilation and lighting (50). This was, almost certainly, in response to the polluted atmosphere of the great industrial city, which was most graphically described by Friedrich Engels in *The Condition of the Working-class in England* (51). Colin Cunningham and Prudence Waterhouse observe that:

> Waterhouse was fortunate that many of the early experiments had already been made for structures such as the Houses of Parliament; and he was able to benefit from the second generation of inventions. He was able to select and apply the most up-to-date systems, and, once a system was proved, could safely apply it elsewhere.
>
> (52)

This effectively confirms that in the latter part of the nineteenth century the provision of building services was on a firm footing of technical expertise and architectural integration.

In his Manchester projects Waterhouse had collaborated with George (G. N.) Haden of Trowbridge, who we encountered in the discussion of the installations at the New Reading Room of the British Museum (page 140).

In total, Haden worked with Waterhouse on no less than 92 projects. The 'campanile' that rises high above the Manchester Assize Courts was equally an essential part of the ventilation system and an important component of the picturesque silhouette of the building. The building was praised by Ruskin as being 'much beyond everything yet done in England on my principles' (53). At Strangeways the extensive plenum system remains in use to the present day. The spiral staircases that are an important feature of Manchester Town Hall act as vent shafts for warm air and the elaborate detailing of the Great Hall roof incorporates extract vents (54). Waterhouses's unbuilt design for the Law Courts in the Strand (1866) would have been a tour de force in the integration of extensive services systems into the fabric of a building of immense size and spatial complexity. The silhouette of the building – what Colin St J. Wilson described as its 'tumultuous roofscape' – was dominated by towers and pinnacles, most of which had some purpose in

5.16
Alfred Waterhouse,
Natural History Museum,
London: view from
Cromwell Road.

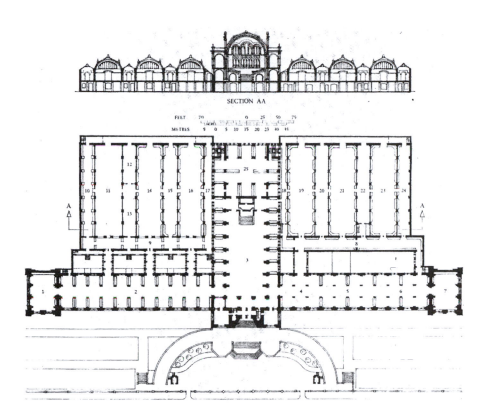

SECTION AA

5.17
Alfred Waterhouse,
Natural History Museum:
principal-floor plan and
cross-section.

relation to the heating and ventilation (55). It must be noted, however, that all the other designs submitted in the competition, which included contributions from E. M. Barry, William Burges, J. P. Seddon, G. Gilbert Scott and G. E. Street (who was eventually appointed as architect), had similarly extravagant, silhouettes, partly in conformity with the prevailing taste for a romantic Gothic, but equally in acknowledgment of the utility of these elements in providing for the latest in environmental management (56).

Waterhouse's Natural History Museum survives relatively unchanged to the present day, albeit with a number of more recent additions (Fig 5.16). The layout, which was deeply influenced by Owen's anti-Darwinist strictures regarding the representation of nature, consists of a three-storey range of side-lit galleries, facing Cromwell Road to the south of the site, behind which are ranged a series of top-lit galleries, on either side of the central hall (Fig. 5.17). The cross-section strongly pre-echoes Louis Kahn's structure of alternate 'served' and 'servant' spaces in the cross-section of his Kimbell Art Museum at Fort Worth, Texas, which was completed in 1972 (57). It is in this cross-section that Waterhouse translated Owen's ideas about gallery lighting. The glazing is located in the lower parts of the arched roof form, with the apex being of solid construction. This avoids excessive glare and solar heat

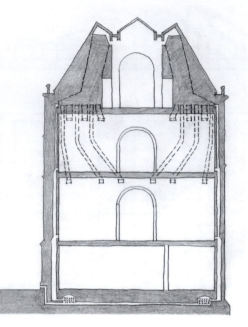

5.18
Alfred Waterhouse,
Natural History Museum:
diagrammatic section
showing the heating and
ventilating ducts and
channels.

gain and achieves a good distribution of light across the space. This arrangement also allows the void at the apex to be used as part of the ventilation system. It may be surmised that the experience of the effects of solar heat gain through highly glazed structures that had been experienced in the Crystal Palace at the 1851 Great Exhibition lived on in the memory of London architects (58) and led to a more prudent understanding of these effects.

In the design and installation of the heating and ventilating system there was a high degree of collaboration and integration of the work of the architect and the engineer. Olley and Wilson (59) show that, some time before the appointment of George Haden, Waterhouse had already made a number of decisions regarding the composition and detail of the building that dictated the general configuration of the mechanical systems. Almost every turret and tower of the building was to accommodate a ventilation shaft or smoke flue, and in some cases both of these. The pair of 'campanile' located to the north of the body of the museum acted as extract ducts for the vitiated air and the easterly one also contained the boiler flue. The heating installation used three boilers, located in the basement. These supplied heat exchangers that converted the steam heat into hot water for circulation around the building via a network of pipes running in ducts formed beneath the floor of the basement. In winter fresh air was warmed as it passed over batteries of pipes placed along the external walls of the south wing and was distributed through ducts to enter the galleries above through floor grilles (Fig. 5.18). Extraction from the south wing was at high level to outlets incorporated in the corner towers, and the top-lit galleries were vented through ceiling grilles into the void below the apex of the roof (60). As an essay in what later became known as 'the integration of structure and services' the building was as thoroughly realized as almost any of its twentieth-century descendants.

Conclusion

In the preceding essays the relationship between the buildings described and the climate in which they stand has been almost exclusively benign. The climate, even when severely hostile in the depth of the winters of the Little Ice Age, has been regarded as an agency to be worked with, rather than to be rejected, kept at bay, filtered. With the arrival of the nineteenth century this relationship changed. In *The Architecture of the Well-Tempered Environment*, Reyner Banham firmly established that the development of environmental services in buildings was a direct response to the climate of what he characterized as 'A dark satanic century' (61). The centuries-long dismay at the polluted atmosphere of the capital was exacerbated by the population growth and industrial development of the nineteenth century. It is as a response to this perception of the urban climate as a profound danger to health and well-being that architects turned to the newly emerging technologies of warming and ventilating as they sought to create more agreeable and healthier internal environments for the users of many types of building.

Sir John Soane is now generally seen as one of the pioneers in experimenting with these new systems in, most significantly, his own house in London, but also in many of his large-scale public commissions. His installations in buildings such as the Bank of England and the Westminster Law Courts were brave, with their technical boldness, in combination with his continual experimentation with the design of rooflighting arrangements, implying a vision of an ideal internalized world of 'fairy halls' that offered the greatest contrast to the conditions outside. The story of the heating and ventilating of the new Palace of Westminster had its roots in the long history of discomfort experienced in the overcrowded debating chambers of the old palace. The scale and complexity of the project were significant causes of its many trials and shortcomings, not least in its environmental aspects. Nonetheless, the building was one of the first to fully incorporate extensive networks of air ducts and pipeways unobtrusively into its fabric and details. At the Reform Club Charles Barry was able to achieve a virtually perfect synthesis of architectural language and technical invention in the transformation of the palazzo type from the climate of renaissance Rome to that of fog-ridden London. Within the almost hermetically sealed envelope, Barry, in collaboration with the engineer John Oldham, created an almost unprecedented standard of resistance to the horrors of the urban microclimate.

The New Reading Room of the British Museum was the product of the growth in the thirst for knowledge amongst the new urban population. Although the initial refusal of the museum authorities to consider gas lighting restricted the use of the room to daylight hours, its scale and its provisions for year-round temperature control made it a model for future innovations in urban building.

As the century entered its last two decades, Alfred Waterhouse and George Haden achieved a mature relationship between architect and engineer in their work at the Natural History Museum. From this point onwards it was almost invariably assumed that large urban buildings would be equipped with the full apparatus of heating and ventilating plant and that these, particularly following the availability of electric lighting after 1879, would allow urban dwellers to enjoy a welcome respite from the dark climate of the city.

Notes

1. John Summerson, 'London, the artifact', in *The Victorian City: Images and Realities.* Volume II: *Shapes on the Ground/A Change of Accent* (ed. H. J. Dyos and Michael Wolff), Routledge & Kegan Paul, London, 1973.

2. Data from Eric E. Lampard, 'The urbanizing world', in *The Victorian City: Images and Realities.* Volume I: *Past and Present/Numbers of People* (ed. H. J. Dyos and Michael Wolff), Routledge & Kegan Paul, London, 1973.

3. Henry-Russell Hitchcock, *Architecture: Nineteenth and Twentieth Centuries*, Penguin, Harmondsworth, 1st edition, 1958; 1st paperback edition, 1971.

4. Summerson, 'London, the artifact', cited in Note 1.

5. Hitchcock, *Architecture*, cited in Note 3.

6. Siegfried Giedion, *Mechanization Takes Command: A Contribution to Anonymous History*, Oxford University Press, Oxford, 1948. Lewis Mumford, *Technics and Civilization*, Harcourt, Brace, New York, 1934.

7. Reyner Banham, *The Architecture of the Well-Tempered Environment*, The Architectural Press, London, 1969; 2nd revised edition, Chicago University Press, Chicago, 1984.

8. Peter Brimblecombe, *The Big Smoke: A History of Air Pollution in London since Medieval Times*, Methuen, London, 1987; paperback edition, Routledge, London, 1988.

9. Brimblecombe, *Ibid.*, provides a detailed account of the emergence of the smoke abatement movement.

10. The best outline of Howard's life and work is the obituary in *Proceedings of the Royal Society*, 1865, Vol. 14, pp. x–xii.

11. Luke Howard, *The Climate of London*, London, 2 vols, 1818; 2nd edition, 3 vols, 1833.

12. Luke Howard, 'On the classification of clouds', *Philosophical Magazine*, Vols 16 and 17, 1803–1804.

13. *Luke Howard, 1772–1864: his correspondence with Goethe and his continental journey of 1816.* Reprint, William Sessions, York, 1976.

14. Brimblecombe, *The Big Smoke*, cited in Note 8.

15. Essay 1: 'Climate described'.

16. Gustave Doré and Jerrold Blanchard, *London, A Pilgrimage*, Grant, London, 1872; reprinted, Dover Publications, New York, 2004.

17. See Brimblecombe, *The Big Smoke*, cited in Note 8, and John E. Thornes and Gemma Metherell, 'Monet's "London Series" and the cultural climate of London at the turn of the twentieth century', in *Weather, Climate, Culture* (ed. Sarah Strauss and Benjamin S. Orlove), Berg, Oxford, 2003.

18. Jacob Baker and John E. Thornes, 'Solar position within Monet's Houses of Parliament', in *Proceedings of the Royal Society A*, Vol. 462, 2006, pp. 3775–3788.

19. See Thornes and Metherell, 'Monet's "London Series"', cited in Note 17.

20. See, for example, Walter Bernan, *On the History and Art of Warming and Ventilating Buildings*, London, 1845 (reprinted Kessinger Publishing Company, 2008); David Boswell Reid, *Illustrations of the Theory and Practice of Ventilating*, Longman, London, 1844; and Thomas Tredgold, *On the Principles and Practice of Warming and Ventilating Buildings*, Josiah Taylor, London, 1824.

21. See Todd Willmert, 'Heating methods and their impact on Soane's work: Lincoln's Inn Fields and Dulwich Picture Gallery', *Journal of the Society of Architectural Historians*, Vol. 52, 1993, pp. 26–58, and Dean Hawkes, *The Environmental Imagination: Technics and Poetics of the Architectural Environment*, Routledge, London, 2008. An excellent international review of these early developments is Robert Bruegman, 'Central heating and forced ventilation: origins and effects on architectural design', *Journal of the Society of Architectural Historians*, Vol. 37, 1978, pp. 143–160. See also Robert Brucemann and Donald Prowler, '19th century mechanical system designs', *Journal of Architectural Education (JAE)*, Vol. 30, 1977, pp. 11–15.

22. Charles James Richardson, *A Popular Treatise on the Warming and Ventilation of Buildings: Showing the Advantage of the Heated Water Circulation*, John Weale: Architectural Library, London, 1837.

23. A more detailed commentary on the general environment and, in particular, of the daylighting at Lincoln's Inn Fields can be found in Hawkes, *The Environmental Imagination*, cited in Note 21.

24. Daniel M. Abramson, *Building the Bank of England: Money, Architecture, Society, 1694–1942*, Yale University Press, New Haven, CT, 2005, locates Soane's work at the Bank in the widest context. See Willmert, 'Heating methods and their impact on Soane's work', cited in Note 21, for a detailed description of Soane's various heating proposals at the Bank.

25. This was the work of John Oldham, who also collaborated with Charles Barry in the warming and ventilating of the Reform Club. The world of building services design and installation in early-nineteenth-century London had many interconnected actors.

26. Arthur Calder Marshall, in his Introduction to *Bleak House*, Pan, London, 1976, suggests that the events described in the novel may have taken place in the 1840s or earlier, not in the 1850s, the decade of its publication. This does not, however, invalidate Dickens' description of the climate of the city as relevant to much of the nineteenth century.

27. The Law Court project is excellently illustrated in Margaret Richardson and Mary Ann Stevens (eds), *John Soane: Architect, Master of Light and Space*, Royal Academy of Art, London/Yale University Press, New Haven, CT, 1999.

28. Richardson, *A Popular Treatise on the Warming and Ventilation of Buildings*, cited in Note 22.

29. M. H. Port (ed.) *The Houses of Parliament*, Paul Mellon Centre for British Art/Yale University Press, New Haven, CT, 1976, is a major reference for any study of this building. In this, Denis Smith's essay, 'The building services', provides an extensive account of the development of the service installations in the building and is the principal source of the technical detail included in the present essay. A further important source of background material is Christine Riding and Jacqueline Riding (eds), *The Houses of Parliament: History, Art, Architecture*, Merrell, London, 2000.

30. Richardson, *A Popular Treatise on the Warming and Ventilation of Buildings*, cited in Note 22.

31. Reid, *Illustrations of the Theory and Practice of Ventilating*, cited in Note 20.

32. Reid, as cited in Smith, 'The building services', cited in Note 29.

33. See Smith, 'The building services'.

34. *Ibid*.

35. John Olley, 'The Reform Club', in *Timeless Architecture* (ed. Dan Cruickshank), The Architectural Press, London, 1985.

36. *Ibid*.

37. See *Dictionary of National Biography*, Oxford University Press, Oxford, 2004–2009. An outline description of Oldham's system may be found in C. W. Williams, 'Mr Oldham's system of warming and ventilating', *Civil Engineer and Architect's Journal*, Vol. 2, 1839, pp. 96–97.

38. Tredgold, *On the Principles and Practice of Warming and Ventilating Buildings* (cited in Note 20), as cited by Olley, 'The Reform Club' (cited in Note 35).

39. P. R. Harris, *A History of the British Museum Library 1753–1973*, British Library, London, 1998, which provides a comprehensive history of the institution and the buildings of the library in its first two centuries. J. Mordaunt Crook, *The British Museum: A Case-Study in Architectural Politics*, Allen Lane/Penguin, Harmondsworth, 1972; Pelican, Harmondsworth, 1973. For an account of the buildings of the museum see Marjory Caygill and Christopher Date, *Building the British Museum*, British Museum Press, London, 1999.

40. Caygill and Date, *Ibid*. A concise description of the Reading Room is given in P. R. Harris, *The Reading Room*, British Library, London, 1979.

41. The Appendix to Richardson's *A Popular Treatise on the Warming and Ventilation of Buildings*, cited in Note 22, records that Smirke had installed a Perkins system at his home, Stanmore House, in Middlesex.

42. See Harris, *A History of the British Museum Library 1753–1973*, cited in Note 39, for a detailed account of the various heating and ventilation systems employed in the museum as the building developed.

43. Crook, *The British Museum*, cited in Note 39.

44. *Ibid*.

45. *British Museum. New Reading Room and Libraries: with a Plan*, John Murray, London, 1867. This was based upon an article first published in the *Times* on 21 April 1867.

46. This information is taken from G. F. Barwick, *The Reading Room of the British Museum*, E. Benn, London, 1929.

47. *Builder*, 29 July 1865, pp. 537–538, as cited in Barwick, *The Reading Room of the British Museum*, cited in Note 46.

48. See Hawkes, *The Environmental Imagination*, cited in Note 21.

49. The most extensive descriptions of the design and construction of the Natural History Museum are Mark Girouard, *Alfred Waterhouse and the Natural History Museum*, British Museum (Natural History), London, 1981; John Olley and Caroline Wilson, 'The Natural History Museum', in *Timeless Architecture* (ed. Dan Cruickshank), The Architectural Press, London, 1985, and F. H. W. Sheppard (ed.), *The Survey of London*, Volume 38: *The Museums of South Kensington and Westminster*, Royal Commission on Historic Monuments (now English Heritage), London, 1975. For a general history of the museum see William T. Stearn, *The Natural History Museum at South Kensington*, William Heinemann, London, 1981. A particularly detailed architectural study of the Natural History Museum is J. B. Bullen, 'Alfred Waterhouse's Romanesque "Temple of Nature": The Natural History Museum, London', *Architectural History*, Vol. 49, 2006, pp. 257–285.

50. The standard critical study of Alfred Waterhouse's work is Colin Cunningham and Prudence Waterhouse, *Alfred Waterhouse, 1830–1905: Biography of a Practice*, Clarendon Press, Oxford, 1992. Waterhouse's Manchester projects are placed in the social and architectural context of the city in Cecil Stewart, *The Stones of Manchester*, Edward Arnold, London, 1956.

51. Friedrich Engels, *The Condition of the Working Class in England* (ed. David McLellan), Oxford University Press, Oxford, 2009.

52. Cunningham and Waterhouse, *Alfred Waterhouse, 1830–1905*, cited in Note 50.

53. John Ruskin, as cited in Cecil Stewart, *The Stones of Manchester*, cited in Note 50.

54. *Ibid.*

55. See Colin St J. Wilson, 'The Law Courts Project by Alfred Waterhouse', in *Architectural Reflections: Studies in the Philosophy and Practice of Architecture*, Butterworth Architecture, Oxford, 1992, for a detailed account of this design, albeit omitting detail of the services installations.

56. See M. H. Port, 'The New Law Courts Competition, 1866–1867, *Architectural History*, Vol. 11, 1968, pp. 75–120, and John Summerson, 'A Victorian Competition: The Royal Courts of Justice', in *Victorian Architecture: Four Studies in Evaluation*, Columbia University Press, New York, 1970.

57. See Hawkes, *The Environmental Imagination*, cited in Note 21, for a discussion of the environmental qualities of this building.

58. See Henrik Schoenefeldt, 'The Crystal Palace, environmentally considered', *Architectural Research Quarterly*, Vol. 12, 2008, pp. 283–294.

59. Olley and Wilson, 'The Natural History Museum', cited in Note 49.

60. See Olley and Wilson, *Ibid.*, for a fuller description of the installation.

61. Banham, *The Architecture of the Well-Tempered Environment*, Chapter 3, cited in Note 7.

Essay 6
The Arts and Crafts house climatically considered

The English house in its present form cannot be explained simply in terms of its historical development . . . There have always been other forces at work moulding it, forces deep within these trends but more stable and more easily measured. They are the local determinants of the English house.

The strongest of these influences always lie in a country's climatic and geographical conditions. The English climate is fundamentally different from that of the continent; in particular, it is milder, the air is extremely damp and it is generally inhospitable – all, basic characteristics of the maritime climate of the country. It is extremely rare for snow and ice to persist in England, and the day-time temperature in winter seldom falls below freezing point. There are short spells of great heat during the summer, but in general summers are rather cool, so that in both seasons the temperature remains much closer to the annual average . . . than it does on the continent.

Herman Muthesius's *Das Englische Haus* (1904/1905) (1) was the first substantial study of the domestic architecture of the English Arts and Crafts movement. Published in German, and not translated into English until 1979, this work stands to the present day as the most comprehensive documentation of this significant phase of the architecture of these islands. Muthesius, who was himself an architect of some distinction, lived in London from 1896, as cultural attaché to the German embassy. His identification of the influence of the climate on this architecture is clearly important in the present discussion and, as we will see, was a matter that was explicitly addressed by many of the architects of the movement in both their practices and writings.

In describing the effect of the climate on the architecture of the English house, Muthesius writes first on the importance of the open fire:

Open fires are the only means of heating the house. The many advantages the fireplace is deemed to possess . . . so completely convince the Englishman of its superiority to all other forms of heating ... One presumes that the mild climate is also responsible for the fact that the English have made scarcely any use of central heating. And even when it is installed it never replaces the open fire, for to the English a room without a fire is like a body without a soul.

Every fireplace has a flue of its own, which accounts for the immense chimney-stacks on English houses.

(2)

He then discourses on the English preoccupation with ventilation, the role of fireplaces in promoting this, and its negative consequence – draughts.

The English are more or less impervious to the draught, partly because they take the precaution of wearing warm underclothing.

(3)

Muthesius's description of the English climate casts it in an unattractive light, 'inhospitable'. He notes, disapprovingly, its mildness and absence of extremes and its pervasive dampness. This view must come from his direct experience of the country as he journeyed about in his quest for notable houses. It is also coloured by comparison with the continental climate of his native Germany, with its seasonal extremes of winter cold and summer heat. The evidence of contemporary weather data for the period of Muthesius's stay in Britain, as represented by the Central England Temperature (CET) series and studies of precipitation (4), shows that the climate had recovered from the sequence of very cold winters that occurred in the first decades of the nineteenth century, as the Little Ice Age ended, and was in a relatively quiet period, so far as temperature and rainfall were concerned, neither unusually hot or cold, nor particularly wet.

There are, however, more positive, even romantic, impressions and descriptions of the climatic setting of Arts and Crafts architecture. E. M. Forster's *Howards End* (5) was first published in 1910, shortly after the date of *Das Englische Haus*, but exactly at the time when many of the major architects of the movement built their best houses. 'Howards End', the house that serves as both location and metaphor for the narrative, is based on 'Rooksnest', an old farmhouse in Hertfordshire where Forster spent ten idyllic years as a boy. In a letter to her sister Helen, Margaret Schlegel, the book's protagonist, writes:

It is old and little, and altogether delightful – red brick. ...
From the hall you go right or left into dining-room or

drawing-room. Hall itself is practically a room. You open another door in it, and there are the stairs going up in a sort of tunnel to the first floor. Three bedrooms in a row there, and three attics in a row above. That isn't all the house really, but it's all one notices – nine windows as you look up from the front garden.

Forster himself later described the house in the following terms:

It certainly was a lovable little house, and still is . . . The garden, the overhanging wych-elm, the sloping meadow, the great view to the west, the cliff of fir trees to the north, the adjacent farm through the high tangled hedge of wild roses . . .

(6)

This is precisely the kind of vernacular house that, in its setting in response to topography and climate, became a reference point for the architects of the Arts and Crafts movement.

The house survives to the present day. It is located just outside the new town of Stevenage, 35 miles north of London on the Great North Road, and on the Great Northern Railway's main line to King's Cross station. The façade of nine windows described by Margaret is oriented to the west of due south, as was commonly the practice of the vernacular houses in this region and was to become the basis of much Arts and Crafts site and garden planning. This lyrical vision of the ideal residence, in which house and garden become a unity in providing for year-round comfort and leisure in the English climate, is in striking contrast with Muthesius's more prosaic description. A similar vision of benign nature, and, by inference, climate, is conjured by the title, *Gardens of a Golden Afternoon*, chosen by Jane Brown for her account of the partnership of Edwin Lutyens and Gertrude Jekyll in making houses and gardens in later Victorian and Edwardian England (7). The reference to 'a golden afternoon' is borrowed from the poem 'All in the golden afternoon' that begins Lewis Carroll's *Alice in Wonderland* (8).

In contrast to the environmental defences constructed by the nineteenth-century urban buildings that were our concern in Essay 5 – what we may call design *against* climate – the country and suburban houses of the Arts and Crafts movement embraced the climate's positive qualities, proposing, therefore, design *with* climate (9). Muthesius notes that, from the 1860s onwards, the English middle classes, who were to become the most important clients for Arts and Crafts architects, began to move further from the city and to use the expanding railway network to travel daily from home to work and back (10). This was particularly the case in London, but the same practice could be found in relation to the industrial cities of the Midlands and the north of England. There, in the smaller towns, local industrialists built quite close to the town, but invariably in locations free from the worst effects of the polluting industries that they owned. Sites were chosen on high land, upwind, usually westward, from the town and its factories. In these favourable situations the Arts and Crafts architects were able to bring climate and building into a wonderfully symbiotic relationship.

Muthesius begins his account of English domestic architecture by describing buildings by a generation of architects born in the 1830s: Philip Webb (1830), Eden Nesfield (1835), Norman Shaw (1831), J. D. Sedding (1837) and Ernest George (1839). These, all prolific builders, established the essential nature of the new domestic architecture. Muthesius wrote of Norman Shaw's plans:

> They are models of utility and convenience yet at the same time, to the eye accustomed to plans, they promise comfort to the highest degree.
>
> (11)

In almost all instances these designs were scrupulous in observing the dictates of orientation as an important aid to providing comfort, with the principal rooms enjoying southerly aspects. A particularly good example is Philip Webb's late design for Standen near East Grinstead (1891–1898), where the drawing and dining rooms face just to the west of south and the morning room enjoys both south-east and south-west windows to capture the sun in the early part of the day. Standen is relatively unusual in having a conservatory, and this beautiful, bright space provides ideal conditions on the cool but sunny days that frequently occur in England (12).

In Muthesius's analysis, 'An important phase of English architecture ends with the architects we have been discussing' (13). For him this phase, whilst seeing the construction of many houses of great quality, proceeded in parallel with, but in relative isolation from, the emergence and definition of William Morris's Arts and Crafts movement. The notable exception was Webb, the architect of Morris's own Red House (1858–1860), 'who is anyway and in all respects exceptional as an architect [and] was the only one who was fully involved in both movements' (14).

But a younger generation of architects – those born in the 1850s and 1860s – had a new and deeper relationship with Arts and Crafts theories and practices and transferred these into the development of their architecture:

> New aims now arose; by and large they were the ones proclaimed . . . by Ruskin and Morris, which concerned the

qualities of material and labour. The idea began to take root that the value of a piece lay mainly in its execution, which must be technically correct and appropriate to the material and workmanship. All the pre-requisites for every man-made object should lie in its material, purpose and construction, its form should be consequent upon these prerequisites and not upon an independent preconceived idea.

(15)

Muthesius catalogues an array of architects whose work satisfies his demanding criteria. These remain noteworthy to the present day and are amongst those identified by Peter Davey in his *Arts and Crafts Architecture: The Search for Earthly Paradise* (16), which has become the standard reference in the field. Davey identifies three of the older members of this company as, respectively, 'the guide', William Richard Lethaby (1857–1931); 'the explorer', Edward Schroeder Prior (1852–1932); and 'the pathfinder', Charles Francis Annesley Voysey (1857–1941). All three feature in Muthesius's study and, as Davey shows, laid the ground rules that were to be followed and elaborated by many others. Amongst these Muthesius identified M. H. Baillie Scott (1865–1945) as one of 'the poets among the domestic architects'. He also drew attention to 'the Glasgow movement' of Charles Rennie Mackintosh (1868–1928) and his 'circle'. Surprising omissions from Muthesius's list are Barry Parker (1867–1947) and his partner Raymond Unwin (1863–1940). At the publication date of *Das Englische Haus* their practice partnership was still located at Buxton in the north of England, but they had already built some notable houses in many parts of the country. They went on to be the architects of the first Garden City at Letchworth and, later, of Hampstead Garden Suburb, in effect the Arts and Crafts city, but at the same time, they continued to design significant individual houses.

Charles Francis Annesley Voysey

Voysey's practice covered the length and breadth of Britain and produced many houses of the highest quality. Throughout his career Voysey made regular written statements of his ideas and practices, and these invariably inform our understanding of his buildings (17). One of the most emphatic themes of these texts is their emphasis on the need to embed building into its context, particularly of tradition and culture, and he frequently made explicit reference to the English climate:

We are not Greeks, nor have we a Grecian climate, or Grecian materials and conditions. Moreover, an attentive study of local material and conditions will greatly aid us in securing harmony and rhythm, making our building look as if it grew where it stood in loving co-operation with its immediate surroundings.

The knowledge of foreign architecture has done much to destroy the full and complete harmony in modern work which is the characteristic feature of all the finest buildings throughout the world. The more we study the conditions under which we build the better.

(18)

Voysey made wide-ranging observations on the design of the English house in the second of two lectures that he gave at the Carpenters' Hall in London, which were published in 1909 (19). He began with an appeal to the innate 'affections' of men as the basis for considering the nature of building:

My dear architects, let me . . . marry your spirits to my own, and see what broad principles of thought and feeling are there already, to work in unison with me – affections common to all men.

The lecture quickly moved to a fascinating exploration of what we now regard to be environmental themes – questions of orientation and the dimensions and positioning of windows – and these are given a profoundly poetic perspective:

Will it not be better for soul and body to capture the early morning sun, which is never too hot in England, and is a great purifying influence.

My architect . . . will not make my rooms high, and thus deceive me into thinking them healthy. Height must be controlled by the length of my rooms. Because we are seeking the feeling of repose, low rooms will help us greatly, and give us the benefit of reflected light, and allow of smaller windows. You will tell me, small windows, when rightly placed, in conjunction with white ceilings and friezes, may produce very light rooms, and have the advantage of preserving equable temperature throughout the year. You will save me the expense of elaborate blinds and curtains, and give me all the sun I need without the scorching or glare on the hottest summer days . . .

It is pleasant to feel well protected when the weather is disturbed and angry; so you will not give me great sheets of plate glass . . . I much appreciate your regarding me and suggesting to others that I am to be regarded as a precious thing, to be protected from all violent intrusion.

Towards the end of the essay Voysey made an eloquent statement on the lighting of buildings, 'by day and by night':

> We all like abundance of light for work or play. . . . Precious as the light is, we must not be blind to the soothing mystery and charm of shadow and twilight. The suggestions of repose and mystery are sublime, and as necessary as the brilliant light. To light up an ordinary room all over at night is to destroy all sense of repose. Again observe nature, how she lights by day and by night. There is always some dominating point most brilliant and never more than one, attended by countless degrees of subordinate brilliancy in reflections around it.

Throughout this essay, and in much of his other writing, whilst conveying a substantial body of practical guidance, Voysey stresses '. . . the needs of the sprit over the needs of the flesh'. From this principle flow the distinctive qualities of his work and the particular response to the conditions of England that it so eloquently expresses.

To illustrate Voysey's translation of principle into practice I have chosen two houses in the north of England. The Lake District in the north-west of the country is outstandingly beautiful and, with the coming of the railways during the nineteenth century, became a weekend and summer retreat for the industrialists of the northern towns. The local climate is characterized by its variety and unpredictability. The height of the mountains, which rise over 900 metres into the moist, westerly airstream that flows from the Atlantic, results in heavy rain in all seasons, but there are frequent and rapid changes from bright sun to rain and back. The temperature typically falls by one degree for every one 150 metres of elevation above the valley floor.

John Ruskin was a resident of the Lake District, living at Brantwood near Lake Coniston from 1871 until his death in 1900. There he made numerous notes of the dramatically unpredictable summer weather of the area. These are vividly illustrated in two extracts from his diary, written only four days apart in June 1876:

> *22nd June 1876.*
> Thunderstorm; pitch dark, with no blackness, but deep, high filthiness of lurid, yet not sublimely lurid, smoke-cloud; dense

manufacturing mist; fearful squalls of shivery wind, making Mr. Severn's sail quiver like a man in a fever fit – all about four, afternoon – but only two or three claps of thunder, and feeble, though near, flashes. I never saw such a dirty, weak foul storm. It cleared suddenly, after raining all afternoon, at half-past eight to nine, into pure natural weather, low rain-clouds on quite, clear, green, wet hills.

26th June 1876
Yesterday an entirely perfect summer light on the Old Man [This is the mountain that overlooks Coniston]; Lancaster Bay all clear; Ingleborough and the great Pennine fault as on a map. Divine beauty of western colour on thyme and rose – then twilight of clearest warm amber far into the night, of pale amber all night long; hills dark clear against it.

(20)

In 1898 Voysey received commissions for two houses: Moorcrag, for the Buckley family, and Broadleys for the Briggs. The sites on the east bank of Lake Windermere are very close, but presented very different challenges and opportunities to the architect. Moorcrag sits high on the hill above the road that winds along the shore of the lake. Voysey used this elevated location to give the house a panoramic prospect over the lower reaches of the lake and to order its apartments to enjoy the benefits of an unobstructed southern orientation. The house is approached from the north by a winding drive. It sits on a platform excavated from the wooded hillside, with an open meadow to the south. The long, narrow plan, with a spine wall running almost its entire length, allows all of the principal rooms on both floors to enjoy a southerly aspect, with the large dining room cutting across the entire plan to allow a view to the north (Fig. 6.1). Noting Voysey's strictures on avoiding overlarge windows, those to the south are generally larger that those on the entrance façade, with the exception of the generous, stone-mullioned window that lights the staircase.

In his essay, 'The quality of fitness in architecture' (21), Voysey wrote that:

> . . . a careful study of our climate makes us emphasise our roofs to suggest protection from weather. Large, massive chimneys imply stability and repose. Long, low buildings also create a feeling for restfulness and spaciousness.

Moorcrag comprehensively exemplifies these principles with its sweeping roof, with strongly expressed gables, two to each façade, and its three groups

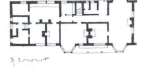

6.1
C. F. A. Voysey, Moorcrag, Windermere: ground-floor plan.

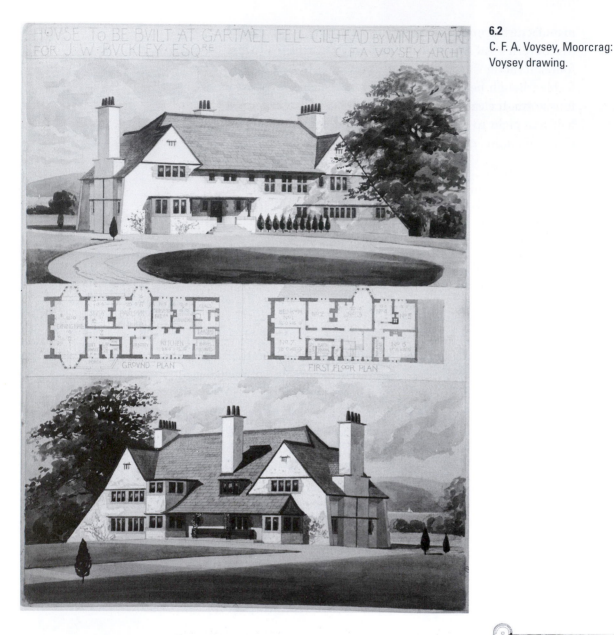

6.2
C. F. A. Voysey, Moorcrag:
Voysey drawing.

6.3
C. F. A. Voysey, Broadleys,
Windermere: ground-floor
plan.

of chimneys. To the south the roof is penetrated by a dormer and a flat-roofed bay and sweeps down to cover a generous verandah and to cap the bay window of the living room at the eastern end of the house. These complex layers of the southern façade create a variety of relationships between the house and its setting (Fig. 6.2). The bay windows capture the sun throughout the day and provide warm places from which to enjoy the prospect of the lake and the distant hills. The overhang of the verandah creates a microclimate sheltered from the breezes and showers of the elevated site. It is curious that

6.4

C. F. A. Voysey, Broadleys:
Voysey drawing.

Voysey disregarded the opportunity to allow the owners of the house to enjoy the view to the mountains across the lake, by positioning the service quarters at the west end of the house.

Just to the north and closer to the lakeshore, Voysey's Broadleys represents a very different interpretation of a similar domestic programme. Here the westerly view proved an irresistible influence on the design, and the plan takes an L-shaped form with the principal wing orientated north–south, parallel to the shore, with a service wing to the east and defining a protected entrance court (Fig. 6.3). The house is entered from the east, first under an open porch and then into an enclosed vestibule. This leads straight into a double-height hall with a two-storey-high, curved bay window, from which there is a beautifully framed view across the lake and to the mountains. This space is a clear response to the compelling character of the site and evokes memories of the hall spaces of earlier English vernacular houses and may be seen as hinting at the similar rooms that became a feature of later designs of the Modern Movement, although it must be said that this prospect was far from Voysey's mind (22). The dining room is to the north, where it connects directly to the service wing, and the sitting room lies to the south of the hall. Both dining and sitting rooms have similar bay windows to that of the hall, but here they are only a single storey in height and also serve the principal bedrooms above. At the southern end of the plan the first floor oversails the ground and, supported on cast iron columns, forms a covered verandah, which is directly accessible from the sitting room, to provide a protected, sunny extension. In this way Voysey elegantly reconciles the conflict between aspect and prospect. The main part of the garden lies to the south of the house and a wide terrace occupies the whole west front, providing a place to enjoy both the view and the evening sun.

The great roof, this time hipped rather than gabled, but again penetrated by massive chimneys, once more speaks of the shelter and comfort that the house promises in this unpredictable, rainy climate. Its scale is exaggerated by the manner in which it springs from a low wall plate with wide eaves that protect the rendered walls. The height of the three bay windows of the lake frontage is emphasized by the manner in which they cut through the eaves (Fig. 6.4).

M. H. Baillie Scott

Muthesius referred to Baillie Scott as 'one of the poets' amongst the architects of the Arts and Crafts movement. His houses are a particularly lyrical variant on the general themes of the movement and an essential aspect of this lyricism may be found in the specific responses he exhibits to questions of climate and comfort. Like Voysey he committed his thoughts about the nature of the house to print. He was a frequent contributor to the pages of *The Studio*, the principal organ of publication for the Arts and Crafts movement, and his most notable written work is the book *Houses and Gardens*, published in 1906 (23). This volume, which is itself a work of art and craft, with fine binding and typography and numerous reproductions of watercolour images of houses and their gardens, is a wide-ranging statement of belief and practice. It offers a commentary on the design of every conceivable room in the house, even discussing accommodation for family pets, and goes to some length in discussing the response to the site and the relation of the house to its garden.

The essence of the house is declared in chapter one:

The house which, for want of a better word, we must continue to differentiate from the ordinary house as 'artistic', bases its claims not on its frillings and on its adornments, but on the very essence of its structure. The claims of common-sense are paramount in its plan, and its apartments are arranged to secure comfortable habitation for its inmates.

Baillie Scott shared Voysey's aversion to large window openings and to large single pieces of glass:

> The beauty of glass depends entirely on its use in small
> pieces, in a setting which, allowing of a slight variation in
> their planes, will make them sparkle and twinkle.

Baillie Scott does not offer a clear-cut prescription for the orientation of the house, but, in the chapter discussing the dining room, states that 'Modern science has shown that sunlight is the great health-giver and germ destroyer, and few rooms should be deprived of it.' He recommends that kitchens should preferably have a northerly exposure, to keep them cool in summer, but accepts the south-east as a compromise in a small house, where 'a more cheerful aspect is desirable'. Larders, in those pre-refrigeration days, should always face north. Later, in a discussion of the relation of the house to its site, he wrote '. . . windows to the south should be introduced to admit the sunlight'.

When writing about the fireplace, Baillie Scott overwhelmingly supports Muthesius's observations regarding the English obsession with the open fire:

> I suppose it must be conceded that the open fire is an
> extremely unscientific and unsatisfactory arrangement. But
> the modern scientist satisfies himself with putting the matter
> to the test of the thermometer, and the value of the system
> is judged by its effects on mercury, rather than on the complex
> human . . .
>   In the house the fire is practically a substitute for the sun,
> and it bears the same relation to the household as the sun
> does to the landscape. It is one of the fairy-tale facts of
> science that the heat and brightness from the burning coal is
> the same that was emitted from the sun on the primeval
> forests; and so the open fire enables us to enjoy to-day the
> brightness and warmth of yesterday's sunshine . . .

Further in this chapter Baillie Scott makes a clear statement of the relationship between a house and the climate:

> In considering the house . . . as a winter dwelling, I am
> assuming those conditions which test its real qualities. The
> main function of a house is that it affords a retreat from the
> cold or a shelter from the rain. In fine warm weather its
> occupation is gone, and its tenants should live, if not in the
> garden, at least in an open verandah. In the English climate
> the apartments of the house can be quite adequately heated
> by means of open fires alone . . .

Here Baillie Scott also discourses at length on the merits and detailed design of the ingle-nook fireplace, found in many English vernacular houses and revived, with a combination of sentimentality and utility, in many Arts and Crafts houses, not least those by Baillie Scott himself.

The idea that the garden is a natural extension of the dwelling is developed in a short chapter on the garden-room:

> Human life, like plant life, flourishes in sun and air and grows pale and anæmic when it is deprived of these.
>
> And so the garden is conceived as an outdoor extension of the house, with its sheltered apartments for sunshine or for shade.
>
> But in our inconsistent climate it is not always possible to use the garden entirely. It is desirable, for instance, that meals should be taken in summer weather out of doors. . . . and so the need for a wide verandah or garden-room is increasingly felt. . . . On summer mornings breakfast in such a room will have much of the charm of breakfast in the garden without its disadvantages, and in the evening it will be pleasant to sit there and enjoy the prospect of the garden after a day spent perforce indoors.

Houses and Gardens is extensively illustrated with descriptions of some of the many houses that Baillie Scott had designed by the date of its publication. One of the most striking of these is Blackwell (1898–1899), which is another of the great Lake District houses built by Arts and Crafts architects for their industrialist clients (Fig. 6.5). Larger than Voysey's two houses lower down the slope, Blackwell is one of the finest examples of the L-shaped Arts and Crafts plan (Fig 6.6). The principal block, which is entered from the north, faces just to the west of due south and the service wing to the east projects to provide shelter to the main entrance. The entry sequence is similar to that at Broadleys, with an enclosed porch leading into a double height hall with a large ingle nook (24). As at Broadleys, the hall has dining room and drawing room to either side and there are also striking parallels between Blackwell and Moorcrag. But Baillie Scott, on his more elevated site, could not resist the prospect across the lake towards Ruskin's Coniston mountains, and the drawing room captures these with a square bay window, with window seat, projecting through its west wall, high above the sloping ground (Fig. 6.7). This room also has a large ingle nook and a principal splayed bay facing south to the long view down the lake. It is difficult to imagine a better place in which to enjoy in comfort the drama of the terrain and climate of the Lake District.

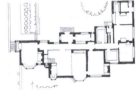

6.5
M. H. Baillie Scott,
Blackwell: view from
south-west.

6.6
M. H. Baillie Scott,
Blackwell: ground-floor
plan.

6.7
M. H. Baillie Scott,
Blackwell: drawing room,
bay window.

Nikolaus Pevsner described the area to the northwest of the centre of Cambridge as 'Cambridge's *Villenviertel*' (25). Baillie Scott built a number of houses there in the years between 1897 and 1926. Two of these serve to illustrate his work in its full maturity. The house at 48 Storey's Way, which was built in 1912, is identified by Diane Haigh as the design that most comprehensively embodies the principles that Baillie Scott so eloquently expressed in *Houses and Gardens* (26).

The site offers an almost ideal orientation with the road to the north-east of the long site, which slopes very gently to the south. The plan is a perfect example of the rectangular type adapted to the needs of an academic family; the client H. A. Roberts was secretary to the Cambridge University Appointments Board (Fig. 6.8). The design fully exemplifies Baillie Scott's principle that house and garden should be conceived as a whole. The garden at the street front is organized into three distinct parts separated by tall hedges. A central formal garden leads to the main entrance and to either side are a service entry that allows access directly to the owner's study and a bicycle entry, in a cycling city, that leads to the kitchen (Fig. 6.9). The house itself is very clearly planned, with staircase and service rooms in a narrow band to the north and all the principal rooms, on both ground and first floors, facing southwards over the garden. The steep tiled roof contains extensive, interconnected rooms. The garden is a sequence of outdoor rooms that progress from the relative formality of the first space close to the house, with garden-rooms and pergolas to east and west, to the rose garden and thence to wild and vegetable gardens and, finally, the orchard (Fig. 6.10). It is easy to imagine how this garden, absolutely a 'garden of a golden afternoon', sustained Baillie Scott's idea of outdoor domestic life in the English climate at all seasons (27).

The two principal apartments of the ground floor together constitute one of Baillie Scott's finest domestic compositions. Living room and dining room each have a wide, splayed bay window that captures the sun. The living room has an ingle nook in its east wall, with a tiny south-facing window to deliver reading light to the fixed settle (Fig. 6.11). The room extends to the north to form a library overlooking the front garden. A secret door behind the ingle nook leads to the study. The smaller, rectangular dining room is connected to the living room by a pair of wide, hinged doors, which open back to the wall to create, in effect, a single room. But there is a subtle and wonderful difference between the two spaces. The living room presents the Arts and Crafts ideal of expressed construction, with exposed ceiling joists and subtle asymmetries of composition. Turning around to look into the dining room (Fig. 6.12), we see floor-to-ceiling oak panelling and a richly modelled plaster ceiling that cover all evidence of construction and speak of the formality of dining in contrast to the informalities and diversities of the

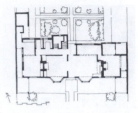

6.8
M. H. Baillie Scott,
48 Storey's Way,
Cambridge: Ground floor
plan.

6.10
M. H. Baillie Scott,
48 Storey's Way:
garden front.

remainder of domestic life. Both rooms are filled with the warm light of the southern sky, which beautifully illuminates their contrasting forms and materiality.

At the time when he designed 48 Storey's Way Baillie Scott was becoming aware that a significant change was occurring in the priorities that conditioned the nature of English domestic architecture. In an essay published in 1910 he wrote:

> There is a peculiar charm about this eighteenth-century manner of building. It has a certain sedate primness. It has a well-behaved and well-drilled aspect, and being somewhat artificial and conventional finds itself more at home in town or suburb than in the country. It does not suffer so much from mechanical workmanship as the older manner of building, and since it imposes some restraint on natural gesture it may be compared to a straight-waistcoat which may be wisely worn by those who have lost the power of natural and graceful movement.

(28)

6.12
M. H. Baillie Scott,
48 Storey's Way:
dining room.

In this poignant paragraph he is describing a design for a house in a modest revived Georgian style, whose virtues seem to derive entirely from a resigned acceptance of the changing taste of clients – 'who have lost the power of natural and graceful movement' – and of the diminishing ability of builders to produce the standard of hand craft required by a full-blown Arts and Crafts house. In Cambridge there are a number of Baillie Scott houses in this 'polite' manner, but there is one late house that shows how, if the opportunity was offered, he could rediscover and further develop all of the subtle complexities of his earlier designs.

Church Rate Corner, built in 1924, is hidden away in a location near the Newnham mill pool, quite close to the centre of Cambridge. Its almost secret site provides the ideal setting in which to deploy all the Arts and Crafts principles of domestic planning. The approach from a discreet entrance gate eventually leads to the house, set at the northern edge of the site, from where it commands a large, but almost completely secluded garden (29). The plan (Fig. 6.13) is a conflation of the rectangular and L-shaped types in which, as

6.13
M. H. Baillie Scott,
Church Rate Corner,
Cambridge: ground
floor plan.

6.14
M. H. Baillie Scott,
Church Rate Corner:
south front.

would be expected, the principal rooms – dining room, drawing room and study – occupy the whole of the south front. The entrance slips in modestly from the north-west and the kitchen and utilities complete the principal rectangle and extend further to the north-east. The south elevation is centred on a double gable, with dormers pushing through a sweeping roof to either side. At the ground floor a large bay window, reaching down to floor level, is asymmetrically placed to light the living room (Fig. 6.14).

In appearance the house could, certainly at first sight, date from one or two decades earlier. There are, however, a number of subtle transformations that confirm that Baillie Scott was alert to new developments in architectural

thought and method. The beams that support the first floor are of steel and a full central heating system was installed from the outset (30). The heating system is an acknowledgement of changes both in the technology of the domestic environment and in the expectations of clients. The house has a full complement of fireplaces, including in all the bedrooms, but the ingle nook has been lost. In the living room, however, there is a clear differentiation between a daytime/summer area related to the bay window and a more enclosed part, close to the fireplace and lit by a small window set flush in the south wall, that suggests nighttime/winter use. Interestingly the fireplace is flush with the east wall, without a projecting chimneybreast. An enormous cast iron radiator sits in the centre of the bay window, served by a large-diameter hot-water pipe (Fig. 6.15). Arts and Crafts principles are here transformed, not by modernist revolution, but, appropriately in Charles Darwin's Cambridge, by subtle evolution. The result is a house that adds new notions of comfort and inhabitation to the deep and enduring qualities of the Arts and Crafts house and its relationship to the English climate.

Edward Schroeder Prior

Edward Prior, Peter Davey's 'Explorer' (31), was both architect and scholar (32). He read Classics at Cambridge and, following his graduation, became an articled pupil in Norman Shaw's office in 1874. There other pupils included Ernest Newton, Mervyn Macartney and, perhaps most important of all, William Richard Lethaby. Prior began his independent practice in 1880 and continued until the early years of the First World War. Concurrently he produced a number of important books on aspects of the history of art and architecture. The most notable of these was *A History of Gothic Art in England* (33), published in 1900. In 1912 he was elected to the Slade Professorship of Art at Cambridge and became a Fellow of Gonville and Caius College. He played a significant role in the early life of the School of Architecture at Cambridge. He remained Slade Professor until his death in 1932.

6.16
Edward Prior, The Barn, Exmouth: garden front.

In *Houses and Gardens* Baillie Scott presents a typology – not a word that he would have used – of 'Some Forms of Plan'. The last of these is what became known as the 'butterfly plan' in which a central block is framed between two splayed wings. Prior adopted this plan type in two of his most important houses: The Barn at Exmouth in Devon, 1896–1897, and Home Place at Kelling in Norfolk, 1903–1905. At The Barn the potential of this type of plan is exploited with great subtlety (34) (Fig. 6.16).

A road climbs up the hill to the east of Exmouth, and Prior adopts the projecting wings of the 'butterfly plan' to form a forecourt from which the house, built of local random-sized stone and originally with a thatched roof, is entered almost exactly from the north (35) (Fig. 6.17). On the axis of the entrance a double-height hall leads under a verandah to a south-facing raised terrace in the garden. To the east of the hall the dining room connects easily to the kitchen and its ancillary spaces, and to the west lie the drawing room and the study. The main window in the dining room faces south-east and a small window in the adjacent wall brings in late-afternoon light. A symmetrically opposite layout serves the drawing room, where a large bay window, under the sweep of the roof, provides a view south-westwards to the sea. The study, at a lower level in response to the contours of the site, is approached by a short flight of stairs and also enjoys a view towards the sea. From there the terraced garden can be entered through a recessed porch.

The 'butterfly plan' is here shown to allow an ingenious and subtle response to the conditions of this quite difficult site. The form allowed Prior to make a clear distinction between the northern and southern aspects and to establish a sheltered place from which to enter the house. All the main rooms enjoy orientations that fit their use and the relationship of house to garden provides a variety of conditions in which to enjoy the best of the south-coast climate, with its balmy summers and mild winters punctuated by squalls and storms at all seasons.

Barry Parker and Raymond Unwin

Peter Davey entitles his chapter on the work of Parker and Unwin, 'Quietly Home'. This is apt, particularly in relationship to their role, as the architects of the first garden city at Letchworth and, later, of Hampstead Garden Suburb, in bringing the ideals of the Arts and Crafts movement to bear on the provision of housing for the wider population (36). The essence of this achievement is beautifully captured in Spencer Gore's painting, dated 1912, of the house that Parker and Unwin built at Letchworth for Harold Gilman, their friend and fellow member of the Euston Road School (Plate 14).

Parker and Unwin were born in the north of England, where they began their practice in the spa town of Buxton in 1896. Following their success, in 1903, in the competition to plan the first garden city at Letchworth, not far north of London and quite close to Forster's *Howards End*, they progressively moved their office to the south, first to Letchworth itself and then to Hampstead. Both partners were sympathetic to the socialism that resided in William Morris' theories of life and art and it was this that promoted their interest in housing and town planning. Nonetheless, throughout the years of their practice, they designed a sequence of fine individual houses.

In 1901 *The Art of Building a Home* was published (37). This consists of the texts of a series of lectures – three by Parker, three by Unwin and two in joint authorship – in which they set out their ideas on the Arts and Crafts house, writing in their Introduction:

> Let us have in our houses, rooms where there shall be space
> to carry out the business of life freely and with pleasure, with
> furniture made for use; rooms where a drop of water spilled
> is not fatal; where the life of a child is not made a burden to
> it by unnecessary restraint; plain, simple, ungarnished if
> necessary, but honest.

In the jointly authored lecture 'The Art of Designing Small Houses and Cottages' they stress the importance of the site in determining the external form and material of a house, but move quickly to a detailed consideration of the significance of orientation in its internal planning. In this they show an acute sensibility to climatic variations within England:

> The position of each room in relation to the points of the
> compass & the outlook should be determined on the spot.
> It is now pretty generally recognised that no sacrifice is
> too great which is necessary to enable us to bring plenty
> of sunshine into all the main living rooms. In the South of

England perhaps some moderation must be observed in applying this rule, there being no inconsiderable number of days on which too sunny a room may become unbearably hot; and, where the size of the house will allow of it, to have an east and west room is often a great boon. But over the greater part of our country, certainly in the Midlands and the North, the importance of arranging for the few days when the sun is oppressive is small indeed compared with that of planning to suit the many days when every hour of sunshine is of the utmost value.

This shows Parker and Unwin in complete accord with Voysey, and they make similar recommendations to his in balancing the sometimes-contradictory demands of aspect and prospect.

The lecture is illustrated by detailed descriptions of three houses, in all of which these 'environmental' principles are demonstrated. One of these is a design for a small cottage, 'near a small Derbyshire town'. The site is described in detail:

6.18
Parker and Unwin, 'Cottage near a small Derbyshire town': ground-floor plan.

> On the north runs a stream, to which the ground falls precipitously; the road is to the west, and there is a steep fall here also; to the east the fall is slight, while to the south the ground rises gently. There are fine views in all directions, most interesting to the north, least so to the south. The client, however, desired the main windows of the living-room to be to the west, having a special liking for the evening light.

The plan is a simple rectangle, with the main entrance in the centre of the south front (Fig. 6.18). This leads directly into the living room, in which all of the elements of the Arts and Crafts room are skilfully, if perhaps over-elaborately, provided. A five-light mullioned window satisfies the client's 'liking for the evening light' and dining takes place by a south-facing window. The entire northern end of the room is given to an ingle nook that is almost a room itself. This has windows to both north and west. The pleasure of the westerly, evening light may also be taken in a recessed external seat set in the wall of the ingle nook.

In 1907–1909 Parker and Unwin designed and built the house that Parker later described 'as the type of home which exemplifies, more than any other I can call to mind in my own practice, the application of principles of architecture and furnishing for which I have been contending' (38).

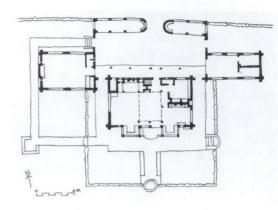

The house, Whirriestone, is at Rochdale, ten miles north-east of Manchester, and, like so many of the houses built by the middle classes of these industrial towns, is on the outskirts to the west and hence in the prevailing westerly breezes upwind of the town's factories.

In comparison with the houses of Voysey, Baillie Scott and Prior, this is relatively small and may be seen in some respects as a development of the Derbyshire cottage design, with all of the principal rooms contained in a simple rectangular block beneath a large, stone-slated, hipped roof. It is, however, flanked to east and west, in an almost Palladian composition, by two pavilions. One houses a billiard room, the other a 'motor house' and engine and generating rooms (Fig. 6.19). These last are an indication of the embrace of modern technologies in the context of Arts and Crafts principles of house design. In his description of the house Parker observed that '. . . as far as possible local building traditions have been observed and local building materials used. . . . All the stone . . . was quarried not far from the site' (39).

The house is approached from the north and the site slopes gently to the south. To the south there is a sweeping view towards Manchester and the Cheshire Plain beyond, and the Pennine hills are visible to the east and north. Parker wrote, '. . . the pleasantest view is toward the south, (so) the two principal rooms have been given a southward "trend" or "direction"' (40). The house is now surrounded by later suburban encroachment, but in 1907 would have been quite isolated. The north entrance is sheltered by a high boundary wall that leads into a protected forecourt with billiard room to the west and motor house to the east. The huge Voyseyan roof of the main house has wide overhanging eaves to the north that provide sheltered access to the side pavilions.

The planning of the main house makes ingenious use of the simple rectangular form. The living room occupies the whole depth of the plan and

has windows to the north, south and west. The quite modest kitchen is at the north-east corner of the plan, where it will be cool, and the south-eastern corner is given to the study. The study may be opened to the living room by operating a beautifully detailed sliding oak screen, so that almost the whole of the ground floor becomes a single, flowing, complex space. A nice environmental detail is the fireplace by this screen that brings additional, warmth to the house beyond the reach of the ingle nook. The spatial complexity is further elaborated by the double-height volume, now, alas, floored in, that rose to a shallow plaster vault beneath the roof. This also brought high-level south light from a clerestory dormer window. Two large square bay windows occupy the south front and between them is a sheltered porch with a seat from which to enjoy the view (Fig. 6.20).

The relationship of the ingle nook and the bay window in the living room together comprise a rich environmental arrangement that responds to all imaginable diurnal and seasonal variations in the climate (Fig. 6.21). The ingle nook, lit in daytime by its tiny north-facing windows, is a comfortable retreat on winter's evenings and the bay windows become warm places on sunny days at all seasons of the year. The house was lit by electric light fittings designed by the architects, supplied originally with electricity from the generating room in the side pavilion.

Charles Rennie Mackintosh

With just one exception all of the buildings discussed in these essays are in England and thereby in the *English* climate, albeit embracing a considerable variation of climate. In conclusion, however, I have chosen to move north to Scotland, where the climate is palpably different from that of the comfortable southern parts of England – Exmouth, Sussex and Cambridge – and even different from that of the northern Pennine hills and the Lake District. We will consider one of the most important house designs of the early twentieth century, The Hill House, by Charles Rennie Mackintosh (41), who featured strongly in Muthesius's review and therefore demands inclusion here.

Unlike most of the other architects discussed here, we have no books or essays on house design by Mackintosh. He did, however, in the early years of his career, deliver a number of public lectures in Glasgow in which he made powerful statements of his beliefs. There are few references to climate in any of these texts. But, in speaking about 'Scotch Baronial Architecture' (1891), Mackintosh refers to visits to '. . . the various castles and palaces in this country, not only under the balmy influences of summer, but along muddy roads and snowy path, and with glowing heart but shivering hand to sketch the humble cottage . . .' (42).

The Hill House was built in 1902–1904 for Walter Blackie, a publisher of children's books, whose offices were in Glasgow. Helensburgh

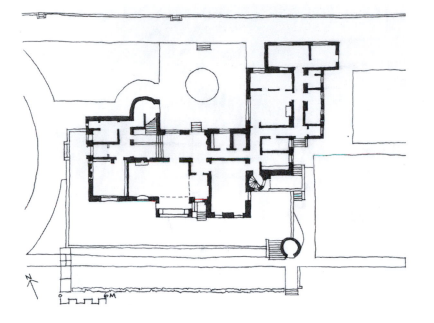

lies 25 miles west of the city, to which it is connected by two railway lines. The first opened in 1858 and the second in 1894. This is another instance in which the wealthier citizens of the great nineteenth-century cities exploited the new transport links to allow them to live in the nearby countryside. In this case the location enjoyed the advantage of overlooking the waters of the Firth of Clyde.

Blackie's site is on the hill above Helensburgh and is conveniently close to the 'Upper' railway station and the direct line to Glasgow. It is an ideal Arts and Crafts site, sloping to the south, here with access from a road to the west. The plan is also the familiar L-shape, with the principal rooms in the main body and servants and services in the secondary wing (Fig. 6.22). The west façade is a complex, almost abstract composition in which the front door sits beneath an asymmetrical bay window and tall chimney to the north side of the large gable end (Fig. 2.23). This play of abstraction continues around the entire form in the placement and detailing of windows and chimneys in relation to the uniform, grey harling render (Plate 5).

Thomas Howarth points out that the garden was laid out, to Mackintosh's design, to provide a precisely calculated setting for the house (43). He also explains that Mackintosh had a particularly acute and individual interpretation of the relationship of a house to its context:

> The architect had explained that, in his opinion, a sense of enclosure, warmth and security was the most desirable

attribute of any dwelling. The house was primarily a place of shelter and refuge, in, but not of the landscape. Furthermore the entire conception of the house was quite distinct from that of the garden: the one artificial and confining space; the other natural, free and virtually boundless. Each possessed distinctive characteristics which should be acknowledged and respected by an architect.

(44)

6.23
Charles Rennie Mackintosh, The Hill House, Helensburgh: west front.

This proposes a keen understanding of the nature of the Scottish climate, as suggested by Mackintosh's observation in his lecture on the baronial style: 'the glowing heart but shivering hand'. The house and garden are not separate entities, but viewed as being in a carefully considered mutual interdependency of microclimate and social order. This may be compared with Baillie Scott's more temperate, primarily English vision in which the house and garden provide a continuity of spaces, open or enclosed, that are easily and necessarily interconnected.

The planning of the ground floor of The Hill House exhibits a masterly manipulation of form, material and tone to create distinct and distinctive settings for the diverse needs of domestic inhabitation (45). From the entrance there is a long perspective view of the hall, dark-panelled and lit by as yet unseen north-facing windows. Immediately to the right is Blackie's library, a dark, but comfortable, book-lined room lit from the south by a large window and, from the west, by two smaller openings either side of the fireplace. In the hall, just beyond the library door, is a hearth, both source and symbol of warmth upon arrival. A short flight of four steps becomes the threshold to the hall proper, a broad, welcoming place well lit by two wide windows. This is a prelude to the house's greatest moment, stepping into the drawing room.

The door of the drawing room is directly opposite the wide, low bay window that floods the room with south light and frames a view of the Clyde estuary at the foot of the hill. On bright days the surface of the almost invariably choppy surface of the water produces glittering light that is seemingly transmitted into the room. The main body of the room is a simple rectangle that is extended southwards by the bay window and to the east by the proscenium-like space that houses the piano. To the right on entry is the 'winter area', as it was known in the family (Fig. 6.24) (46). Lit by a relatively small south-facing window, this contains the fireplace on its north wall and becomes a comfortable refuge from the Scottish winter. The whole is a refined, more spacious reinterpretation of the comforts of an ingle nook and, as such, may perhaps be read as a demonstration of the manner in which Mackintosh more radically interpreted tradition than his English counterparts. The bay window is almost a room in itself (Fig. 6.25). It has floor-to-ceiling windows to the east and west that visually disconnect it from the body of the room. That to the east opens fully and leads to the garden terrace below. Sitting on the window seat, with its solid east and west flanks and wide south window, you inhabit a territory that is poised between the 'refuge' of the interior and the 'virtually boundless' space of the garden and the wide view beyond. Once again this is a refinement of the often-generous bays of most English architects at this time. On bright days in winter the low angle of the sun, just above 10° at this latitude, floods this and the other south-facing rooms with warming light. Next door the plain panelled dining room is a very understated place. The Blackies wished to re-use an older table and dining chairs, and Mackintosh provided a simple unassertive setting for these. One of the most perceptive observations about the light of Mackintosh's interiors was made by Alison and Peter Smithson:

Light pouring into the dwelling, to lift the spirit towards hope; Mackintosh introduced, the Modern Movement

6.24
Charles Rennie
Mackintosh, The Hill
House: living room.

6.25
Charles Rennie
Mackintosh, The Hill
House: living-room bay
window.

celebrated. Mackintosh harnessed light inside white rooms; delineated the enlivened space by black ladders, pewter lines; accented with pink or mauve petals: a sparing use of colour as punctuation in his language.

(47)

On the first floor the principal bedroom is comparable in its originality to the drawing room. Once again Mackintosh subtly shapes the room to create distinct territories in the one space. On entering, you are in a boudoir-like space. With its white-fronted wardrobes and corner seat and fireplace, this is both dressing room and sitting room. This is all brightly illuminated by two tall, south-facing, sliding sash windows. To the right lies a barrel-vaulted alcove containing the white bed, an intimate place lit discreetly by a small, shuttered window in a projecting curved masonry bay directly above the library window.

When the house was completed in 1904, electricity was not available at the site and nighttime illumination was provided by gas lamps in fittings all designed by Mackintosh. The only exception was the library, where oil was burned, reportedly to protect the books. The gas lighting was not a success. The ceiling-mounted gasolier fittings in the living room produced condensation and were replaced by gas-burning wall lights (48). There are no reports of such problems elsewhere in the house. This engagement with the design of light fittings, notwithstanding the shortcomings of the fuel burned, is another indication of Mackintosh's modernity of intention. The lamps are essential elements of the environmental strategy of the house and, now converted to electricity, take their place in this remarkable *Gesamptkunstwerk*.

Conclusion

In this essay we have examined the relation of architecture to climate in the house designs of a number of the most important architects of the Arts and Crafts movement. It is clear that these share much common ground in the manner in which they take account of the significant characteristics of their sites, with particular emphasis on the value of good, southerly orientation and of the primacy of this – aspect – over prospect. Most of these houses also provide sheltered, outdoor places adjacent to the building, either in porches or verandahs or in garden rooms. Within the houses we consistently find rooms of appropriate complexity to provide sun-filled bay windows and enclosing ingle nooks. These consistencies, however, do not constrain individual expression in responding to a wide range of climate conditions. Prior's 'The Barn' is in a benign coastal setting; the Lake District designs of Voysey and Baillie Scott are exposed to the dramatic diurnal and seasonal changes of the weather so vividly described by Ruskin. The gentle, sheltered suburbs of Cambridge are different from these places and, to some degree, from the outskirts of northern industrial towns, and this is subtly reflected in Baillie Scott's houses there. Finally, we return to more extreme northern conditions above the Firth of Clyde, where Mackintosh built The Hill House with its refined responses to climate and comfort. The latitude of Exmouth in Devon is almost 6° to the south from that of Helensburgh, only a little less than the distance between Calais and Marseilles. Muthesius was correct when he identified the climate as a profound influence on *Das Englische Haus*, but how varied is that climate and how inventive were these architects in their responses to it.

Notes

1. Hermann Muthesius, *Das Englische Haus*, Wasmuth, Berlin, Volumes 1 and 2, 1904, Volume 3, 1905; 1st English edition, abridged (ed. Dennis Sharp, trans. Janet Seligman), Crosby, Lockwood, Staples, London, 1979; 2nd English Edition, full text (ed. Dennis Sharp, trans. Janet Seligman and Stuart Spencer), Frances Lincoln, London, 2007.

2. *Ibid.*

3. *Ibid.*

4. D. E. Parker, T. P. Legg and C.K. Folland, 'A new daily Central England Temperature series, 1772–1991', *International Journal of Climatology*, Vol. 12, 1992, pp. 317–342. T. J. Osborne and Mike Hulme, 'Evidence for trends in heavy rainfall events over the UK', *Philosophical Transactions of the Royal Society of London, Series A*, Vol. 360, 2002, pp. 1313–1325.

5. E. M. Forster, *Howards End*, first published Edward Arnold, London, 1910.

6. From E.M. Forster, *Marianne Thornton*, Edward Arnold, London, 1956.

7. Jane Brown, *Gardens of a Golden Afternoon: The Story of a Partnership: Edwin Lutyens and Gertrude Jekyll*, Allen Lane/Penguin, London, 1982.

8. Lewis Carroll, *Alice in Wonderland*, Everett, London, 1912.

9. This contrast in approach borrows from the title of Victor Olgyay's *Design with Climate: Bioclimatic Approach to Architectural Regionalism*, Princeton University Press, Princeton, NJ, 1963. This major contribution to architectural environmentalism is significant in proposing, at the height of the twentieth century's adoption of the 'technological fix', that we should regard the climate as a positive factor in shaping new architecture.

10. Muthesius, cited in Note 1.

11. *Ibid.*

12. Essential references to Webb's work are W. R. Lethaby, *Philip Webb and His Work*, first published as a series of articles in *The Builder* in 1925 and reprinted by Oxford University Press, Oxford, 1935 (revised reprint, Raven Oak Press, London, 1979) and Sheila Kirk, *Philip Webb: Pioneer of Arts and Crafts Architecture*, Wiley-Academy, Chichester, 2005. The standard work on Shaw is Andrew Saint, *Richard Norman Shaw*, Yale University Press, New Haven, CT, 1976.

13. Muthesius, cited in Note 1.

14. *Ibid.*

15. *Ibid.*

16. Peter Davey, *Arts and Crafts Architecture: The Search for Earthly Paradise*, The Architectural Press, London, 1980; revised edition, Phaidon, London, 1995.

17. A useful list of Voysey's writings is given in David Gebhard, *Charles F. A. Voysey, Architect*, Hennesey & Ingalls, Los Angeles, 1975. The standard critical monograph is Duncan Simpson, *C. F. A. Voysey: An Architect of Individuality*, Lund Humphries, London, 1979. See also Stuart Durant, *C. F. A. Voysey*, Academy Editions, London, 1992.

18. C. F. A. Voysey, 'The quality of fitness in architecture', *The Craftsman*, Vol. 23, 1912, pp. 174–182.

19. C. F. A. Voysey, 'Ideas in things II', in *The Arts Connected with Building* (ed. T. Raffles Davidson), Batsford, London, 1909.

20. John Ruskin, 'The Storm-Cloud of the Nineteenth Century', Two lectures delivered at the London Institution, February 4th and 11th, 1884, *The Complete Works of John Ruskin*, Vol. 24, Project Gutenberg.

21. Voysey, 'The quality of fitness in architecture', cited in Note 18.

22. Voysey was enlisted by Nikolaus Pevsner as one of his 'Pioneers of Modern Design', although Broadleys was not used to illustrate that proposition. There is an interesting, similarity between the plan of Broadleys and that of George Checkley's modernist Thurso House, built at Cambridge in 1932, which is discussed in Essay 7 below.

23. M. H. Baillie Scott, *Houses and Gardens*, George Newnes, London, 1906. Other important references on Baillie Scott's work are James D. Kornwulf, *M. H. Baillie Scott and the Arts and Crafts Movement: Pioneer of Modern Design*, Johns Hopkins Press, Baltimore, 1972, and Diane Haigh, *M. H. Baillie Scott: The Artistic House*, Academy Editions, London, 1995.

24. James D. Kornwulf, *M. H. Baillie Scott and the Arts and Crafts Movement*, writing within the Pevsnerian paradigm of 'Pioneers of Modern Design', offers a speculative comparison between this room and Le Corbusier's Ozenfant Studio of 1922. It is interesting, at this time distant, that these two buildings were constructed only some 23 years apart, but their architects' central pre-occupations must be seen to be almost entirely different.

25. Nikolaus Pevsner, *The Buildings of England: Cambridgeshire*, Penguin, Harmondsworth, 2nd edition, 1970. *Villenviertel* is the German term for the best residential district of a city.

26. Haigh, *M. H. Baillie Scott: The Artistic House*, cited in Note 23.

27. The house is much valued by its present owners, who continue, a century later, to enjoy Baillie Scott's deep insights into how we might live in England.

28. M. H. Baillie Scott, 'A suburban house', in *The Studio Yearbook of Domestic Art*, The Studio, London, 1910.

29. A recent development beyond the southern boundary has, almost incomprehensibly, compromised this seclusion.

30. This information is from Haigh's excellent book, cited in Note 23.

31. Davey, *Arts and Crafts Architecture*, cited in Note 16.

32. In addition to Peter Davey's chapter, a useful overview of Prior's work is, Christophe Grillet, 'Edward Prior', in *Edwardian Architecture and its Origins* (ed. Alistair Service), The Architectural Press, London, 1975. For detailed studies of Prior's important Arts and Crafts church see Dean Hawkes, 'St Andrew's Roker' in *Timeless Architecture* (ed. Dan Cruickshank), The Architectural Press, London, 1985, and Trevor Garnham, *St Andrew's Church, Roker, Sunderland, 1905: Edward Prior*, Architecture in Detail, Phaidon, London, 1990.

33. Edward S. Prior, *A History of Gothic Art in England*, G. Bell, London, 1900.

34. See Jill Franklin, 'Edwardian butterfly houses', *The Architectural Review*, Vol. 157, 1975, pp. 220–225.

35. When first built the house was covered in a thatched roof, which was destroyed in a fire and replaced by the somewhat angular tiled roof that may be seen today.

36. Davey, *Arts and Crafts Architecture*, cited in Note 16. For accounts of Unwin's life and work see Walter Creese, *The Legacy of Raymond Unwin: A Human Pattern for Planning*, MIT

Press, Cambridge, MA, 1967, and Frank Jackson, *Sir Raymond Unwin: Architect, Planner and Visionary*, A. Zwemmer, London, 1985. For an examination of designs for houses in relation to texts by Parker see Dean Hawkes, *Modern Country Homes in England: The Arts and Crafts Architecture of Barry Parker*, Cambridge University Press, Cambridge 1986; reprinted in paperback, 2010.

37. Barry Parker and Raymond Unwin, *The Art of Building a Home: A Collection of Lectures and Illustrations*, Longman, Green, London,1901.

38. This is from the 15th of Parker's essays, 'Modern country homes in England', published between 1910 and 1912 in the American journal *The Craftsman*. See Hawkes, *Modern Country Homes in England*, cited in Note 36, for edited versions of these with an accompanying critical commentary.

39. *Ibid.*

40. *Ibid.*

41. The standard works on Mackintosh's life and work are Thomas Howarth, *Charles Rennie Mackintosh and the Modern Movement*, Routledge & Kegan Paul, London, 1st edition, 1952, 2nd edition, 1977; Robert Macleod, *Charles Rennie Mackintosh*, Country Life, London, 1968; and Alan Crawford, *Charles Rennie Mackintosh*, Thames and Hudson, London, 1995. An excellent monograph on The Hill House is James Macaulay, *Hill House*, Phaidon, London, 1990.

42. These lectures are collected together, with critical commentaries, in Pamela Robertson (ed.), *Charles Rennie Mackintosh: The Architectural Papers*, White Cockade Publishing, Wendlebury, in association with the Hunterian Art Gallery, Glasgow, 1990. It has been pointed out by a number of Mackintosh scholars, notably Robert Macleod, that the extensive passages of these lectures are unacknowledged verbatim quotations from Lethaby's writings, specifically from *Architecture, Mysticism and Myth*, London, 1891; reprinted, The Architectural Press, London, 1974.

43. Howarth, *Charles Rennie Mackintosh and the Modern Movement*, cited in note 41.

44. *Ibid.*

45. The two editions of the guidebook for the house provide important, if different, descriptions of its original and present condition: Charles McKean and Robert Rogerson, *The Hill House*, The National Trust for Scotland, Edinburgh, undated; Anne Ellis, updated by Charlotte Rostek, *Hill House*, The National Trust of Scotland, Edinburgh, 2008.

46. McKean and Rogerson record this description in their guidebook.

47. Alison and Peter Smithson, *The Charged Void: Architecture*, The Monacelli Press, New York, 2001.

48. See both National Trust of Scotland guidebooks cited in Note 45.

Essay 7
The Modern Movement house in the British climate

The status of environmental questions in the theories and practices of the Modern Movement in architecture is not a simple matter. Le Corbusier was seemingly unambiguous when, in one of his 1929 Buenos Aires lectures, he rejected the historic relation of house and climate in favour of a radical, universal solution:

> Every country building its houses in response to its climate. At this moment of general diffusion, of international scientific techniques, I propose only one house for all countries, the house of *exact breathing*.
>
> (1)

By this date the science of meteorology had become a prime example of an 'international scientific technique'. Detailed forecasts were available in the popular print media and were being transmitted by the new medium of radio. In Britain the BBC first broadcast regular weather forecasts in 1922, the year in which the public radio service was inaugurated (2). The beginnings of international air travel, initially by airship, required the production of accurate forecasts along lengthy routes that often traversed a number of distinct climate zones in a single journey.

But, as is often the case, we find quite a discrepancy between theory and practice in the development of Le Corbusier's work in the period between the two world wars, particularly so in his designs for houses. The present author has suggested previously that an analysis of Le Corbusier's house designs shows that their environmental roots lie in the continuation of a long tradition of domestic design, in which questions of orientation and the con-figuration of domestic space in relation to the fireplace play central roles (3). Implicit in this is the need to make a specific response to climate. Additional support for the argument comes from Colin Porteous, who has provided a succinct and elegant résumé of the manner in which Le Corbusier fine-tuned his house designs to the distinct and different climates of Paris (Villa Savoye and Villa Stein at Garches), Bordeaux-Pessac, North Africa (Villa Baizeau, Carthage) and South America (Maison Curutchet, La Plata) (4).

In *Le Poème de l'Angle Droit*, published in 1955, a quarter of a century after the Buenos Aires lectures, the ground had shifted significantly. Here Le Corbusier was emphatic in connecting architecture to the annual and diurnal cycles of the sun and hence of the seasons (5). The first five stanzas of this important lyric poem are entitled *Milieu* (Environment), and in the first of these he declares:

Ponctuelle machine tournante	Punctual machine turning
depuis l'immémorial il fait	since time immemorial
naître à chaque instant des	engenders every instant of the
vingt-quatres heures la	Twenty-four hours cycle of the
gradation	gradation
le nuance l'imperceptible	the nuance of the imperceptible
presque leur fornissant	almost providing
une mesure. Mais il la rompt	a rhythm. Yet brutally
à deux fois brutalement le	he breaks it twice –
matin et le soir. Le continu	morning and evening. Continuity
lui appartient tandis qu'il	is his but he
nous impose l'alternatif –	imposes an alternative –
le nuit le jour – les deux temps	night and day – these two phases
qui règlent notre destinée:	rule our destiny:
Un soleil se lève	A sun rises
un soleil se couche	a sun sets
un soleil se lève à nouveau	A sun rises anew

The colour lithograph that accompanies this stanza is one of the most poetic of representations of the solar cycle (Plate 17).

The relationship between internationalism and local influences was an important theme in the emergent theories and practices of the modern movement in Britain. A particularly valuable insight was offered by J. M. Richards in *An Introduction to Modern Architecture* (6), first published in 1940:

We have referred to modern architecture as still being in the international stage. That is true today, but it is only a temporary stage. The new architecture, in that it is a way of approaching architectural problems based on reason instead of sentiment, is not concerned with frontiers. . . . The kind of civilization that has produced modern architecture . . . is much the same in all countries where it has flourished, but countries also have their own different temperaments and ideals, and different climates, habits and raw materials. They also have a past, and the national culture of which their modern architecture is part and is not separable from its roots . . . So, as modern architecture matures, a new differentiation according to national characteristics is inevitable . . . this kind of development should be described as *regionalism* rather than *nationalism*, to suggest that the geographical boundaries are the important ones.

In 1936 Nikolaus Pevsner published his influential *Pioneers of the Modern Movement*, later to become *Pioneers of Modern Design* (7). The book's subtitle is *From William Morris to Walter Gropius*, and this explicitly proposes a historical continuity between the English Arts and Crafts movement and European Modernism. Pevsner's proposition was adopted by Richards in *Introduction to Modern Architecture* (8) and underpinned some of the seminal studies of individual architects of the Arts and Crafts movement, such as Thomas Howarth on *Charles Rennie Mackintosh and the Modern Movement* and James D. Kornwulf in *M. H. Baillie Scott and the Arts and Crafts Movement: Pioneer of Modern Design* (9). More recent scholarship has led to a reappraisal of the Pevsnerian paradigm to bring other perspectives to bear on the Arts and Crafts movement – in terms of both its sources and its influences – but the continuity of cultural and physical context between British architecture of the nineteenth and twentieth centuries proposed by Richards may be seen to have played a part in shaping the specific characteristics of the modern house as it evolved in Britain.

A note on climate and the Modern Movement

The relation of architecture and nature assumed a new interpretation and significance in the modern movement when slogans such as 'light, space and air' acquired wide currency. Paul Overy in *Light, Air and Openness: Modern Architecture Between the Wars* (10) has given the subject comprehensive consideration. In reviewing works by architects including the major figures of European modernism, among them Le Corbusier, Eileen Gray, Mies van der Rohe, Walter Gropius and Jan Duiker, along with the work of émigrés to the United States, such as Marcel Breuer, Richard Neutra and Rudolf Schindler, Overy demonstrates the universality of the theme. The warm, coastal climates of the south of France and California were ideal locations for an architecture that was conceived to achieve the maximum, beneficial exposure to sunlight and fresh air. Nice lies at a latitude of 43°N and the annual daily mean temperature is 15.5° Celsius. Los Angeles lies even further south at 33°N latitude and there the annual daily mean temperature is over 17° Celsius. At Nice there is an annual average of just 63 days when precipitation occurs and there are merely 35 such days in Los Angeles.

These are ideal climates for an architecture of light, space and air, but very similar principles were also adopted by the great figures of European modernism in the less congenial climates of northern and central Europe. There it is possible to enjoy summers not very different from those of the Mediterranean coast or even of southern California, but the continental winters are less agreeable. Paris is at a latitude of 48°N and Berlin at 52°N. The respective annual average temperatures are in striking contrast with Nice and Los Angeles: Paris 8.5° Celsius and Berlin 9.6°. But averages do not tell the whole story and 24-hour average temperatures in the summer months are in excess of 21° Celsius in both cities, in stark contrast to 24-hour average winter temperatures of 2° or 3° in December and January in Paris and even lower, at −1.9° for January, in Berlin.

The effect of these variations of climate on the designs of the major architects of European modernism was reflected in their adoption of means by which to achieve winter comfort. The works of Le Corbusier and Mies van der Rohe made much play of their central heating installations and they made sophisticated use of artificial lighting to bring brightness to the dark evenings. In the summer months, even in conditions more temperate than those of southern Europe and California, these designs were often similar, with open terraces, balconies and roof gardens. The 'solarium' on the roof of the Villa Savoye is a striking symbol of this, as are the completely openable south-facing windows at the Tugendhat House, with their retractable canvas awnings (11).

The climate of the British Isles is, in broad geographical terms, not unlike that of the near continent, London is at the same latitude as Berlin, 52°N, but the shift from a central continental location to an island condition tempers both summer and winter conditions. In comparison with Berlin, the July 24-hour average temperature in London is a relatively cool 18.9° Celsius and the January 24-hour average is much milder at 5.9°. Beyond the physical facts, these data translate into a very different context within which to make architecture, as Hermann Muthesius had observed at the beginning of the century (12). The British summer offers the prospect of warm, sunny days to compare with the continent, when the pleasures of balconies and roof terraces may be enjoyed. It also carries the threat of cold and wet spells, when a house must provide sheltering comfort. The winter is seldom very cold and sunny days may occur with sufficient frequency to justify the use of glazed, south-facing façades that bring warmth and bright light to the interior.

As we noted when discussing the houses of the Arts and Crafts movement in Essay 6, the climate within the British Isles is quite diverse, with noticeable variations between south and north and west and east. The synopsis of data that are presented in the Met Office's fact sheet on the climate of the United Kingdom (13) succinctly conveys this. For example, mean average temperatures in January range from between 5° and 9° Celsius in the south to between 0.5° and –4° on the uplands of Scotland and northern England. In July the comparative average temperatures lie between 16.5° and 19° in the south and between 6° and 11.5° in the north. The distribution of sunshine, expressed as average annual hours duration, is correspondingly in the favour of the south, with the coastal fringes of southern England enjoying a noticeable advantage over even their immediate hinterland.

Unlike the geography of the Arts and Crafts house, where significant examples are found across the length and breadth of Britain, it is striking that the majority of notable early modern houses in Britain are located in the southern counties (14). This may be more a consequence of social and economic factors than of climate, but nonetheless is important in establishing the background to a review of the influence of climate on the design of these houses.

Berthold Lubetkin and Tecton

The attractions of the sunny southern coast of Britain are probably no more clearly demonstrated than at Aldwick Bay. This is an estate of vacation houses on the outskirts of the resort of Bognor Regis in Sussex and in easy reach of London. The estate had been developed in 1927 and was promoted by explicitly publicizing the number of sunshine hours enjoyed on this part of the coast. The climate there is rather subdued in comparison with the south of France or California, but it would have obvious attractions to the architects who were seeking to introduce the new architecture into Britain. In the summer of 1933 Berthold Lubetkin (1901–1990) and Anthony Chitty (1907–1976), who were members of the group practice Tecton, bought a site on the edge of the estate on which to build a speculative house (15). The house, which they sold upon completion in 1934, is a wonderful essay in modern design, with an *in situ* concrete frame and walls (Fig. 7.1). The plan at ground-floor level is a sophisticated play upon symmetry and asymmetry (Fig. 7.2). The principal orientation is to the south-east and this brings copious amounts of sunlight into all the principal rooms. The Corbusian *plan-libre* creates an eastward covered terrace off the dining room – ideal for breakfast – and an extensive roof terrace wraps around all four principal bedrooms. John Allan tells us that the design was entirely the work of Lubetkin, who had arrived in Britain in 1931, following a decade when he had travelled first to Germany and then to Paris. The modernity of the design was in extreme contrast to the sentimental vernacularism of the other houses on the estate at that date. Lubetkin's own metaphor was 'a ship beached by the storm' (16). John Betjeman continued the metaphor when he wrote that the house possessed '. . . a nautical efficiency one associates with

7.1
Berthold Lubetkin and
Anthony Chitty, House at
Aldwick Bay, Sussex:
principal elevation.

coastal building. . . . This is not an ordinary seaside villa with "modernistic" trappings. . . . The house at Bognor is truly modern' (17).

The familiar association of modern architecture with nautical style and detail would have been irresistible to both designer and critic in the 1930s, but there are important distinctions that have to be drawn between a sea-going vessel and a building, whatever the architect's own metaphor may have been. A building, rooted in one place, has an obligation to respond to its specific context in a manner that a ship may not. This house clearly exemplifies this with its meticulous attention to good orientation and providing full opportunities to enjoy the microclimate of the sunniest region of the country. These qualities confirm its modernity more than mere stylism.

At the same date as the construction of the house at Bognor, Lubetkin was at work on the design of two small, single-storey houses on the large estate of the London Zoological Society at Whipsnade in Bedfordshire. One was for himself, to use as a weekend and summer refuge from London, the other, slightly smaller, was for a friend, Dr Ida Mann (18). The zoo site is in the very middle of southern Britain, on the west-facing escarpment of the Chiltern Hills at an altitude of over 120 metres. In general form and construction the houses are similar. The plans are T-shaped, with a principal wing housing the daytime rooms, and the other wing the bedrooms (Figs 7.3 and 7.4). Lubetkin's house is on the edge of the escarpment, and this dictates that the dayrooms face almost due west to enjoy the remarkable view. Dr Mann's house is set to the east, in a less dramatic setting, and here the orientation is adjusted to face south-west, bringing the day rooms more directly towards the sunlight.

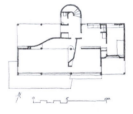

7.2
Berthold Lubetkin and
Anthony Chitty, House at
Aldwick Bay: ground-floor
plan.

The Lubetkin house sits at the northern end of a platform that was elaborately carved from the chalk of the hilltop. To the south this establishes a quite formal, flat terraced garden. The planning is a sophisticated essay in response to microclimate. John Allan beautifully explains Lubetkin's approach to the site:

> The house was neither an outgrowth of the landscape, as advocated by Frank Lloyd Wright, nor – as Le Corbusier's formula of pilotis would imply – was it placed insouciantly over and above it. The relationship was to imply neither camouflage nor conquest: it was a dialogue, a benign intervention suggesting, in Lubetkin's favourite phrase, the vision of 'nature tamed, not with a fist but with a smile.'
>
> (19)

To the north the body of the house is wrapped by an ensemble of free-standing structures that, at first sight, may appear to be purely sculptural. But closer attention shows that they have important environmental functions. They subtly modify the impact of the exposed site at the point of entry to the house and form a series of sheltered places in relation to the kitchen. Most dramatic is the 'sun-catch' in a curved enclosure that is reminiscent of the solarium on the upper roof terrace of Le Corbusier's Villa Savoye (20). Placed at the north-east corner, this is particularly effective as a sun-trap from midday onwards until late afternoon. The beautiful early image by Dell and Wainwright shows, as the shadow tells us, this place at about solar noon on a summer's day (Fig. 7.5). Opposite the kitchen window the enclosing wall is penetrated by a wide opening to allow both light in and a view out beneath a pergola of concrete beams. The sequence ends in a low, short return wall.

The west front of the house is a seemingly simple construction of a prefabricated modular concrete frame with panel infill (Fig. 7.6). But observation shows that, once again, subtle environmental considerations are at work. Opposite the kitchen the two-bay wide frame becomes a roofed, unenclosed loggia, which serves mainly as a circulation route. But the next two bays, which lie in front of the small dining room, project forward to become an outdoor room where we find a fireplace on the dividing wall to the dining room. The remainder of the west front, four bays wide, is the principal glazed wall of the living room. The dining room loggia is an environmentally intriguing place. External fireplaces are relatively unusual in British architecture, but interesting parallels may be found in the works of Alvar Aalto. One may be found at both the house and studio he built for himself in Helsinki in 1936 and at the celebrated Villa Mairea that he built shortly afterwards at Noormarkku in south-western Finland (21). In the Helsinki house the

7.3
Berthold Lubetkin, own house at Whipsnade: plan.

7.4
Berthold Lubetkin, Dr Mann's house at Whipsnade: plan.

7.6
Berthold Lubetkin,
own house at Whipsnade:
west front.

fireplace is under a canopy roof off the first-floor roof terrace and that at the Villa Mairea is also sheltered beneath a canopy above an external dining place. At the high latitude of Finland these places have a particular environmental *raison d'être* insofar as they provide warmth as the temperatures fall in the long Nordic summer evenings. But, even at Whipsnade, in a somewhat different climate, the fireplace will similarly warm the occupants of the loggia when the sun is falling towards the western horizon. Perhaps Lubetkin's Russian origins carried some memory of similar arrangements in northern climates. One remaining feature of the exterior environment of the house is the pair of south-facing, covered sleeping porches off the two bedrooms, intended for summer siestas.

John Allan observes that in its use as a weekend retreat the house would be relieved of some of the expectations that are placed upon permanent dwellings, suggesting that its servicing arrangements were 'distinctly spartan' (22). The heating system in the living room consisted of removable electric panel heaters mounted behind 'Thermolux' insulating glass infill panels in the lower part of the wall frame. In the 1930s there were few concerns with the inefficiency of this kind of heat source and they would have provided almost instantaneous warmth for someone arriving on a cold winter's evening. In the summer months the living room will be bright and sun-filled from early afternoon, with copious ventilation provided, if required, by the array of centre-pivot opening lights.

Dr Mann's house is similar to Lubetkin's villa, except that it is slightly reduced in scale. The most significant difference is the orientation. Set away from the attraction of the view enjoyed by Lubetkin's site, the living room here faces just to the west of south, giving it an almost Arts and Crafts emphasis on aspect over prospect. The design of the free-standing wall is simplified and the roofed loggias are missing. The difference in orientation may explain the later installation of external canvas awnings that are noted by John Allan (23). These would provide shade from the high summer sun.

George Checkley

George Checkley (1893–1960) was a New Zealander who came to Britain in 1918, following service in the First World War, and spent two years as a student at the Liverpool School of Architecture. In 1928 he began teaching in the Cambridge school, where he would certainly have encountered the Arts and Crafts architect Edward Prior, who was Slade Professor at the university until his death in 1932 (24). The Cambridge connection also brought him into contact with Raymond McGrath, a young Australian architect who arrived in England in 1926 and became a research student at Clare College, Cambridge. McGrath became an important figure in the development of modernism in Britain and went on to undertake a number of interesting architectural projects and make a particularly significant contribution through his books and architectural journalism (25). In 1934 he published his important book, *Twentieth Century Houses* (26), which predates Pevsner's *Pioneers* by two years and is a particularly important document in the literature of the Modern Movement in Britain, presenting a survey of houses from 20 different countries. In seeking to bring a comprehensive modernity to the book McGrath chose to write it entirely in 'Basic English'. This was developed in Cambridge by the English language scholar, C. K. Ogden in an attempt to render the language more 'international' (27). In an appendix to the book Ogden contributed 'A note on Basic English', where he drew a parallel between language and architecture:

> In building with words there is the same pull between the science of structure and the art of ornament as there is in building with steel and stone and wood.

7.7
C. F. A. Voysey, Broadleys: plan as shown in Raymond McGrath, *Twentieth Century Houses*, Faber and Faber, London, 1934.

One of the most important attributes of the book is the adoption of a systematic mode of presentation of the house plans. They are all drawn in a consistent format upon scaled grids and standard graphic conventions are adopted to denote the uses of rooms.

One of the houses illustrated in McGrath's book is Voysey's Broadleys. McGrath shows the L-shaped plan, with the main body of the house that contains the principal rooms and the attached service wing (Fig. 7.7). A little further in the book is Thurso House, now Willow House, built in 1932 in the suburbs of Cambridge by George Checkley (Fig. 7.8). In 1930 Checkley had built a house for himself, known as the White House, in the part of west Cambridge that Pevsner, in discussing the city's Arts and Crafts houses, described as 'Cambridge's *Villenviertel*'. This was one of the very first examples of the new architecture in Britain and clearly attracted attention in the university city, where in the 1920s and 1930s a new young generation of academics, many of them scientists, chose to build modern houses. Very soon after the completion of the White House, Checkley was commissioned to build a house on a nearby site by one of these dons, Hamilton McCombie, who was a reader in chemistry at the university and a fellow of King's College. The house, first known as The Thurso House and now as Willow House, is on quite a large, but relatively featureless suburban plot, although now, in its maturity, magnificent trees surround the site (Plate 6). Just as at Broadleys, the plan is L-shaped, but here the scale and content of the service wing are more modest, accommodating just a garage and utility rooms. At Broadleys the lakeside site fundamentally influences the orientation. The principal rooms face west towards the view, rather than observing the Arts and Crafts convention of a predominant southerly aspect. At The Thurso House the suburban site offered no such distraction and aspect takes priority over prospect, with entry from a protected northern court with the principal rooms orientated to the south.

When we compare the plans of the two houses in more detail a number of significant similarities emerge. In each a sheltered entrance porch leads directly into a double-height living room with the other apartments disposed to either side. The staircase leads directly to a first-floor gallery overlooking the void of the double-height space. It is perhaps not too fanciful to see the influence, however subliminal, of the older house on its modern successor. In their construction and detail the two houses could hardly be more different. For example, Checkley's adoption of Le Corbusier's *Cinque points d'une architecture nouvelle* is quite explicit, in particular, in the use of a reinforced concrete structural frame, which permitted the realization of *fenêtre en longueur* on the south façade. These create a completely different distribution and quality of light from that of Voysey's tall semicircular bay windows at Broadleys. In combination with its white-painted internal surfaces the interior is vibrantly bright. The house had a full central heating system, which was common practice by this date. This used straightforward cast-iron radiators, which were served by a boiler located in a utility room adjacent to the kitchen. But, as with Le Corbusier's houses (28), Checkley also provided a fireplace in both the main living room and, using a shared chimney-stack, in the adjacent study. These could provide useful supplementary warmth, if required, but, as also with Le Corbusier, they are probably more significant as symbols of the protecting function of a dwelling than as principal sources

7.8
George Checkley, Thurso House, Cambridge: plan as shown in Raymond McGrath, *Twentieth Century Houses*, Faber and Faber, London, 1934.

of warmth. It is noteworthy that the same chimney-stack also serves a fireplace in the original principal bedroom that is suspended over the double-height living room. This bedroom has direct access via a short staircase to that other essential element of the modernist house, *les toits-jardins*. This would have been an appealing tree-top refuge at all times of day and would also encourage open-air sleeping on balmy summer's nights.

Returning to ground level, the nature of the mature garden establishes particularly happy relationships with the principal ground-floor apartments that are comparable to those of the Arts and Crafts garden that Baillie Scott created a stone's throw away at 48 Storey's Way. In this respect, and in others, it is plausible to suggest a clear continuity between the principles of the Arts and Crafts movement, with their careful observance of the character of the British climate, and this pioneering example of the modern house in Britain.

Wells Coates

Wells Coates (1895–1958) was born in Japan of Canadian missionary parents and returned to Canada in 1913, where he entered university in Vancouver to study engineering. The First World War interrupted his studies and he came to Europe in 1917. Following a period in the trenches, Coates trained in Britain as a pilot with the Royal Air Force, before returning to the continent shortly before the armistice. He returned to Canada and completed his degree studies and then returned to Britain in 1922 to take a PhD in engineering at London University. He then moved into architecture and became one of the most important figures in the development of British modernism, most significantly through the design of the Isokon flats at Lawn Road in Hampstead, completed in 1934 (29).

In addition to Lawn Road, Coates built many projects, including a number of important houses in the south of England. His work attracted the attention of Raymond McGrath in *Twentieth Century Houses* (30), and there it is his project, in collaboration with David Pleydell-Bouverie, for the Sunspan house built at the Ideal Home Exhibition at Olympia in London in 1934 that is illustrated (Figs 7.9 and 7.10). Promoted with the slogan 'the Home of Tomorrow with sunshine laid on', the two-storey design has a square plan that is oriented diagonally on the cardinal points. The principal living room and bedroom above are at the southerly point of the plan, where they enjoy the sun throughout its daily progress. Cantacuzino (31) draws a comparison with 'Edwardian "butterfly" plans', in which the sun also enters the rooms throughout the day, but McGrath offers a contradictory analysis, when he proposes that 'the design is a working out of . . . an international idea'. McGrath proposed that:

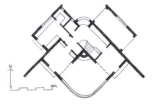

7.9
Wells Coates, Sunspan House, Ideal Home Exhibition, London: ground-floor plan.

. . . it is not a house for any one country, any one town or any one position, but for one sun giving light and heat from a fixed sun path all through the day. In other words it has to do with completely general needs and not with special conditions.

(32)

In 1933 Coates was a member of the first British delegation to attend a meeting of CIAM (Congrès Internationaux d'Architecture Moderne) that took place on the famous sea voyage from Marseilles to Athens. There he met all of the leaders of international modernism, including Le Corbusier, Mies van der Rohe and Walter Gropius. McGrath's reading of the essence of the Sunspan design is close to Le Corbusier's Buenos Aires declaration in 1929 of 'one house for all countries', with which the present essay began, but, as was argued there, that proposition was never upheld in Le Corbusier's own international practice. Perhaps Sunspan – although the work of an immigrant contributor to British architecture – was more closely grounded in an interpretation of the British climate than McGrath would allow. An exhibition house, in particular one built indoors in a large hall, is always unreal, perhaps even surreal. The original images of the exhibition house depict a generalized illumination, both outside and in, with the dynamic and directional quality of natural light completely absent. The construction of the house had a steel frame clad, inside and out, in an interlocking steel sheeting system, which was then plastered. The exhibition house had a curiously heavy brick fireplace at the apex of the living room, with a brick dado extending along the two flanking walls, almost recreating an ingle nook. The living room and principal bedroom had continuous bands of sliding windows that curved around the 'prow' of the house. Those at the ground floor were wider than those above to acknowledge the different needs for both light and view of the two rooms. They had relatively high cill lines and appear to be quite well adapted to the luminous and thermal nature of the British climate.

A number of variants of the house were subsequently constructed in the south of England. Cantacuzino estimates a total of 15, including a single-storey variant at Welwyn Garden City, north of London, and an enlarged three-storey example at Portsdown Hill in Hampshire. The latter has survived in good condition and Cantacuzino reports that its owner at the date of his research in the late 1970s was very satisfied with it (33).

F. R. S. Yorke

An important document of British modernism is *The Modern House* by F. R. S. Yorke (34). Yorke (1906–1962) was an architect who, in the first years of the 1930s, supplemented his income from practice by contributing to the *Architects' Journal*. He also established contacts with a number of European modernists. *The Modern House* was a direct product of this background (35). The book presents a review of designs for houses drawn from around Europe and includes a number of British examples. The intention is clearly to influence and inform the development of British practice. In an important passage Yorke presents a powerful argument for the virtues of bringing copious quantities of sunlight into a house:

> In earlier times sunlight was regarded as harmful rather than beneficial; it was considered a stimulant to the growth of bacteria, and windows were made small deliberately and placed away from the sunny side. It did not occur to people that the effect of this upon garbage and not upon their bodies or their rooms was the real cause of the mischief. Through medical research we have learnt better, and today sunlight is accepted as healthy and desirable; we take sunbaths and even artificial sun-ray treatments, we like large windows and sometimes fill them with special glass to admit the ultra-violet rays.

The purpose of the window is to admit light and air when necessary, and to widen the visual scene, and as part of the wall, to protect the interior from the elements.

(36)

These ideas are clearly demonstrated in Yorke's design for Torilla, a house at Nast Hyde, Hatfield (1934–1935). The house is built from in-situ concrete, with walls just 150 mm thick. The apparently simple T-shaped plan conceals considerable spatial complexity and the whole observes strict principles of orientation (Fig. 7.11). The main entrance is from the east. At the ground floor the east wing houses a study to the south and servant accommodation to the north. The entrance leads directly to the dramatic double-height volume of the living room, with its tall chimney-piece, lit by a high south-facing window and a high glass-brick clerestory to the west (Fig. 7.12). Dining takes place in a lower part of the room to the west, which opens onto

7.11
F. R. S. Yorke, Torilla, Nast Hyde, Hatfield: ground-floor plan.

7.12
F. R. S. Yorke, Torilla: living room.

a terrace facing the evening sun. The north-facing kitchen sits behind the fireplace wall. The first-floor gallery, which is approached via a staircase rising directly from the living room, leads in one direction to the master bedroom above the east wing and in the other to a second west-facing terrace. In addition the master bedroom suite has both south- and north-facing terraces. That to the south is partially covered by the over-sailing roof. In his description of the house in *The Modern House*, Yorke refers to the 'blinds concealed in boxes to windows to the south'. These adjustable canvas awnings, found only on the living-room and study windows, provide effective shade from the greatest heat of the day.

Formally the design does not owe much, if anything, to the precedent of the Arts and Crafts house, nor do we recognize much influence from Le Corbusier's *Cinque points* that Yorke refers to explicitly in *The Modern House*, in which he reproduces Le Corbusier's famous comparison of the virtues of horizontal over vertical window types. Jeremy Melvin, in his monograph on Yorke (37), suggests that the influence may have come from the Czech architects who were personal friends of Yorke and whose buildings appear in *The Modern House*. But the modernist discipline of orientation is meticulously observed for both the site layout and the detailed design of all the rooms. The view from the south-west (Fig. 7.13) illustrates the house at midday in summer. The entire façade is sunlit and the bedroom terrace is

7.13
F. R. S. Yorke, Torilla:
view from south-west.

clearly enjoyed by its occupants. The canvas awnings precisely shade the windows of the study and the living room. All this is beautifully judged.

Elsewhere in *The Modern House* Yorke addresses the question of winter comfort. By this date, it was axiomatic that a house would be centrally heated – that was an important part of being 'modern', and such systems were becoming ever more sophisticated:

> Since, by the use of thermostats, in conjunction with im-proved methods of heating, fuel consumption is not uncon-trolled, as it was with the open fire, and it is possible to maintain a given temperature in a room. Heat loss and its consequent fuel waste may be minimised by the provision of proper thermal insulation. The cost of insulation is recovered in one or two years by saving in fuel consumption.
>
> (38)

An indication of the assumption that would be made about 'proper thermal insulation' may be obtained from the illustration elsewhere in the book of a house in the United States with a mere ½ inch (12 mm) of insulation board as part of a frame wall construction – woefully inadequate by present-day standards.

Connell, Ward and Lucas

The partnership of Connell, Ward and Lucas was responsible for many important modern houses in Britain. Colin Lucas was the sole Englishman; Amyas Connell and Basil Ward, were, like George Checkley, New Zealanders (39). Amongst many important projects, their most notable house is High and Over at Amersham (Fig. 7.14). The design of the house began in 1928 and construction was completed in 1931. This makes the house exactly contemporary with Le Corbusier's Villa Savoye and Mies van der Rohe's Tugendhat House. In the early stages of the design an Australian architect, Stewart L. Thompson, collaborated with Amyas Connell, but, as Dennis Sharp and Sally Rendel record (40), the design should be fully attributed to Connell and all the significant drawings are in his name only.

As in the case of many important works of architecture, the clients had an important influence on the design of the house. Here, Bernard and Dorothy Ashmole were both scholarly and radical. He had been the director of the British School at Rome, where he met Connell, who was a Rome Scholar from 1927 to 1929, and Basil Ward, who also spent a year at the school in the same period. The Ashmoles returned to England in 1928, when he was elected to the chair of classical archaeology at London University. Surprisingly Raymond McGrath does not illustrate the house in *Twentieth*

7.14
Connell, Ward and Lucas,
High and Over, Amersham:
entrance front.

Century Houses, but he offers a quite extended verbal description of it, in which he, again rather surprisingly, declares:

> Here was a house that made no attempt to be a natural growth of English earth.

(41)

In a literal sense this might be the conclusion that one would reach from the early images of the house on its high, bare Chiltern hilltop, and one might recognize some resonance over the centuries with the situation of Hardwick Hall. But with the now mature planting of the garden a different reading might be reached. McGrath, however, acknowledges the importance of good orientation and his description of the house implies a deeply considered response to the nature of the English climate:

> Its three-pointed plan, its far from regular spacing of windows, its wing-like covers over the flat roof-terraces, its general cardboard quality – these were all an outcome of the hard reasoning put into the design, *reasoning in the interests of sunlight, outlook and general comfort* [my italics]

Bernard Ashmole, perhaps in a reference to the principles of classical design given by Vitruvius, recalled that the design observed:

> . . . the principles well known in antiquity, that a building facing south gains heat when the sun is low, in spring, autumn and winter, yet is particularly shaded inside when the sun is at its highest in summer.
>
> (42)

Dennis Sharp makes a connection with Arts and Crafts house design when he suggests that the Y-shaped plan of High and Over is a development of the butterfly plan and specifically cites Edward Prior's The Barn, which he describes as:

> . . . a progressive (plan) designed to catch the sun.
>
> (43)

The Y-shaped plan is oriented so that the house is approached almost exactly from the north (Fig. 7.15). It is set in a garden that, in its layout and carefully calculated relationship to the house, could almost be by Baillie Scott (Fig. 7.16). On entering the house the hexagonal, double-height hall opens directly to the dining room to the east, with the kitchen and service wing beyond, the drawing room to the west, while straight ahead to the south lies the library. The hall is lit from the glazed staircase enclosure to the southeast and through windows to the south west. The drawing room and the library thus frame the terraced garden, stepping down to the south-west. The main windows of the drawing room and library face the garden and each room has a fireplace in the opposite wall. On the first floor the Ashmoles' bedroom is above the library, with a guest suite opposite over the drawing room. The third wing contains maids' rooms, which are approached via a service stair. The plans of the two principal bedroom suites – the Ashmoles' and the guest suite – are, symmetrically, almost identical, but they are totally unalike in their window arrangements. The guest suite has a *fenêtre en longueur* filling the whole south-west wall and wrapping around the corner. On the other hand, the Ashmoles' suite has a blind wall to the west; that is, the garden front and its main windows face due east, supplemented by a modern interpretation of an oriel window in the south face. There is a tradition in the design of dwellings that proposes that bedrooms should face east, so that sleepers will be awakened by the morning sun. This conforms to Vitruvius' recommendation that 'Bedrooms (and libraries) ought to have eastern exposures, because their purposes require the morning light' (44). If Ashmole and Connell were observing antique principles in the design of the bedroom,

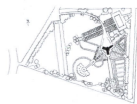

7.15
Connell, Ward and Lucas, High and Over: garden plan.

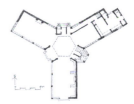

7.16
Connell, Ward and Lucas, High and Over: ground-floor plan.

in the library they were clearly influenced by other priorities. The view over the garden and the landscape would have been irresistible. It should be pointed out that Vitruvius' anxiety that books in a south-facing library would be 'ruined by worms and dampness' would hardly be an issue in twentieth-century Buckinghamshire.

The free disposition of the rooms within the strict geometry of the overall form of the house is quite characteristic of many of the British buildings discussed in this book. The earliest and probably the most striking example is, once again, Hardwick Hall, where the complexity of the internal planning is completely concealed by the mathematical symmetries of the exterior. Closer to the twentieth century the houses of the Arts and Crafts movement quite frequently made a play of this disconnection between exterior and interior. Parker and Unwin, at Whirriestone (see page 178), arranged a freely planned interior within the simple roofed pavilion of the main house.

As suggested by Dennis Sharp, the closest precedent for High and Over is probably Edward Prior's The Barn. In both houses we find the windows freely and asymmetrically disposed upon the geometrically disciplined form. At High and Over this is more strikingly apparent when set against the pristine clarity of the white-painted mass (Fig. 7.17). But, as with Prior, this is no mere formal game. The sizes and positions of the windows are precisely calculated to serve the needs of the interior, whether a drawing room, a library or a bedroom suite, and are practically and poetically attuned to the conditions of the English light and climate.

E. Maxwell Fry

One of the most important figures in early British modernism was Edwin Maxwell Fry (1899–1987). Like George Checkley, Fry was educated at the Liverpool School of Architecture and moved to London to seek work in practice in 1925 (45). His early buildings, carried out when he was a partner in the practice of Adams, Thompson and Fry, were in the neoclassical mode that was the hallmark of the Liverpool School in the 1920s, under the direction of Professor C. H. Reilly (46). In the Adams and Thompson office he met Wells Coates and there began his gradual conversion to modernism. He became a member of the influential Design and Industries Association and in 1933 was a founder member of the Modern Architectural Research Group (MARS).

By the mid-1930s Fry had become an assured exponent of the new architecture and this is demonstrated in his designs for two of the most important houses built in Britain at that time: the Sun House at Frognal Way, Hampstead, completed in 1936 (Fig. 7.18) and Miramonte at Kingston-upon-Thames in the following year (Fig. 7.19). The very name 'Sun House' expresses the environmental emphasis of the design. On a sloping site set above the road the house faces just to the west of due south. The principal

7.18
E. Maxwell Fry, Sun House, Hampstead, London: principal-floor plan.

7.19
E. Maxwell Fry, Miramonte, Kingston-upon-Thames: ground-floor plan.

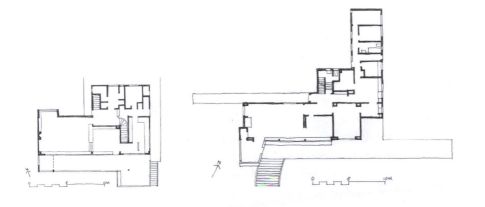

7.20
E. Maxwell Fry, Sun House:
street front.

rooms are at *piano nobile* level, from where they enjoy views across London. Two open balconies extend the study to the east and the living room to the west. The main bedroom, directly above the living room, also enjoys a projecting balcony. The house is, of course, topped with a roof terrace. All of this brings the modernist benefits of copious quantities of sunlight to the interior. Writing later, Fry made an important observation on the benefits of sunlight in the British climate:

> Sunlight, not necessarily sunshine, is a form of heating that costs nothing. If dwellings are planned so that the living quarters face the sun, which in England travels across the sky from east to west in a high curve in the summer and a low one in the winter, sunlight entering through generous-sized windows will heat throughout most days of the year, and the large windows will, on balance, let in more heat than they let out.
>
> (47)

To assist in fine tuning its relationship with the climate, the house had an array of retractable blinds and awnings to protect the south-facing windows from the greatest heat of the sun, and areas of the roof terrace were sheltered by hanging shades to provide protection against the wind and to create comfortable microclimates (Fig. 7.20). The house was equipped with a gas-fired underfloor heating system (48). Miramonte, on a relatively flat site oriented to the east of due south, not surprisingly explores the same themes and repeats the idea of a projection beyond the main façade at the south-western corner, this time with an enclosed sun room that opens off the living room and a roofed terrace above to serve the principal bedroom (Fig. 7.21).

By the date of these two houses Fry was a convinced devotee of modernism and the designs clearly show the influence both of Le Corbusier's 'white' villas in the Paris suburbs and of Mies van der Rohe's Tugendhat House at Brno. They share the emphasis on a southerly orientation of these recent exemplars and almost didactically apply Le Corbusier's *Cinque points*. But they have a freer approach to planning and composition than most of their European contemporaries. In their planning both houses may be as much associated with the Arts and Crafts movement as with modernism. The L-shaped plan at Miramonte, with its clear differentiation of the principal apartments from the service wing, and the organization of the entrance and staircase, could almost be by Baillie Scott at his most lyrical. The relation of the hearth and sun room, between day-to-night and summer–winter conditions, operates in a similar way to the juxtaposition of ingle nook to bay window of the Arts and Crafts movement – although the presence of the bar might have offended the Spartan tastes of some of the earlier generation.

Later, in the post-war years, in collaboration with his second wife, Jane Drew, Fry's work became deeply concerned with the relation of architecture and climate. Fry and Drew built many buildings in Ghana and Nigeria in which they meticulously adapted modern architecture to the conditions of the tropics. Here they paid careful attention to orientation, in this case to avoid and exclude the extremes of solar heat gains, and the proper use of devices such as *brise soleil*. This experience led to the publication of two important manuals on design in the tropics (49). In 1951 Fry and Drew were invited to become members of the team that was assembled to design the capital of the Punjab at Chandigarh. There they played an important part in seeking the appointment of Le Corbusier to design the capitol buildings.

Leslie Martin and Sadie Speight

As we noted at the outset of this essay, the large majority of important modernist houses in Britain are located in southern England, with major concentrations in the London suburbs and the Home Counties and others by or close to the sea on the south coast. In *Modern* (50), his valuable survey of British architecture before the second world war, Alan Powers includes just four houses that lie to the north of the River Trent, a useful line of demarcation between the south and the north of the country. These are, in date order, Kirkby House in north Yorkshire (1931), by the Leeds-based architect John Proctor; a house in Dick Place, Edinburgh (1932), by William Kinmouth; Harry Weedon's almost exotic Villa Marina (1936) at Llandudno in north Wales; and Brackenfell in Cumberland (1937). Here the architects were Leslie Martin (1908–2000) and Sadie Speight (1906–1992).

Martin and Speight met as students at Manchester University in the late 1920s. The married in 1935 and began a joint practice. At the same time Martin was head of the School of Architecture at Hull. He later became deputy architect at the London County Council, where he led the design team for the Royal Festival Hall, and in 1956 became Professor of Architecture at Cambridge (51).

In the 1930s Martin and Speight were closely associated with the leading figures of the 'constructive art' movement in Britain, including the painter Ben Nicholson and the sculptor Naum Gabo. In 1937 Martin, Nicholson and Gabo were joint editors of *Circle: International Survey of Constructive Art* (52). Through their friendship with Ben Nicholson, Martin and Speight were introduced to Alastair Morton, a progressive designer and manufacturer of textiles, whose company was located in Carlisle. In 1937 Morton commissioned the architects to design a house, which would include a studio and would be a setting for his collection of contemporary art and design works (53).

The house, known as Brackenfell, is on the crest of a hill to the south of the village of Brampton, which has a number of fine buildings by Philip Webb, most notably St Martin's Church (1877–1878) (54). Louise Campbell has comprehensively charted the development of the design (55). The early sketches show an L-shaped form, but, as built, the house consists of a simple, strong, two-storey rectangle, oriented with its long axis just to the north of east-west (Fig. 7.22). An obviously striking difference between Brackenfell and the other houses discussed here is that the main body of the house is constructed of brick. This is a sand-faced local product and is a deep red colour. Louise Campbell suggests that this materiality endows the house with 'a markedly regionalist flavour'. It should be recalled that Le Corbusier had, from the late 1920s, produced designs that used local materials to forge a kind of modern regionalism. William Curtis (56) cites the Maison de Mandrot at Le Pradet in the south of France (1929–1932), the house at Mathes on the Atlantic coast of France (1934–1935) and the unbuilt Maison Erazuris in Chile (1930) as examples of this phase. In addition to their use of local materials and low-technology construction, each of these houses also exhibits a precise response to the regional climate (57).

At Brackenfell it is clear that, whilst the architects and their client are striving to make an entirely *modern* house, other concerns and, perhaps influences, were also at play. Leslie Martin frequently asserted the importance of the Arts and Crafts movement in his thinking. In his essay 'Background and belief' (58) he wrote of the 'English Free School', often a synonym for the Arts and Crafts movement:

> [The English Free School] method, with its informality, its planning arranged around use, site and aspect that had done so much to produce a new open ended approach and which was to leave such a rich legacy for the future of English domestic architecture. For my generation it opened up the possibility of a continuing and developing process of design related to different needs and changing conditions.

7.22
Leslie Martin and Sadie Speight, Brackenfell, Brampton: ground-floor plan.

This statement is reinforced by the immediate juxtaposition on the page of the ground-floor plan of Voysey's Broadleys with a cut-away axonometric drawing of Brackenfell.

The house is approached from the north, from where it presents a striking silhouette (Fig. 7.23). The long plane of brickwork at the first floor is punctured by a group of three quite small rectangular windows, but at the west end the surface is cut away and filled by the slightly sloping, enormous window to the studio, with a punctuation point just to its left of a small circular opening. The foreground is occupied by the overlapping stone and concrete planes of the porch and *porte cochère*. The ground-floor plan has many of the characteristics of an Arts and Crafts house, with the principal rooms – living, dining and nursery – facing south and the kitchen at the cooler north-east corner. The living room, with a stone fireplace on the northern wall, and the dining room project forward from the main body of the south front and have continuous windows above a relatively low cill (Fig. 7.24). To the east the dining room opens onto a sheltered terrace, covered by the projecting upper floor. This is reminiscent of a similar arrangement at Alvar Aalto's own house in Helsinki, completed in 1936 just before work began on Brackenfell. Service spaces, bathrooms and a box room are placed to the north of the first-floor plan and the bedrooms enjoy the southerly prospect and aspect. A recessed and roofed-over sleeping balcony separates the bedrooms from the studio. This is probably the most significant room in the house and its design was the subject of a great deal of discussion

with Morton. The great north window meets the conventional needs for consistent illumination, but there are also windows in the west and south walls. Sadie Speight made a cut-away perspective drawing of this space, looking to the south (Fig. 7.25). This shows how the room was carefully organized into distinct territories. The brightly and functionally lit studio proper is at the north, and at the southern end, with its extensive views over the Cumbrian countryside, is a study with a desk placed under the west-facing window. A wide storage cupboard occupies a part of the south wall; a large, frameless window fills the remainder. The cill is above the floor level and the lintel is quite low, both to frame the view and to control the amount of south light entering the room.

A very important part of the environmental conception of the house was the use of colour in the interior. The living-room walls were white and Quaker grey and the ceiling primrose yellow. The carpet was grey haircord and the curtains, woven by Alastair Morton's company Edinburgh Weavers, were saxe blue chenille, with a vertical white line every eight inches (200 mm). A Barbara Hepworth sculpture, 'Conoid, Sphere and Hollow II' (1937), stood above the fireplace. Louise Campbell suggests, perceptively, that these and the other colour schemes throughout the house reflect a sensitivity perhaps derived from Winifred Nicholson, Ben's first wife and a native of Cumbria – that they were a response to 'the clear, cool fugitive light of northern England and to the effectiveness of small accents of bright colour in this environment' (59).

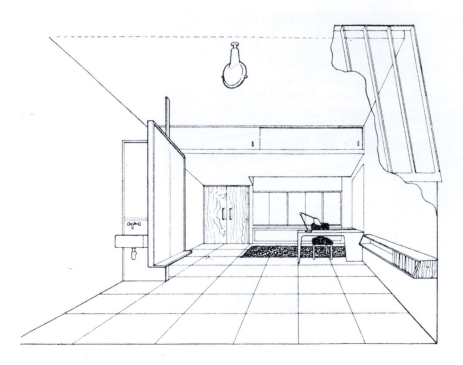

7.25
Leslie Martin and Sadie
Speight, Brackenfell:
cut-away perspective of
the studio.

Brackenfell emerges as a particularly British interpretation of the nature of the modern house. In comparison with its more southerly cousins, it exhibits a more overt response to its context, both through its materiality and in its environmental character and climate response. This owes much to its architects' deep understanding of the houses of the Arts and Crafts movement, and, in particular, the northern examples with which they were directly familiar. In the taxonomy of modern architecture it should perhaps be placed in the category of 'regional' rather than with the 'international' allegiance of all our other British examples. Nonetheless it should be recognized that the 'international' style in Britain was consistently quite carefully and subtly adapted to the British condition, not least to the demands of climate, and that this invests these designs with their distinctive character.

Notes

1. Le Corbusier, *Precisions on the Present State of Architecture and City Planning*, Crès, Paris, 1930; English translation MIT Press, Cambridge, MA, 1991.
2. The Met Office, Exeter, 'History Timeline', www.metoffice.gov.uk/news/in-depth/overview
3. See Dean Hawkes, 'Essay 2: Le Corbusier and Mies van der Rohe: continuity and invention', in *The Environmental Imagination: Technics and Poetics of the Architectural Environment*, Routledge, London, 2008.
4. Colin Porteous, *The New eco-Architecture: Alternatives from the Modern Movement*, Spon, London, 2002.

5. Le Corbusier, *Le Poème de L'Angle Droit*, editions Verve, Paris, 1955. Reprinted, Fondation Le Corbusier/Editions Connivences, Paris, 1989.

6. J. M. Richards, *An Introduction to Modern Architecture*, Penguin, Harmondsworth, 1st edition, 1940.

7. Nikolaus Pevsner, *Pioneers of the Modern Movement: From William Morris to Walter Gropius*, Faber and Faber, London, 1936; 2nd edition, Museum of Modern Art, New York, 1949; revised edition, Penguin, Harmondsworth, 1960.

8. Richards, *An Introduction to Modern Architecture*, cited in Note 6.

9. Thomas Howarth, *Charles Rennie Mackintosh and the Modern Movement*, Routledge & Kegan Paul, London, 1st edition, 1952, 2nd edition, 1977. James D. Kornwulf, *M. H. Baillie Scott and the Arts and Crafts Movement: Pioneer of Modern Design*, Johns Hopkins Press, Baltimore, 1972.

10. See Paul Overy, *Light, Air and Openness: Modern Architecture Between the Wars*, Thames and Hudson, London, 2007.

11. See Hawkes, 'Essay 2: Le Corbusier and Mies van der Rohe', cited in Note 3 and Porteous, *The New eco-Architecture*, cited in Note 4.

12. Hermann Muthesius, *Das Englische Haus*, Wasmuth, Berlin, Volumes 1 and 2, 1904, Volume 3, 1905; 1st English edition, abridged (ed. Dennis Sharp, trans. Janet Seligman), Crosby, Lockwood, Staples, London, 1979; 2nd English Edition, full text (ed. Dennis Sharp, trans. Janet Seligman and Stuart Spencer), Frances Lincoln, London, 2007.

13. Met Office, *Fact Sheet No. 4 – Climate of the United Kingdom*, National Meteorological Library and Archive, Exeter, 2007.

14. This is confirmed by the examples included in Alan Powers' survey of British modernism in *Modern: The Modern Movement in Britain*, Merrell, London, 2007.

15. The standard and authoritative study of the work of Berthold Lubetkin is John Allan, *Berthold Lubetkin: Architecture and the Tradition of Progress*, RIBA Publications, London, 1999. John Allan's later *Lubetkin*, Merrell, London, 2002, nicely supplements this; the book has good modern colour photographs of the buildings by Morley von Sternberg. A valuable earlier study is Peter Coe and Malcolm Reading, *Lubetkin and Tecton: Architecture and Social Commitment*, Arts Council of Great Britain/University of Bristol, 1981.

16. Lubetkin, as cited by Allan, *Berthold Lubetkin: Architecture and the Tradition of Progress*, cited in Note 15.

17. John Betjeman, 'Airflow house by the sea', *London Evening Standard*, 20 June 1936, as cited by Coe and Reading, *Lubetkin and Tecton*, cited in Note 15.

18. As before, the invaluable secondary sources here are Alan Powers, *Modern*, cited in Note 14, and Coe and Reading, *Lubetkin and Tecton*, cited in Note 15.

19. Allan, *Berthold Lubetkin: Architecture and the Tradition of Progress*, cited in Note 15.

20. See Hawkes, 'Essay 2: Le Corbusier and Mies van der Rohe', cited in Note 3.

21. See Dean Hawkes, 'Essay 3: The "other" environmental tradition: Erik Gunnar Asplund and Alvar Aalto', in *The Environmental Imagination: Technics and Poetics of the Architectural Environment*, Routledge, London, 2008.

22. Allan, *Berthold Lubetkin: Architecture and the Tradition of Progress*, cited in Note 15.

23. *Ibid.*

24. See Powers, *Modern*, cited in Note 14, for a brief biographical note on Checkley.

25. For an account of the foundations of English modernism see Elizabeth Darling, *Re-forming Britain: Narratives of Modernity Before Reconstruction*, Routledge, London, 2006.

26. Raymond McGrath, *Twentieth Century Houses*, Faber and Faber, London, 1934.

27. C. K. Ogden, *Basic English: A General Introduction with Rules and Grammar*, Kegan Paul, Trench, Trubner, London, 1930. 'Basic' is an acronym for British American Scientific International Commercial (English).

28. Le Corbusier's almost universal adoption of fireplaces in his house designs was identified by Todd Willmert; see 'The "ancient fire, the hearth of tradition": combustion and creation in Le Corbusier's studio residences', *arq: Architectural Research Quarterly*, Vol. 10, 2006, pp. 57–78.

29. Sherban Cantacuzino, *Wells Coates: A Monograph*, Gordon Fraser, London, 1978. This is a good survey of Coates' life and works. Other important references are *Wells Coates: Architect and Designer, 1895–1958* (exhibition catalogue), Oxford Polytechnic Press, Oxford, 1979, and Laura Cohn, *The Door in a Secret Room: A Portrait of Wells Coates*, Scolar Press, Aldershot, 1999.

30. McGrath, *Twentieth Century Houses*, cited in Note 26.

31. Cantacuzino, *Wells Coates*, cited in Note 29.

32. McGrath, *Twentieth Century Houses*.

33. Cantacuzino, *Wells Coates*.

34. F. R. S. Yorke, *The Modern House*, The Architectural Press, London, 1934.

35. Information from the entry on Yorke in the *Oxford Dictionary of National Biography*, online edition, Oxford University Press.

36. *Ibid*.

37. Jeremy Melvin, *F. R. S. Yorke and the Evolution of English Modernism*, Wiley-Academy, Chichester, 2003.

38. Yorke, *The Modern House*, cited in Note 34.

39. See Dennis Sharp and Sally Rendel, *Connell, Ward and Lucas: Modern Movement Architects in England 1929–1939*. Frances Lincoln, London, 2008.

40. *Ibid*.

41. McGrath, *Twentieth Century Houses*, cited in Note 26.

42. Bernard Ashmole, *Bernard Ashmole 1894–1988: An Autobiography* (ed. Donna Kurtz), Oxbow Books, Oxford, 1994, as cited in Sharp and Rendell, *Connell, Ward & Lucas*, cited in Note 37. Ashmole's summary of solar effects in buildings is in many respects a paraphrase of Book VI of Vitruvius.

43. Sharp and Rendel, *Connell Ward & Lucas*, cited in Note 39.

44. Vitruvius, *Ten Books on Architecture*, Book VI, Chapter V.

45. Biographical information on Fry from Alan Powers in the *Oxford Dictionary of National Biography*, Oxford University Press, Oxford, online edition.

46. See Peter Richmond, *Marketing Modernisms: The Architecture and Influence of Charles Reilly*, Liverpool University Press, Liverpool, 2001.

47. E. Maxwell Fry, *Fine Building*, Faber and Faber, London, 1944.

48. The house is illustrated in Colin Davis, *Key Houses of the Twentieth Century: Plans, Sections and Elevations*, Laurence King, London, 2006.

49. E. Maxwell Fry and Jane Drew, *Tropical Architecture in the Humid Zone*, Batsford, London, 1956, and *Tropical Architecture in the Dry and Humid Zones*, Reinhold, New York, 1964.

50. Alan Powers, *Modern*, cited in Note 14.

51. For a comprehensive representation of Martin's works see Leslie Martin, *Buildings and Ideas 1933–1983: From the Studio of Leslie Martin and His Associates*, Cambridge University Press, Cambridge, 1983. A critical review of Martin's work is in Peter Carolin and Trevor Dannatt (eds), *Architecture, Education and Research: The Work of Leslie Martin: Papers and Selected Articles*, Academy Editions, London, 1996. Biographical information is from the *Oxford Dictionary of National Biography*, online edition, Oxford University Press: on Sadie Speight by Jill Seddon and on Leslie Martin by Peter Carolin.

52. Leslie Martin, Ben Nicholson and Naum Gabo (eds), *Circle: International Survey of Constructive Art*, Faber and Faber, London, 1937. Contributors included Piet Mondrian,

Le Corbusier, Barbara Hepworth, Henry Moore, Siegfried Giedion, Walter Gropius, Leonide Massine and Lewis Mumford.

53. For a detailed account of the genesis of Brackenfell see Louise Campbell, 'Constructivism and contextualism in a modern country house: the design of Brackenfell (Leslie Martin and Sadie Speight, 1937–38)', *Architectural History*, Vol. 50, 2007, pp. 247–266. The relation of the design to the architects' other early projects is elegantly discussed in Trevor Dannatt, 'Early years: towards a new order', in Carolin and Dannatt, *Architecture, Education and Research*, cited in Note 51.

54. Philip Webb's buildings at Brampton are comprehensively described in Sheila Kirk, *Philip Webb: Pioneer of Arts and Crafts Architecture*, Wiley-Academy, Chichester, 2005.

55. Campbell, 'Constructivism and contextualism in a modern country house', cited in Note 51.

56. William Curtis, *Le Corbusier: Ideas and Forms*, Phaidon, London, 1986.

57. See Hawkes, 'Essay 2: Le Corbusier and Mies van der Rohe', cited in Note 3.

58. In Martin, *Buildings and Ideas, 1933–1983*, cited in Note 51.

59. Campbell, 'Constructivism and contextualism in a modern country house', cited in Note 53.

Essay 8
The environmental architecture of Alison and Peter Smithson

Alison and Peter Smithson (1928–1993 and 1923–2003) were amongst the most important figures in the theory and practice of architecture in Britain in the second half of the twentieth century. The full scope and substance of their work is best captured in the two volumes of *The Charged Void*, published in 2001 and 2005 with the respective subtitles of *Architecture* and *Urbanism* (1). In chronological, parallel narratives these books record the Smithsons' life work, illustrating all of their projects, built and unbuilt, with related texts and commentaries that identify recurrent and developing themes. These embrace the social obligations of architecture, a deep regard for history, and a complex and evolving exploration of the tectonic essence of buildings and, the theme most directly relevant to the present discussion, of the connection of architecture and climate.

Quasi-scientific reductivism was not the Smithsons' method. The categories with which they 'ordered' their work are poetic rather than prosaic, qualitative rather than quantitative. Yet, throughout these two volumes, the significance of the environmental dimension of architecture is rarely absent. In the first book, *Architecture*, Chapter 10 has the title 'The harnessing of light' and Chapter 12 is 'Sun acceptance/energy containment'. In the second book, *Urbanism*, Chapter 9, 'and again the sun (1976–1992)' has sub-divisions into the themes of, 'Aspect and prospect responsive' and 'Climate responsive'. These themes are both explicit and implicit in many of the Smithsons' architectural and urban projects. A particularly striking example is the competition entry for the Bibliotheca Alexandrina (1989) (2). The drawings include explicit 'sun studies' of the overall form of the building and detailed investigations of the twin-skinned façade design.

Almost inconspicuously present in the first book are two pages of sketches made by Peter Smithson, dated 6 June 1957, for an 'English Climate House' (Fig. 8.1). These show an idea for a group of stepped-section, two-storey houses in which south-facing private terraces are laid out in echelon formation in relation to common gardens. A diagrammatic sun appears in both the plan and the section sketches. They later reinforced the ideas represented in the sketches when they wrote, 'The climate house subjects the British house to a climate analysis' (3). A reading of both the substance of the

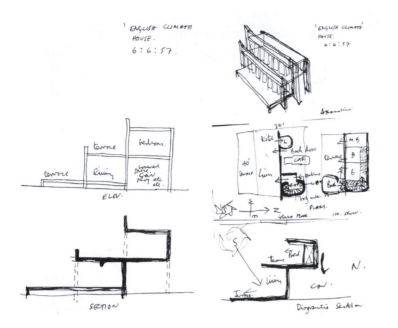

volumes of *The Charged Void* and other writings and statements by the Smithsons provides emphatic demonstration of their deep understanding of the nature and architectural potential of their native climate.

In the introduction to Essay 2, on the works of the 'other' significant Smythsons of British architecture, I cited Peter's description of Hardwick Hall from his keynote paper at the 1987 European Conference on Architecture (4). Throughout his writings Peter made numerous references to this building; for example, in a discussion with students at Arizona State University in 2001 (5) he described the plan of the house in the following terms:

> In Hardwick New Hall there is a gallery which runs the whole extent of the house. What's nice about this drawing is that it indicates the thick spine wall, where the fireplaces are, as well as the heating apparatus and the perimeter bay windows that let in the light. In the wintertime the family would pull back to the fireplaces. The organization of the house was based on the available coal. In this part of England coal was produced at the time. Fuel found formal expression in the organization of houses, so that in winter you have screens around the gallery against the fireplaces, and in the summer you moved into the bay windows. The organization of the plan was a consequence of thinking about the way in which it could be used – that is the pleasures of winter and summer.

Whilst the more detailed study of Hardwick in Essay 2 reveals yet more richness in the relationship between the organization and inhabitation of the house and the seasonal variations of the English climate, Smithson's analysis is an accurate paraphrase of these relationships and a clear indication of his sensibility to the link between architecture and climate.

The Smithsons grew up in the north-east of England, Peter in Stockton-on-Tees and Alison in South Shields. They studied architecture at what was then the King's College School of Architecture in Newcastle upon Tyne (6). It is possible that their formative years in a region of Britain with a relatively hostile climate had a subliminal influence on their later alertness to climate in their professional lives. The English landscape was a constant preoccupation in their lives and work and this sensibility was, again, shaped in their early years by events such as Peter's annual cycle ride with his father from Stockton to Whitby, along a route that traversed rugged terrain in often-inclement weather (7). Climate and landscape are most poetically and comprehensively represented in *AS in DS: An Eye on the Road*, a so-called 'sensitivity primer' published by Alison in 1983 (8). In the Preface she wrote:

> This is a diary of car-movement recording the evolving sensibility of a passenger in a car to the post-industrial landscape.
>
> To the eighteenth century's inherited consciousness of nature and landscape Jane Austen's novels added her generation's perception of distance and time; a response to the news of movement of ships and armies in the Napoleonic Wars and, within England, to the ease of communication on trunk roads.
>
> In the last quarter of the twentieth century, we have inherited a literature of man and machine in nature but there is as yet no equivalent of the eighteenth century's understanding which penetrated all levels of society through the work of writers, artists, landscape designers and architects.
>
> This Primer is a document reaching out towards such an understanding.

In the 'After-papers' to the book Alison included, as a kind of precedent study, extracts from William Cobbett's *Rural Rides* (9). Cobbett was an almost exact contemporary of Jane Austen and both were born in the county of Hampshire, Austen in the village of Chawton and Cobbett not far away in Farnham. Cobbett wrote eloquent descriptions of the English landscape in the southern counties, mainly in the autumn months between 1822 and 1826 (10). He makes occasional reference to the climate, but the emphasis is upon topography and, even more, on 'Economical and Political Observations'. The majority of the Smithsons' journeys, in the years between the mid 1960s and the early 1980s, were between their London home and Upper Lawn Pavilion, their weekend house at Fonthill in Wiltshire. But they frequently ventured further afield, in particular on trips to their home territory in the north of the country. The journeys were made at all seasons of the year and the commentaries are full of detail on the quality of the light, by day or night, temperature, precipitation and visibility. The verbal descriptions are complemented by numerous sketches, mainly by Alison from the passenger seat, and photographs, by Peter, taken, of course, when the car was stationary. Just a few fragments will convey the environmental richness of this text:

London to Fonthill: night
. . . the night sky showing water-washed clouds of grey . . . A threatening sky of a type favoured for Victorian sea-scapes, complete with ominous, lighter horizon.

Fonthill to Oxford
. . . the light is very good for looking at the countryside patchworked by the ripening season . . .
Sun behind the car, rain-full-grey sky ahead; the landscape resonates in all the green-based range of tones . . . Before the rain lashes the road . . .

Leaving London by M4
. . . circular red sun is misted over by muddy, ill-profiled obscuration . . . The sun is low enough to be cerise . . . After forty miles the sun's face is clear apart from a stray wisp of mist; quite Japanese . . .

London to Sheffield
. . . The expansive outlook from the passenger seat is chill, the overall sky overcast; the wind catching the car still blustery . . . Bracing weather?

Further evidence of the significance of climate in the Smithson's work is to be found in *Climate Register* (11). This is an analysis of four Smithson projects, based on studies made by students of Diploma Unit 6 at the Architectural Association School of Architecture in London, under the direction of Peter Salter. The projects are:

1. The Economist Building, London (1959–1964)
2. The Second Arts Building, University of Bath (1979–1981)
3. The Kuwait Government Building (the Mat-Building) project (1970)
4. The Bibliotheca Alexandrina competition entry (1989)

The analysis is more concerned with the effect of climate on the physical weathering of the fabric of a building than with the environmental effects that are the primary concern here. Nonetheless there is a particularly poetic description of the 'Qualities of Light' that underpin the design of the Bibliotheca Alexandrina project and there are geometrically precise graphical solar shading studies of the façades of the Second Arts Building at Bath. Yet another connection is made with the Smithsons' sensitivity to the environmental qualities of Elizabethan architecture, when Peter Salter writes:

> . . . I remember walking with them (the Smithsons) through
> . . . Kirby Hall [(12)], and entering a room with a large bay
> window. The window faced south and was fully glazed, with
> a timber seat at its sill. Sitting there in the morning, you
> could feel the sun streaming through the window to warm
> your back. The height of the window allowed the sun deep
> into the room and the hearth of the fireplace was positioned
> at the margin where the sun gave way to shade.

The term *Climate Register* accords precisely with the proposition that underlies the present book – that buildings may become instruments that represent and interpret the climate in which they are located. The buildings of the Smithsons do just this, and I will examine two English houses by them in order to illustrate the relevance of this idea in the twentieth century. These are the Sugden House at Watford to the north of London (1955–1957) and the Upper Lawn Pavilion (1959–1962), the weekend house built for the Smithsons' own use at Fonthill in Wiltshire.

The Sugden House

In 1955 Derek Sugden of the Ove Arup office was working with the Smithsons as a structural engineer. He had just found a piece of land at Watford upon which to build a house for himself and his wife Jean. One evening he asked Peter Smithson if he could find a young architect to design the house. To his surprise, and no doubt pleasure, Peter said that he and Alison would do the job (13). At first sight the house is disarmingly simple (Fig. 8.2), but careful study reveals its tectonic sophistication and environmental sensitivity (14). The site is hidden away in the midst of typical British suburbia. By the usual standards of these places the more or less rectangular site is relatively large

and rises gently from south-west to north-east. The site layout makes the most of the topography, and the house, in its now mature setting, sits comfortably on what the Smithson's described as 'an earthwork apron, whose facets effect the transition between the natural dished contours and the squareness of the house' (15). The site entrance is at the southern corner and a driveway leads along the eastern edge to the house that sits on its excavated platform at the northern corner of the site.

The design was constrained by a number of conservative requirements imposed by the former owners of the site and the local authority. These stipulated that it should be made of brick and have a pitched roof. The first design sketches show a compact rectangular plan with a complex cross-section under an inverted pitched, butterfly roof. Derek Sugden describes his and Jean's response, in which they liked the plan, but had reservations about the butterfly roof, with its internal gutter, and the relatively small dimensions of the windows, because they wished to have views over the garden that they hoped to develop. He records that, at the end of the discussion, 'Peter gathered up the drawings and sketches and said, "I'll have another go, if we can't design something for the Sugdens, we can't design anything for anybody"' (16). The final design retains the compact rectangular plan, but now is covered by a simple, if asymmetrical, pitched roof. The plan has three distinct parts, defined by two load-bearing cross walls that support the first-floor structure and the simple timber-joisted roof, whose boarded underside is exposed in the first-floor rooms (Fig. 8.3).

This seemingly simple arrangement forms an armature upon which a subtle response to the Sugdens' brief and the potential of the site are developed. In the half a century since it was completed the house has acquired celebrity, in particular, and justifiably, with reference to its clarity of form, its materiality and, perhaps most of all, the apparently complex disposition of the windows. The distinguished British architect Peter St John has written that:

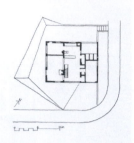

8.3
Alison and Peter Smithson, Sugden House: ground-floor plan.

> Many associations come in and out of focus when considering this little house: a cottage, a Palladian villa and the products of mass suburban house-building are all involved. In the tradition of the English Arts and Crafts house, there are windows to the garden on all sides. On the flanks of the compact volume they adopt a wild scattered arrangement within the wall, as if pushed around by some natural accident. On the front of the house, at the top of the garden, the windows are arranged almost symmetrically, making the building appear grand at the entrance to the site. Regarding the house from its garden, its image is not clear but is instead ambiguous, unstable and vital.
>
> (17)

On close analysis it is possible to uncover an underlying logic in the location, shapes and dimensions of the windows in response to the relationship between inside and out. Here Peter St John's reference to the Arts and Crafts house becomes particularly apt as parallels with that tradition that we explored in Essay 6 become apparent. The relatively strict observance of north and south orientation of the Arts and Crafts movement is rejected in favour of a north–south axis laid diagonally across the plan. The service functions, garage, storage and so on occupy the north-eastern edge of the ground floor, and the main daytime rooms take up the remainder of this floor. The discipline of the load-bearing masonry structure is dissolved at key points by the insertion of *in situ* concrete beams. These allow the living and dining rooms and the kitchen to become interconnected. The kitchen, as in Arts and Crafts precedent, is at the cool northern corner. It is directly connected to the dining room by a range of elegant and practical kitchen units designed by Alison, which remain in use to the present (Fig. 8.4). The dining room, or 'dining hall' in a reference to the tradition of the English vernacular house,

faces south-east and the living room at the southern corner has windows facing both south-east and south-west. On the first floor the principal bedrooms have large windows facing south-west with views over the garden. The living room has carefully contrived 'light' and 'dark', winter and summer areas – again reminiscent of Arts and Crafts practice, most particularly as found in Mackintosh's arrangement in the living room at The Hill House. The 'light' area is defined by the large floor-to-ceiling window that casts light deep into the heart of the plan and allows the sweeping views of the garden that the Sugdens wanted. The 'dark' zone is focused on the hearth and its light comes from the timber-framed French window to the south-west and the high-cilled window in the south-easterly flank wall. The load-bearing walls are left as exposed brick, but all others are finished, exactly as originally, with white-painted plaster. The dining-room and kitchen floors have black-and-white chequerboard tiles and the living-room floor has hardwood boards.

8.4

Alison and Peter Smithson, Sugden House: dining hall.

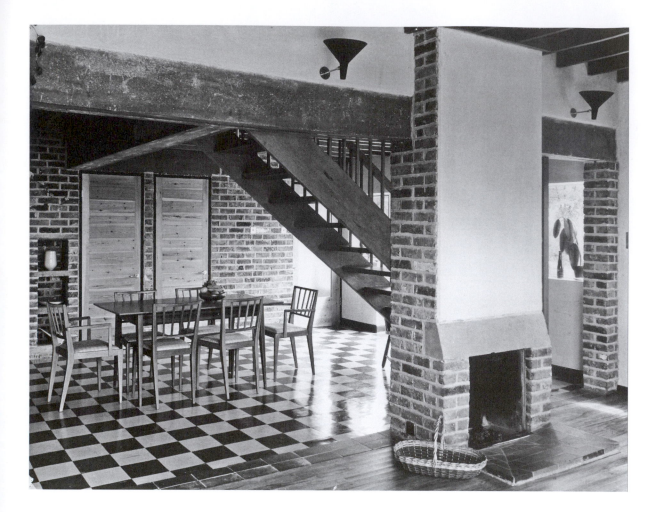

The Smithsons wrote that the 'imposed' materiality of the exterior suggested representations of houses 'as seen in Dutch paintings' (18). The same may also be said of the interiors, where the play of light on material and form carries similar associations (Fig. 8.5).

Early photographs of the house show the site as raw ground, scarred by the construction process. After half a century this is changed almost beyond recognition. There is none of the geometrical order and English prettiness of a Baillie Scott garden. Here it is more of a miniature fragment of the English landscape, achieved by Jean Sugden's loving attention to the selection and positioning of lawns, shrubs and trees in relation to the house to create an ideal setting for it. Moving from room to room in the house, the logic of the windows as frames to the garden, as specified by the Sugdens in their early conversations with the Smithsons, becomes clear. From every room there is a vista that captures a fragment of the garden, expanding the

8.5
Alison and Peter Smithson, Sugden House: living room, looking into dining hall.

perceived dimensions of the relatively small rooms (19). In 1984 the Smithsons published an essay, 'Thirty years of thoughts on the house and housing' (20) in which they stated that '. . . the window positioning [is] based on views and the sun . . .'.

For the Smithsons these environmental qualities were part of the larger architectural conception. As was suggested earlier, 'scientific' reductivism was not their way. In 1955, around the time they began work on the Sugden House, they wrote, 'We see architecture as the direct result of a way of life' (21). That is the true quality of this remarkable small house. For over half a century it has sustained the Sugden family through all of the cycles of domestic life. Probably the best summary of the Smithsons' insight into domestic architecture is to be found in a short essay 'Beatrix Potter's places', which Alison published in 1967 (22). There she wrote:

> Beatrix Potter's interiors are tailored to meet the need of the individual and each individual room is tailored to its function with each group of rooms directly responding to their context in the environment . . . The dwellings of her people fit the landscape with that sort of anonymity that is only achieved through building in a personally consistent language – or an internally consistent imagination.

How better could one describe the essence of the Sugden House?

The Upper Lawn Pavilion

> Here, it is enough to say it is a pavilion in a compound, surfaced half by paving 'as found' and half by lawn; a pavilion in which to enjoy the seasons; a primitive solar-energy pavilion whose thin skin forms a new space against the thick masonry north walls of the original eighteenth century and earlier farmstead cottages.
>
> (23)

In this simple statement the Smithsons establish the fundamentals of their design for the small house that they built as a weekend retreat for themselves and their children. It is a building that has attracted much well-merited critical attention and analysis in the 50 years of its existence (24), but, surprisingly, relatively little of this has concerned the building's environmental credentials, which were so strongly expressed by its authors and owners when it was just completed. Writing in 1963 in the *Architectural Review* (25), they described the house almost in the terms of an experiment in building science:

This is to some extent an experimental building, designed to discover whether, as a house presenting glass walls to the south, east and west, enough solar heat can be obtained through most of the year and its build-up can offset heat losses.

This proposition was taken further a few months later in *Architectural Design* (26):

The ideas behind the building are several and diverse:

An attempt at a simple 'climate house'; being able to open up the service areas on the ground floor onto the old paved areas of the garden, and as rapidly close them up again when the weather changes.

To find out what it is like to live in a house in England all the year round which presents glass walls to the entire south, east and west.

... and if it is so that solar heat can be obtained most of the year round and its build up noticeably offset heat loss.

And a further elaboration was offered when they wrote, 20 years later:

A thin-skinned structure in a compound, openable-up at garden level ... like a 'scena' changeable for the acts of inhabitation at the different seasons of the year. ... This is a true solar pavilion designed to capture the sun from its rise to its setting, especially in winter ... a theme which reappeared at the end of the 1970s.

(27)

The site of the house is in Wiltshire, close to the location of Fonthill Abbey (1795–1807), a neo-gothic fantasy of a house built by James Wyatt for the eccentric William Beckford (28). The house partially collapsed a quarter of a century after it was built and soon after was demolished. Nothing remains today, but the fact of its existence lends a magical quality to the location that appealed to the Smithsons. Their house is positioned to the south of the Fonthill estate at the northern edge of an ancient farmyard and on the site of an old cottage that was partially incorporated into the new house, with only the northern boundary wall and a chimney-stack retained (Fig. 8.6). Tectonically a pair of *in situ* concrete columns and a beam provide intermediate support for the principal structure, which is otherwise a simple timber 'balloon-frame'. As the Smithsons stated in their descriptions of the house,

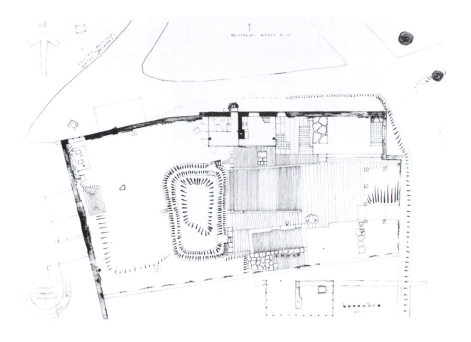

8.6
Alison and Peter Smithson,
Upper Lawn Pavilion,
Tisbury: site plan.

8.7
Alison and Peter Smithson,
Upper Lawn Pavilion:
opened up for summer.

the south, east and west walls are fully glazed with large planes of glazing set in teak frames (Fig. 8.7). The ground-floor glazing runs on beautifully detailed tracks that provide wide openings in all directions on fine days. The first-floor glazing is in fixed frames. Above the retained north wall at ground floor level the structure has aluminium sheet cladding, lined with plywood and with insulation between the timber frames (Fig. 8.8). At the north-west corner of the plan a large window provides a view across open terrain towards the site of Fonthill. The ground floor accommodates the practical functions of entrance hall, kitchen with dining, and bathroom; the main enclosed living and sleeping places are on the first floor.

The enclosure of the house is, however, only part of the place that the Smithsons made at Fonthill. The relationships between the interior and the surrounding open spaces are essential elements of their intention to create 'a "scena" changeable for the acts of inhabitation at the different seasons of the year . . .'. The area immediately to the east of the building is, in essence, a room. Close by the house a window in the north wall of the original cottage is retained, complete with glazing, wooden shutters and window seat (Fig. 8.9) and in the north-eastern angle of the boundary wall there is a large open fireplace beneath a raised concrete slab that is itself approached by a flight of steps (Fig. 8.10). This sheltered south-facing territory thereby becomes habitable to some degree at all seasons. Other, less precisely differentiated, open spaces to the south and west offer other opportunities for outdoor life, particularly so in the days when the Smithsons' three children were growing up, when they became a wonderful playground.

8.9
Alison and Peter Smithson,
Upper Lawn Pavilion: yard,
Fonthill Woods.

8.10
Alison and Peter Smithson,
Upper Lawn Pavilion: yard
in summer.

The 'experimental' aspect of the house centred on the possibility of achieving thermal comfort in the English climate, from the capture of solar heat gain within a highly glazed enclosure. A small coke-burning stove connected to the chimney retained from the old cottage provided the only permanent supplementary heating. This can be seen to the left in an early photograph (Fig. 8.11). This image also provides important information about other aspects of the house's environmental equipment. The kitchen consists of a small worktop with shelves above. A free-standing bowl is served by a water tap, and a portable gas camping stove is the only means of cooking. This accords with Peter Smithson's frequent references to life at Upper Lawn as 'camping out'. In the image two candlesticks are seen on the folding legged dining table. After dark, dining at the house was always by candlelight. From the beginning there was a mains electricity supply, which supplied a lamp over the kitchen worktop and 'Anglepoise' lamps that were used for reading and writing in the evenings. There was also an electric immersion heater in a water cylinder that served the bathroom shower. This was used sparingly since 'we didn't wash a lot'. There was also a portable electric convection heater to back up the coke stove and this was joined later by a second. A major luxury was a 'Miele' dishwasher because, although the ethos was 'camping', the family didn't like washing-up. There was, however, no refrigerator. Food was usually purchased at the nearby village shop and was kept cool by being stored in 'Dunlop' rubber dustbins, with tightly fitting lids, that were placed in the shelter of the roof of the external fireplace enclosure (29).

The Smithsons kept an extensive photographic record, mainly taken by Peter, of the construction and inhabitation of Upper Lawn in the years between 1961 and 1982. These images, which were meticulously dated, show the house at all seasons of the year and thereby become vital data in relation to their experiment in solar design. Because they visited intermittently, the family adopted the use of Japanese flags, hoisted on a mast on the boundary wall, to inform the milkman when they were in residence. One snowy, but sunny, image shows one of these billowing in a stiff easterly breeze, and from this we may infer that the closed-up house was providing a true test of the hypothesis of solar heating. Other winter images (Figs 8.12 and 8.13), one taken on an overcast day in 1963, the other at the sunny Christmas of 1970, convey the wonderful and challenging variability of the British winter climate. Summer views show how the house opened up, plant-like at this season, as life extended out into the surrounding open spaces. The area by the external fireplace becoming the focal point in the first summer of 1962. In the early summer of 1978, as the site and planting matured, the blossom added a new enchantment to the place (Plate 7, Figs 8.14 and 8.15). An image taken in May 1973 shows the setting sun reflected in the west-facing glazing of the upper floor (Fig. 8.16).

Simon Smithson recalls (30) that the house was sometimes very cold in winter or very hot in summer, but that it was also comfortable on cold, sunny days, in some confirmation of the underlying environmental hypothesis. He also has memories of summertime family enactments of the rustics' play-within-a-play from *A Midsummer's Night's Dream*, in yet another resonance of Alison's and Peter's affinity with their first Elizabethan forebears.

Peter's photographic record was complemented by the detailed diaries kept by Alison throughout their occupancy of the house. Below I present extracts from that for 1964, which, in Gilbert White-like prose, record the weather and other observations for each month of the year (31):

1964

JANUARY 17–20. Hoar frost. No wind.

FEBRUARY 15–22 or 23. (School half term). Bund re-modelling to ease slope for grass cutting. Bulbs in grass round the Fonthill stone* not up yet although those round

the walls are up to various heights. Crocuses by sand platform* are orange and mauve. Wood chippings and clips collected from the start of the cutting-down and grubbing-out of the hazel copse* badly overgrown with elder.

*Found on triangle of grass before door, a carved vault springing.

*Orange bricks from ruined wash-house later removed as never used.

*When property first seen, old coppice to left of view had been felled.

MARCH 13–15. Sun, bright cloud, no wind, dark nights. Daffodils and narcissi in bud in three splendid patches.

MARCH 26 to APRIL 1. Sun on Good Friday, sufficient to take lunch and tea outside. Chives usable length*. Sunday spitted large piece of lamb on wood forks.

*Under fig. Still there until 1987.

8.12
Alison and Peter Smithson, Upper Lawn Pavilion: snow in the yard.

8.13
Alison and Peter Smithson, Upper Lawn Pavilion: garden side, Christmas 1970.

8.14
Alison and Peter Smithson,
Upper Lawn Pavilion: fully
open in summer.

8.15
Alison and Peter Smithson,
Upper Lawn Pavilion: yard.

8.16
Alison and Peter Smithson,
Upper Lawn Pavilion:
sunset, May 1973.

APRIL 25–28. Sun on Saturday morning, all day Sunday; evening mist. Pear, greengage, plum, cherry, loaded with flowers. First time ever walnut flowered in quantity. Bird nesting again in old fireplace.

MAY 9–11. Wind in night, dewy, sunny morning. Apple blossom.

JUNE 11–16. Sun, summer showers.

JUNE 29–JULY 13. First hot week, although dull towards weekend. Lilies about to flower. Cherries picked.

JULY 30–AUGUST 5. (Thursday evening to Wednesday tea-time). Too much thin growth and too many leaves on fig therefore second culling and leaf-pluck necessary to keep it to wall and so prevent it being ripped away by winds.

AUGUST 28 to SEPTEMBER 4. Sun all week, occasional chill wind sounding in trees. Wasps at apples, must be a nest near. Walnut really growing.

October 29–31. (School half term). Misty with fine rain. Not down since September. Right hand coppice cut down gives impression of road being moved much nearer and grass triangle dwarfed into insignificance.

NOVEMBER 27 to DECEMBER 1. Sun and showers, mild; much wild life seen on night journey down. View of Fonthill woods fully exposed (coppice's removal). First flying of September birthday fish*; long weekend; to Salisbury Saturday Market day, for Christmas crackers*.

*Japanese carp bought in Liberty's in replacement of those bought in Japan 1960.

*Became a ritual for many years.

DECEMBER 25–30. (Late Christmas morning to Wednesday). Bright sun, clear, snow on Sunday, excellent dry, over ice: sledging in sun on road to Lower Lawn. Snow house burrowed in banked up snow on Hatch Newtown lane verge*.

*Gone by next day.

A more 'scientific' record of the house as experiment is to be found in a typescript note made by Alison in 1963 (32). This frank, self-critical document is reproduced here in full:

TESTING OF THE 'CLIMATE HOUSE' – FIRST TWO YEARS

1. The solar heat can be obtained all the year round in England – and inside the glass it can be extremely 'close' even on one of our typical overcast days with glaring-grey sky. This too bright unpleasant sky effect we also found in Japan and the overhang of their roofs seems to be functional in this respect as well as from the rainfall/protection aspect. We had, we thought, protected ourselves from this sky glare effect by lowering window head height on the upper floor to 5'10". But it could come much lower – to bridge of nose level at 5'3". Even then sitting positions are unprotected. Yet overhang does not seem predictable since traditional Japanese houses are very dark and particularly in inclement weather conditions the country cottage user does an immense amount of reading so needs all the natural light he can get. Another side effect of so much glazing is condensation. Double glazing in England is so expensive that a great many modern houses suffer from this. At certain times of day in certain seasons it is impossible to see out.

2. In the country, particularly in our hill crest situation, wind conditions work against any free open-or-closed idea. This we also found true of the Aalto Maison Carré where our whole tour was conducted to the accompaniment of slamming doors. Our heavy teak glazed doors therefore mean we live in the house as a boat: every ingress or egress becomes a routine of precise actions. The children find no difficulty in this, but we would not dare lend the house to another family. To make a 'climate house' workable as an every day proposition and not as a game it would have to be openable at a touch as Japanese screens indeed are.

The aluminium cladding has stayed bright in the unpolluted atmosphere. But in gales the crack of the sheeting recalls the descriptions of noises on big sailing ships.

AMS
12:7:63

Although the Smithsons regarded Upper Lawn Pavilion and their inhabitation of it to be in the nature of an 'experiment', their method was not that of conventional building science. Like their sixteenth-century antecedents, they had no quantitative measuring devices, but, on the other hand, the immersion of themselves and their family in the direct experience of the seasons, in all their English unpredictability and diversity, through the delicate filter of this simple enclosure and its carefully arranged surroundings, would certainly have increased their personal understanding of both the English climate and the potential of architecture both to register and transform it for domestic life.

In the chapter, 'Sun acceptance/energy containment' in *The Charged Void: Architecture* (33), the Smithsons state that 'In the "Solar" Pavilion at Upper Lawn the energy containment is in the "as found"'. They summarized their environmental philosophy in the light of their experience of this and other buildings in the following terms:

> The stress is on the needs for immediacy of response and reaction to the changeable weather of England: the almost constant need for full or partial weather protection from one quarter or another, a need that can change several times throughout an afternoon. . . . Northern Europe involves us inevitably in sun acceptance, amelioration of climate and, above all of exclusion of rain.

The elements of this analysis were eloquently and concisely summarized in the 'replenishment' image that they made in 1977 (Fig. 8.17), which beautifully captures the essential qualities of Upper Lawn.

It was Peter Smithson's conference paper presented in Munich in 1987 (34) that first opened to me the environmental qualities of Robert Smythson's buildings and thereby provoked the line of thought that eventually led to the present book. Hardwick Hall and Upper Lawn are at first sight totally dissimilar, the one grandiose and formal, the other understated and informal. But, beyond such superficial descriptors, it may be argued that the two houses have much in common and that Upper Lawn is in some senses, most particularly in its environmental sensibility, a direct descendent of Hardwick. In their fundamentals both houses offer deeply considered responses to the British, or more precisely in the thinking of their architects, the *English*, climate. The relative moderation but unpredictability of this may be seen to inform the form, materiality and detail of both buildings. They become not simply responses to, but *expressions* of the climate. They provide relative shelter against its extremes of cold and damp and accommodate the occurrence of its most generous and life-affirming moments. At Hardwick,

8.17
Alison Smithson,
replenishment image.

Bess and her grand entourage would promenade in the long gallery, sit close to log or coal fires, with the light of few and dispersed candlesticks, and celebrate midsummer on high on the 'leads' with their banqueting houses. At Upper Lawn the Smithsons with their children and friends enacted less formal rituals. In winter they would be warmed by the coke stove or convection heaters, dining, as did Bess, by candlelight and reading in the circles of light from their 'Anglepoise' lamps. In summer their life expanded, as the house opened up, to inhabit the surrounding open spaces, the outdoor fireplace almost becoming the equivalent of the renaissance banqueting turrets at Wollaton and Hardwick as the place for summer pleasures.

In the half-century since the Sugden House and Upper Lawn were constructed, the art of designing houses, and other building types, to capture the benefits of solar heat in the British climate has developed to a point where it is now commonplace in much of the best practice. But these buildings continue to serve as invaluable paradigms. They evince their architects' deep understanding of the relationship between architecture and climate in Britain and remind us that 'environmental', 'climate-responsive', 'sustainable' design in architecture must be as much a cultural enterprise as it is the mechanical observance of technical principle.

Notes

1. Alison and Peter Smithson, *The Charged Void: Architecture*, The Monacelli Press, New York, 2001, and *The Charged Void: Urbanism*, The Monacelli Press, New York, 2005.

2. This project is illustrated in both volumes of *The Charged Void*: *Architecture*, pp. 564–570 and *Urbanism*, p. 259.

3. Alison and Peter Smithson, 'Thirty years of thoughts on the house and housing', in *Architecture in an Age of Scepticism* (ed. Denys Lasdun), Heinemann, London, 1984.

4. Peter Smithson, 'Territorial imprint', in *Proceedings of 1987 European Conference on Architecture* (ed. W. Palz), H. A. Stephens & Associates, Bedford.

5. Published as Catherine Spellman and Carl Unglaub (eds) *Peter Smithson: Conversations with Students*, Princeton Architectural Press, New York, 2005.

6. At that time King's College was part of Durham University and became part of the University of Newcastle upon Tyne upon its foundation in 1963.

7. In a conversation with the author in London on 17 June 2010, Simon Smithson, Alison and Peter's son, suggested that the experience of the cold microclimate of South Shields would have had some effect on Alison. He also recalled Peter's stories about cycling with his father.

8. Alison Smithson, *AS in DS: An Eye on the Road*, Delft University Press, Delft, 1983; reprinted by Lars Müller Publishers, Baden, Switzerland, 2001. The 'DS' in the title is a reference to the much loved Citroen DS car owned by the Smithsons, in which they regularly travelled across England.

9. William Cobbett, *Rural Rides*, London, 1830. Alison Smithson cites the enlarged 1853 edition, published by James Paul Cobbett.

10. The book describes 19 rides in total, only four of which were outside the months between September and November.

11. Peter Salter and Peter Smithson, *Climate Register: Four Works by Alison and Peter Smithson* (selected and interpreted by Lorenzo Wong and Peter Salter), Architectural Association Publications, London, 1994.

12. Kirby Hall is an Elizabethan mansion in Northamptonshire, completed in 1570. The house is not formally attributed to any architect, but Girouard proposes that the master mason was Thomas Thorpe of Kingscliffe. See Mark Girouard, *Elizabethan Architecture*, Yale University Press, New Haven, CT, 2009.

13. The evolving relationship between clients and architects in the design of the Sugden House is recalled by Derek Sugden, 'The Sugden House', in *Architecture is Not Made with the Brain: The Labour of Alison and Peter Smithson*, Proceedings of a symposium held at the Architectural Association, London, November 2003, AA Publications, London, 2005.

14. Descriptions and analyses of the house are to be found in Alison and Peter Smithson, *Upper Lawn: Solar Pavilion Folly* (foreword by Enric Miralles), Barcelona, 1986; Alison and Peter Smithson, *The Charged Void: Architecture*, cited in Note 1, pp. 150–156; Dirk van den Heuvel and Max Risselada (eds), *Alison and Peter Smithson – From the House of the Future to a House of Today*, 010 Publishers, Rotterdam, 2004; and Dean Hawkes, 'A celebration of domestic life', in *The Architects' Journal*, 26 June 1997, pp. 45–50.

15. Alison and Peter Smithson, *The Charged Void: Architecture*, cited in Note 1.

16. Sugden, 'The Sugden House', cited in Note 13.

17. Peter St John, 'An Emotional Architecture', in *Architecture is Not Made with the Brain*, cited in Note 13.

18. Alison and Peter Smithson, *The Charged Void: Architecture*, cited in Note 1.

19. The author, who has visited the house on a number of occasions, had this reading reinforced on a visit made on 6 June 2010, enjoying these framed views into the now mature landscape surrounding the house.

20. Alison and Peter Smithson, 'Thirty years of thoughts on the house and housing', cited in Note 3.

21. Alison and Peter Smithson, 'The New Brutalism: An editorial', *Architectural Design*, Vol. 25, 1955, p. 1.

22. Alison Smithson, 'Beatrix Potter's places', *Architectural Design*, Vol. 37, 1967, p. 573; reprinted in van den Heuvel and Risselada (eds), *Alison and Peter Smithson*, cited in Note 14.

23. Alison and Peter Smithson, *The Charged Void: Architecture*, cited in Note 1.

24. The principal texts are the Smithsons' own essay, *Upper Lawn: Solar Pavilion Folly*, cited in Note 14; Claude Lichtenstein and Thomas Schregenberger (eds), *As Found: The Discovery of the Ordinary*, Lars Müller, Baden, 2001; Bruno Krucker, *Complex Ordinariness: The Upper Lawn Pavilion by Alison and Peter Smithson*, Verlag ETH, Zurich, 2002; and van den Heuvel and Risselada (eds), *Alison and Peter Smithson*, cited in Note 14.

25. Alison and Peter Smithson, 'Architects' own house', in *Architectural Review*, Vol. 133, 1963, pp. 135–136.

26. Alison and Peter Smithson, 'Architects' own house at Fonthill', *Architectural Design*, Vol. 33, 1963, pp. 482–483.

27. Alison and Peter Smithson, 'Thirty years of thoughts on the house and housing', cited in Note 3.

28. See John Summerson, *Architecture in Britain: 1530–1830*, Penguin, Harmondsworth, 1953; 9th revised edition, Yale University Press, New Haven, CT, 1993, pp. 462–464.

29. Information from the author's conversation with Simon Smithson on 17 June 2010.

30. *Ibid*.

31. The diaries are kept at the Smithson Family Collection. This and other extracts were previously published in Alison and Peter Smithson, *Upper Lawn: Solar Pavilion Folly*, cited in note 14.

32. Typescript from the Smithson Family Collection.

33. Alison and Peter Smithson, *The Charged Void: Architecture*, cited in Note 1.

34. Peter Smithson, 'Territorial imprint', cited in Note 4.

Illustration credits

7.13   Architectural Press Archive / RIBA Library Photographs

7.14   Morley von Sternberg/RIBA Library Photographs

7.17   Morley von Sternberg/RIBA Library Photographs

7.21   © Architectural Press Archive / RIBA Library Photographs

7.23   RIBA Library Photographs Collection

7.24   RIBA Library Photographs Collection

7.25   RIBA Library Photographs Collection

8.4   © Architectural Press Archive / RIBA Library photographs

8.5   © Architectural Press Archive / RIBA Library photographs

Plate 5   All images reproduced with kind permission of the National Trust for Scotland

Plate 8   Jan Siberechts, 'Landscape with Rainbow, Henley-on-Thames', 1698 (Tate Images)

Plate 9   Wollaton Hall and Park, Nottinghamshire, Jan Siberechts, Yale Centre for British Art, Paul Mellon Collection B1973.1.52

Plate 10   © Trustees of the Goodwood Collection

Plate 11   © National Gallery, London

Plate 12   © Royal Meteorological Society

Plate 13   © Musee d'Orsay, Paris

Plate 14   © Leicester Arts and Museum Services

Plate 15   Paul Nash, English 1889–1946, Landscape of the summer solstice 1943, oil on canvas 71.8 × 91.6 cm, © National Gallery of Victoria, Melbourne Felton Bequest, 1952

Plate 16   Le Corbusier, 'Lithograph B.4 (mind) from Le Poeme de l'Angle Droit' © FLC / ADAGP, Paris and DACS, London 2010

Selected bibliography

This presents the principal books that are referred to in the text. Citations of essays, articles and other sources are given in full in the Notes to each Essay.

Abramson, Daniel M., *Building the Bank of England: Money, Architecture, Society, 1694–1942*, Yale University Press, New Haven, CT, 2005.

Allan, John, *Berthold Lubetkin: Architecture and the Tradition of Progress*, RIBA Publications, London, 1999.

Allan, John, *Lubetkin*, Merrell, London, 2002.

Allwood, Rosamond, *Spencer Gore in Letchworth*, Catalogue of Exhibition at Letchworth Museum and Art Gallery, Letchworth, 2006.

Ashmole, Bernard, *Bernard Ashmole 1894–1988: An Autobiography* (ed. Donna Kurtz), Oxbow Books, Oxford, 1994.

Austen, Jane, *Emma*, John Murray, London, 1815.

Baillie Scott, M. H., *Houses and Gardens*, George Newnes, London, 1906.

Banham, Reyner, *The Architecture of the Well-Tempered Environment*, The Architectural Press, London, 1969; 2nd revised edition, Chicago University Press, Chicago, 1984.

Barnard, T. C. and Clark, Jane (eds), *Lord Burlington, Architecture, Art and Life*, Hambledon Continuum, Harrisburg, PA, 1994.

Barwick, G. F., *The Reading Room of the British Museum*, E. Benn, London, 1929.

Bate, Jonathan, *The Song of the Earth*, Picador, London, 2000.

Bennett, J. A., *The Mathematical Science of Christopher Wren*, Cambridge University Press, Cambridge, 1982.

Bernan, Walter, *On the History and Art of Warming and Ventilating*, G. Bell, London, 1845.

Boynton, Lindsay (ed.), *The Hardwick Hall Inventories of 1601*, The Furniture History Society, London, 1971.

Brimblecombe, Peter, *The Big Smoke: A History of Air Pollution in London since Medieval Times*, Methuen, London, 1987; paperback edition, Routledge, London, 1988.

Brown, Jane, *Gardens of a Golden Afternoon: The Story of a Partnership: Edwin Lutyens and Gertrude Jekyll*, Allen Lane/Penguin, London, 1982.

Buell, Laurence (ed.), *The Environmental Imagination: Thoreau, Nature Writing and the Formation of American Culture*, Harvard University Press, Cambridge, MA, 1996.

Byron, Lord George Gordon, *The Complete Poetical Works*, The Clarendon Press, Oxford, 1986.

Campbell, Colen, *Vitruvius Britannicus or The British Architect*, 1715, 1717 and 1725. Published in unabridged facsimile (3 vols), Dover, New York, 2006.

Cantacuzino, Sherban, *Wells Coates: A Monograph*, Gordon Fraser, London, 1978.

Carolin, Peter and Dannatt, Trevor (eds), *Architecture, Education and Research: The Work of Leslie Martin: Papers and Selected Articles*, Academy Editions, London, 1996.

Caygill, Marjory and Date, Christopher, *Building the British Museum*, British Museum Press, London, 1999.

Chambers, William, *A Treatise on the Decorative Part of Civil Architecture*, 1759. Facsimile edition, Dover, New York, 2003.

Clayton, J., *The Works of Christopher Wren: The Dimensions, Plans, Elevations and Sections of the Parochial Churches of Sir Christopher Wren. Erected in the Cities of London and Westminster*, Longman, Brown, Green & Longman, London, 1848–1849.

Cobbett, *Rural Rides*, London, 1830; reprinted in paperback, Penguin, Harmondsworth, 1967.

Coe, Peter and Reading, Malcolm, *Lubetkin and Tecton: Architecture and Social Commitment*, Arts Council of Great Britain/Bristol University, 1981.

Cohn, Laura, *The Door in a Secret Room: A Portrait of Wells Coates*, Scolar Press, Aldershot, 1999.

Colvin, Howard, *The Sheldonian Theatre and the Divinity School*, Oxford University Press, Oxford, 1981; reprinted 1996.

Crawford, Alan, *Charles Rennie Mackintosh*, Thames and Hudson, London, 1995.

Creese, Walter, *The Legacy of Raymond Unwin: A Human Pattern for Planning*, MIT Press, Cambridge, MA, 1967.

Crook, J. Mordaunt, *The British Museum: A Case-Study in Architectural Politics*, Allen Lane/Penguin, Harmondsworth, 1972.

Cruickshank, Dan (ed.), *Timeless Architecture*, The Architectural Press, London, 1985.

Cunningham, Colin and Waterhouse, Prudence, *Alfred Waterhouse, 1830–1905: Biography of a Practice*, Clarendon Press, Oxford, 1992.

Curtis, William, *Le Corbusier: Ideas and Forms*, Phaidon, London, 1986.

Dahl, Thorben (ed.), *Climate and Architecture*, Routledge, London, 2010.

Darley, Gillian, *John Evelyn: Living for Ingenuity*, Yale University Press, New Haven, CT, 2006.

Darling, Elizabeth, *Reforming Britain: Narratives of Modernity Before Reconstruction*, Routledge, London, 2006.

Davey, Peter, *Arts and Crafts Architecture: The Search for Earthly Paradise*, The Architectural Press, London, 1980; revised edition, Phaidon, London, 1995.

Davis, Colin, *Key Houses of the Twentieth Century: Plans, Sections and Elevations*, Laurence King, London, 2006.

De Beer, E. S. (ed.), *The Diary of John Evelyn*, Clarendon Press, Oxford, 1955.

Deakin, Roger, *Wildwood: A Journey Through Trees*, Penguin, Harmondsworth, 2008.

Deakin, Roger, *Waterlog: A Swimmer's Journey Through Britain*, Vintage, London, new edition, 2009a.

Deakin, Roger, *Notes from Walnut Tree Farm*, Penguin, Harmondsworth, 2009b.

Dickens, Charles, *Little Dorrit*, first published 1855–1857; BBC Books edition, London, 2008.

Doré, Gustave and Jerrold, Blanchard, *London: A Pilgrimage*, Grant, London, 1872; facsimile edition, Dover Publications, New York, 2004.

Downes, Kerry, *Christopher Wren*, Allen Lane/The Penguin Press, London, 1971.

Durant, David N., *Bess of Hardwick: Portrait of an Elizabethan Dynast*, Peter Owen, London, 1977; revised paperback edition, 1999.

Durant, Stuart, *C. F. A. Voysey*, Academy Editions, London, 1992.

Dyos, H. J. and Wolff, Michael (eds), *The Victorian City: Images and Realities*, 2 vols, Routledge & Kegan Paul, London, 1973.

Eliot, T. S., *The Waste Land*, Faber and Faber, London, 1922.

Engels, Friedrich, *The Condition of the Working Class in England* (ed. David McLellan), Oxford University Press, Oxford, 2009.

Evelyn, John, *Fumifugium or The Inconveniencie of the Aer and the Smoak of London Dissipated. Together With some Remedies humbly Proposed*, Printed by W. Godbid for Gabriel Bedel and Thomas Collins, London, 1661.

Evelyn, John, *Sylva, or a Discourse on Forest Trees*, London, 1664.

Fagan, Brian, *The Little Ice Age: How Climate Made History, 1300–1850*, Basic Books, New York, 2000.

Forster, E. M., *Howard's End*, first published Edward Arnold, London, 1910.

Fowler, Alastair, *The Country House Poem: A Cabinet of Seventeenth-Century Estate Poems and Related Items*, Edinburgh University Press, Edinburgh, 1994.

Friedman, Alice T., *House and Household in Elizabethan England: Wollaton Hall and the Willoughby Family*, University of Chicago Press, Chicago, 1989.

Fry, E. Maxwell, *Fine Building*, Faber and Faber, London, 1944.

Fry, E. Maxwell and Drew, Jane, *Tropical Architecture in the Humid Zone*, Batsford, London, 1956.

Fry, E. Maxwell and Drew, Jane, *Tropical Architecture in the Dry and Humid Zones*, Reinhold, New York, 1964.

Garnham, Trevor, *St Andrew's Church, Roker, Sunderland, 1905: Edward Prior*, Architecture in Detail, Phaidon, London, 1990.

Gaskell, Philip and Robson, Robert, *The Library of Trinity College, Cambridge: A Short History*, Trinity College, Cambridge, 1971.

Gebhard, David, *Charles F. A. Voysey, Architect*, Hennesey & Ingalls, Los Angeles, 1975.

Golinski, Jan, *British Weather and the Climate of Enlightenment*, University of Chicago Press, Chicago, 2007.

Giedion, Siegfried, *Mechanization Takes Command: A Contribution to Anonymous History*, Oxford University Press, Oxford, 1948.

Girouard, Mark, *Life in the English Country House: A Social and Architectural History*, Yale University Press, New Haven, CT, 1978; paperback edition, Penguin, Harmondsworth, 1980.

Girouard, Mark, *Robert Smythson and the Elizabethan Country House*, Yale University Press, New Haven, CT, 1983.

Girouard, Mark, *Elizabethan Architecture: Its Rise and Fall, 1540–1640*, Yale University Press, New Haven, CT, 2009.

Givoni, Baruch, *Man, Climate and Architecture*, Elsevier, Amsterdam, 1969.

Haigh, Diane, *M. H. Baillie Scott: The Artistic House*, Academy Editions, London, 1995.

Harris, John, *The Palladian Revival: Lord Burlington, His Villa and Garden at Chiswick*, Yale University Press, New Haven, CT, 1994.

Harris, P. R., *A History of the British Museum Library 1753–1973*, British Library, London, 1998.

Harrison, William, *The Description of England*, 1587, reprint edition, Georges Edelen (ed.), Dover, New York, 1994.

Hawkes, Dean, *Modern Country Homes in England: The Arts and Crafts Architecture of Barry Parker*, Cambridge University Press, Cambridge, 1986; Reprinted in paperback, 2010.

Hawkes, Dean, *The Environmental Tradition: Studies in the Architecture of Environment*, E. & F. N. Spon, London, 1996.

Hawkes, Dean, *The Environmental Imagination: Technics and Poetics of the Architectural Environment*, Routledge, London, 2008.

Hawkes Dean, with Jane McDonald and Koen Steemers, *The Selective Environment: An Approach to Environmentally Responsive Architecture*, Spon, London, 2002.

Henderson, Paula, *The Tudor House and Garden*, Paul Mellon Centre for Studies in British Art/Yale University Press, New Haven, CT, 2005.

Hitchcock, Henry-Russell, *Architecture: Nineteenth and Twentieth Centuries*, Penguin, Harmondsworth, 1st edition, 1958, 1st paperback edition, 1971.

Hopkinson, R. G., *Architectural Physics: Daylighting*, HMSO, London, 1963.

Hoskins, W. G., *The Making of the English Landscape*, Hodder & Stoughton, London, 1953; paperback edition, Pelican, Harmondsworth, 1970.

Howard, Ebenezer, *Tomorrow: A Peaceful Path to Real Reform*, London, 1898; reprinted as *Garden Cities of Tomorrow*, S. Sonnenschein, London, 1902.

Howard, Luke, *The Climate of London*, 2 vols, 1818; 2nd edition, 3 vols, 1833.

Howarth, Thomas, *Charles Rennie Mackintosh and the Modern Movement*, Routledge & Kegan Paul, London, 1st edition, 1952; 2nd edition, 1977.

Jackson, Frank, *Sir Raymond Unwin: Architect, Planner and Visionary*, A. Zwemmer, London, 1985.

Jardine, Lisa, *On a Grander Scale: The Outstanding Career of Sir Christopher Wren*, Harper Collins, London, 2002.

Jardine, Lisa, *The Curious Life of Robert Hooke: The Man Who Measured London*, Harper Collins, London, 2003.

Jeffrey, Paul, *The City Churches of Sir Christopher Wren*, Hambledon Continuum, London, 1996.

Jenkins, David Fraser, *Paul Nash: The Elements*, Scala Publishers, London, 2010.

Kirk, Sheila, *Philip Webb: Pioneer of Arts and Crafts Architecture*, Wiley-Academy, Chichester, 2005.

Knowles, C. C. and Pitt, P. H., *The History of Building Regulations in London, 1189–1972*, The Architectural Press, London, 1972.

Knowles Middleton, W. E., *Invention of the Meteorological Instruments*, Johns Hopkins University Press, Baltimore, 1969.

Kornwulf, James D., *M. H. Baillie Scott and the Arts and Crafts Movement: Pioneer of Modern Design*, Johns Hopkins Press, Baltimore, 1972.

Lamb, H. H., *Climate, History and the Modern World*, 2nd edition, Routledge, London & New York, 1995.

Le Corbusier, *Precisions: On the Present State of Architecture and City Planning*, Crès, Paris, 1930; English translation, MIT Press, Cambridge, MA, 1991.

Le Corbusier, *Le Poème de l'Angle Droit*, editions Verve, Paris, 1955; facsimile edition, Fondation Le Corbusier/Editions Connivences, Paris, 1989.

Lethaby, W. R., *Architecture, Mysticism and Myth*, London, 1891; reprinted by The Architectural Press, London, 1974.

Lethaby, W. R., *Philip Webb and His Work*, Oxford University Press, Oxford, 1935; Revised reprint, Raven Oak Press, London, 1979.

Lichtenstein, Claude and Schregenberger, Thomas (eds), *As Found: The Discovery of the Ordinary*, Lars Müller, Baden, 2001.

Lovell, Mary S., *Bess of Hardwick: First Lady of Chatsworth*, Little Brown, London, 2005; paperback edition, Abacus Books, London, 2007.

Macaulay, James, *Hill House*, Phaidon, London, 1990.

McGrath, Raymond, *Twentieth Century Houses*, Faber and Faber, London, 1934.

McKitterick, David (ed.), *The Making of the Wren Library*, Cambridge University Press, Cambridge, 1995.

Mackmurdo, A. H., *Wren's City Churches*, G. Allen, Orpington, 1883.

Macleod, Robert, *Charles Rennie Mackintosh*, Country Life, London, 1968.

Marshall, Pamela, *Wollaton Hall: An Archaeological Survey*, Nottingham Civic Society, Nottingham, 1996.

Martin, Leslie, *Buildings and Ideas 1933–1983: From the Studio of Leslie Martin and His Associates*, Cambridge University Press, Cambridge, 1983.

Martin, Leslie, Nicholson, Ben and Gabo, Naum (eds), *Circle: International Survey of Constructive Art*, Faber and Faber, London, 1937.

Melvin, Jeremy, *F. R. S. Yorke and the Evolution of English Modernism*, Wiley-Academy, Chichester, 2003.

Moore, Andrew (ed.), *Houghton Hall: The Prime Minister, the Empress and the Heritage*, Philip Wilson, London, 1996.

Morris, Robert, *Lectures on Architecture: Consisting of Rules Founded Upon Harmonic and Arithmetical Proportions in Building*, 1734; facsimile edition, Kessinger, Whitefish, MT, 2009.

Mowl, Timothy, *Elizabethan and Jacobean Taste*, Phaidon, London, 1993.

Mumford, Lewis, *Technics and Civilization*, Harcourt, Brace, New York, 1934.

Muthesius, Hermann, *Das Englische Haus*, Wasmuth, Berlin, Volumes 1 and 2, 1904, Volume 3, 1905; 1st English edition, abridged (ed. Dennis Sharp, trans. Janet Seligman), Crosby, Lockwood, Staples, London, 1979; 2nd English edition, full text (ed. Dennis Sharp, trans. Janet Seligman and Stuart Spencer), Frances Lincoln, London, 2007.

Ogden, C. K., *Basic English: A General Introduction with Rules and Grammar*, Kegan Paul, Trench, Trubner, London, 1930.

Olgyay, Victor, *Design with Climate: Bioclimatic Approach to Architectural Regionalism*, Princeton University Press, Princeton, NJ, 1963.

Oliver, Paul (ed.), *Encyclopedia of Vernacular Architecture of the World*, Cambridge University Press, Cambridge, 1997.

Overy, Paul, *Light, Air and Openness: Modern Architecture Between the Wars*, Thames and Hudson, London, 2007.

Palladio, Andrea, *I quattro libri dell'architettura*, Venice, 1570; English translation, Isaac Ware, London, 1738; facsimile edition, Dover, New York, 1965.

Palladio, Andrea, *The Four Books of Architecture* (eds Robert Tavernor and Richard Schofield), MIT Press, Cambridge, MA, 2002.

Parham, John (ed.), *The Environmental Tradition in English Literature*, Ashgate Publishing, Farnham, 2002.

Parker, Barry and Unwin, Raymond, *The Art of Building a Home: A Collection of Lectures and Illustrations*, Longmans, Green, London, 1901.

Pevsner, Nikolaus, *Pioneers of Modern Design: From William Morris to Walter Gropius*, Museum of Modern Art, New York, 1949; revised edition, Penguin, Harmondsworth, 1960; first published as *Pioneers of Modern Movement* by Faber and Faber, London, 1936.

Pevsner, Nikolaus, *The Englishness of English Art*, first published by The Architectural Press, London, 1956, reprinted by Peregrine, Harmondsworth, 1964.

Pevsner, Nikolaus, *The Buildings of England: Cambridgeshire*, Penguin, Harmondsworth, 2nd edition, 1970.

Plot, Robert, *The Natural History of Oxfordshire*, printed at the Theatre, Oxford, 1677.

Port, M. H. (ed.), *The Houses of Parliament*, Paul Mellon Centre for British Art/Yale University Press, New Haven, CT, 1976.

Porteous, Colin, *The New eco-Architecture: Alternatives from the Modern Movement*, Spon, London, 2002.

Powers, Alan, *Modern: The Modern Movement in Britain*, Merrell, London, 2005.

Price, Martin, *The Renaissance and the Eighteenth Century*, The Oxford Anthology of English Literature, Oxford University Press, Oxford, 1973.

Prior, Edward, *A History of Gothic Art in England*, G. Bell, London, 1900.

Reid, D. B., *Illustrations of the Theory and Practice of Ventilating*, London, 1844.

Richards, J. M., *An Introduction to Modern Architecture*, Penguin, Harmondsworth, 1st edition, 1940.

Richardson, Charles James, *A Popular Treatise on the Warming and Ventilation of Buildings: Showing the Advantage of the Improved System of Heated Water Circulation*, John Weale, Architectural Library, London, 1837.

Richardson, Margaret and Stevens, Mary Ann (eds), *John Soane: Architect, Master of Light and Space*, Royal Academy of Art, London/Yale University Press, New Haven, CT, 1999.

Richmond, Peter, *Marketing Modernisms: The Architecture and Influence of Charles Reilly*, Liverpool University Press, Liverpool, 2001.

Riding, Christine and Riding, Jacqueline (eds), *The Houses of Parliament: History, Art, Architecture*, Merrell, London, 2000.

Robertson, Pamela (ed.), *Charles Rennie Mackintosh: The Architectural Papers*, White Cockade Publishing, Wendlebury, in association with the Hunterian Art Gallery, Glasgow, 1990.

Rykwert, Joseph, *The First Moderns: Architects of the Eighteenth Century*, MIT Press, Cambridge, MA, 1984.

Saint, Andrew, *Richard Norman Shaw*, Yale University Press, New Haven, CT, 1976.

Salter, Peter and Smithson, Peter, *Climate Register: Four Works by Alison and Peter Smithson* (selected and interpreted by Lorenzo Wong and Peter Salter), Architectural Association Publications, London, 1994.

Sebald, W. G., *Rings of Saturn*, Vintage Classics, London, new edition, 2011.

Service, Alastair (ed.), *Edwardian Architecture and its Origins*, The Architectural Press, London, 1975.

Shakespeare, William, *Complete Works* (eds Jonathan Bate and Eric Rasmussen), The Royal Shakespeare Company/Macmillan, London, 2007.

Sharp, Denis and Rendel, Sally, *Connell, Ward and Lucas: Modern Movement Architects in England 1929–1939*, Frances Lincoln, London, 2008.

Simpson, Duncan, *C.F.A. Voysey: An Architect of Individuality*, Lund Humphries, London, 1979.

Sinclair, Iain, *Edge of the Orison: In the Traces of John Clare's 'Journey Out of Essex'*, Penguin, Harmondsworth, 2006.

Smithson, Alison, *AS in DS: An Eye on the Road*, Delft University Press, Delft, 1983; reprinted by Lars Müller Publishers, Baden, Switzerland, 2001.

Smithson, Alison and Smithson, Peter, *Upper Lawn: Solar Pavilion Folly* (foreword by Enric Miralles), Barcelona, 1986.

Smithson, Alison and Peter, *The Charged Void: Architecture*, Monacelli Press, New York, 2001.

Smithson, Alison and Peter, *The Charged Void: Urbanism*, Monacelli Press, New York, 2005.

Snow, C. P., *The Two Cultures and the Scientific Revolution*, Cambridge University Press, Cambridge, 1959.

Soo, Lydia, *Wren's Tracts on Architecture and Other Writing*, Cambridge University Press, Cambridge, 1998.

Stearne, William T., *The Natural History Museum at South Kensington*, William Heinemann, London, 1981.

Stewart, Cecil, *The Stones of Manchester*, Edward Arnold, London, 1956.

Strauss, Sarah and Orlove, Benjamin S. (eds), *Weather, Climate and Culture*, Berg, Oxford, 2003.

Stravinsky, Igor and Craft, Robert, *Conversations with Igor Stravinsky*, Faber Music, London, 1959.

Strong, Roy, *The Renaissance Garden in England*, Thames and Hudson, London, 1979.

Summerson, John, *Architecture in Britain: 1530–1830*, Penguin, Harmondsworth, 1953; 9th revised edition, Yale University Press, New Haven, CT, 1993.

Tavernor, Robert, *Palladio and Palladianism*, Thames and Hudson, London, 1991.

Thomson, James, *The Seasons*, first complete edition, London, 1730.

Thornes, John E., *John Constable's Skies: A Fusion of Art and Science*, University of Birmingham Press, Birmingham, 1999.

Thornton, Peter, *Seventeenth-Century Interior Decoration in England, France and Holland*, Yale University Press, New Haven, CT, 1981.

Upstone, Robert, *The Camden Town Group*, Exhibition Catalogue, Tate Britain, London, 2008.

van Heuvel, Dirk and Risselada, Max (eds), *Alison and Peter Smithson – From the House of the Future to a House of Today*, 010 Publishers, Rotterdam, 2004,

Waterhouse, Ellis, *Painting in Britain, 1530–1790*, Pelican History of Art, 5th edition, with an introduction by Michael Kitson, Yale University Press, New Haven, CT, 1994.

Waugh, Evelyn, *Decline and Fall*, Chapman & Hall, London, 1928.

Whinney, Margaret, *Wren*, Thames and Hudson, London, 1971.

White, Gilbert, *The Natural History of Selborne*, London, 1789, first published 1788–1789, Penguin Classics edition, with Introduction by Richard Mabey, Penguin, Harmondsworth, 1987.

White, Gilbert, *The Journals of Gilbert White* (ed. Walter Johnson), John Routledge and Sons, London, 1931; paperback edition, Futura, London, 1982.

Williams, Margaret Harcourt and Stevenson, John (eds), *'Observations of Weather': The Weather Diary of Sir John Wittewronge of Rothamsted, 1684–1689*, Hertfordshire Record Publications, Hertford, 1999.

Wilson, Colin St J., *Architectural Reflections: Studies in the Philosophy of Architecture*, Butterworth Architecture, Oxford, 1992.

Wilson, Michael I., *William Kent: Architect, Designer, Painter, Gardener, 1685–1748*, Routledge & Kegan Paul, London, 1984.

Woolf, Virginia, *Mrs Dalloway*, The Hogarth Press, London, 1925.

Wright, Lawrence, *Home Fires Burning: The History of Domestic Heating and Cooking*, Routledge & Kegan Paul, London, 1964.

Yorke, F. R. S., *The Modern House*, The Architectural Press, London, 1934.

Index

Page numbers in *italics* denote illustrations